D0966480

LIST OF FIGURES

Figure 1.1 The Breakout Strategy Cycle
Figure 1.2 Breakout Types
Figure 2.1 Companies Getting on the Fast Track
Figure 3.1 Companies Staying Out in Front
Figure 4.1 Types of Capital and the Capital-Accumulation Process
Figure 5.1 The Vision Wheel
Figure 5.2 State Transition for Harley-Davidson: Organization
Figure 5.3 State Transition for Harley-Davidson: Culture
Figure 5.4 State Transition for Harley-Davidson: Relationships
Figure 5.5 State Transition for Harley-Davidson: Markets
Figure 6.1 The Six Pillars of a Value Proposition
Figure 6.2 Leveraging Up the Apple Value Proposition
Figure 6.3 Reconciling Different Value Propositions
Figure 6.4 Leveraging Up Samsung Electronics' Value Proposition
Figure 7.1 Components of a Business Model
Figure 7.2 Aligning the Business Model and the Value Proposition
Figure 7.3 Business Model Needs Analysis
Figure 8.1 Delivering Strategy
Figure 8.2 System Balance and Strategy Delivery at CEMEX
Figure 8.3 Organizational Culture and Cultural Reproduction
Figure 9.1 Breakout Leadership Capabilities

ACKNOWLEDGMENTS

Ten years in the making and three years in the writing, this book is the culmination of a much longer period spent reflecting on and engaging with the elements of strategy and leadership. More to the point, *Breakout Strategy* is the result of a fusion of academic research and business application. Through working with companies large and small and with public, private, and nonprofit organizations across the globe, we have leveraged and honed our scholarly expertise to put together an integrated and practical process for putting strategy to work. We owe an enormous debt of gratitude to all those who have directly or indirectly influenced our thinking during this journey of discovery. At the risk of omission, permit us to thank some of those individuals and organizations by name.

The project had its genesis in an in-house executive MBA program designed by the authors in the mid-1990s. Charles Harvey and Thomas Lawton set up an innovative and tailored course of study to facilitate the fast tracking of the best and the brightest asset managers at Robert Fleming investment bank (later JP Morgan Fleming Asset Management) into leadership roles. The program was global in its reach; we ran sessions in Hong Kong, London, New York, Paris, and Tokyo. During one of the sessions in New York, Sydney Finkelstein gave a guest talk to delegates and at the same time struck up a rapport with his future coauthors. From our experience with asset managers and investment bankers, and subsequently with information technology consultants, health care professionals, industrial lubricant advisors, rail vehicle manufacturers, insurance underwriters, mobile telecommunications providers, transport infrastructure consortia, airline managers, and a host of other executives, we recognized the need for an integrated strategy system that managers could understand easily and use straightaway. Our thanks go out to all those who facilitated and participated in these assorted interventions.

The methods and models on which *Breakout Strategy* is constructed really took shape in a fully logical, structured format only when the actual book project commenced in early 2003. We would like to thank the many executives and leaders who were generous with their time during the subsequent three years of research and writing, granting us access for interviews and discussion. We also benefited tremendously from the many senior executives and managers who participated in executive development programs that we organized all over the world during this period, people who reacted to our ideas and pushed our thinking. We were especially lucky to have met as many breakout leaders as we have, people who have dedicated their professional lives to excelling at their work and have refused to accept below-par effort or performance. We have certainly learned a great deal from all these people.

Many students in the United States and Europe were involved in the breakout project as well. We have tested and integrated many of these ideas in MBA and MSc classrooms and have come away with an even deeper understanding of what it means to be a leader striving for breakout strategy. A particular note of thanks goes to the MBA students of the Tanaka Business School, Strathclyde Business School, and the Tuck School of Business. A special mention also should be made of those entrepreneurs, managers, and leaders who have participated in the Tuck Executive Program, the IBM Business Leader Programme of the Bristol Business School, and the Trinity College Dublin–Enterprise Ireland MSc in International Business Program. Our students helped us to fine-tune our ideas, and in some cases pointed us in the direction of particularly interesting instances of breakout that we have brought into the narrative at various points.

We would like to thank academic colleagues who have shared their thoughts on many of the topics covered in this book. These include Lars Bruzelius, Ming-Jer Chen, Jonathan Doh, Colin Eden, Robert French, Patrick Gibbons, Denis Harrington, Gerry Johnson, Mark Kriger, Richard Lynch, Robert MacIntosh, Mairi Maclean, Margaret Peteraf, Jaideep Prabhu, Tazeeb Rajwani, Richard Schoenberg, Peter Simpson, John Stopford, and Roger Strange.

Invaluable data inputs and feedback on earlier drafts of the book also have been provided by friends in business and elsewhere. A special note of thanks is extended to Jehanbux Edulbehram, Kevin Michaels, Akin Oyesola, and Daniel Ruddy.

Thank you as well to those who labored long and hard directly supporting our research. Kirstin Howgate and Christine Reid deserve a special mention here.

Thomas Lawton would like to thank the Tuck School of Business at Dartmouth College for providing him with a warm welcome and a quiet office on several occasions during the research and writing of this book. The authors also gratefully acknowledge the organizational inputs and support provided by the Bristol Business School, Strathclyde Business School, Tanaka Business School, and Tuck School of Business throughout this project.

We were lucky to have Jeanne Glasser as our editor at McGraw-Hill. Jeanne was inspirational in her support and commitment to the project. Our agent, Helen Rees, likewise provided the clear guidance and sage advice needed to keep the team on the right track at every stage. We are very grateful to Jeanne and Helen for their constant good humor and unfailing professionalism. Thanks also to Sally Glover, Ann Renton, and the McGraw-Hill team for their superb efforts in the production and marketing of this book.

On a personal note, none of us could possibly have completed this project without the energetic and understanding support of our friends and loved ones. For Sydney, all the hard work was made easier by knowing that his wife, Gloria, and his daughter, Erica, were by his side no matter what. For Charles, the book could not have been completed without the constant support of his wife, Mairi, his daughters, Elizabeth and Rebecca, and his stepchildren, Emily and Alex. For Thomas, Kirstin provided a constant source of inspiration and encouragement. This book is dedicated to Gloria, Mairi, and Kirstin, without whom *Breakout Strategy* may not have seen the light of day.

Sydney Finkelstein
Hanover, New Hampshire

Charles Harvey
Glasgow, Scotland

Thomas Lawton
London, England

CHAPTER 1

BREAKOUT STRATEGY

We all want to discover the essential ingredient of outstanding business success, the decisive factor that differentiates exceptional companies from those that are just plain average. However, the goal of finding a panacea for the periodic difficulties that bedevil most businesses has proved elusive. More often than not, the search for a winning commercial formula proceeds more naturally by trial and error. Companies might try a dozen or more combinations before they eventually discover one that delivers growth and sustained profitability. For many, the quest proves fruitless; they never find the right formulation. Perhaps it was not meant to be. Perhaps the original concept for the business was found lacking or was irredeemably flawed. Yet, even when market signals are emphatically negative, business leaders often continue to search obsessively for the elusive X factor, the magic bullet that somehow will eliminate the problems besetting them.

The single-minded pursuit of instant remedies for fundamental business problems is at odds with the strategic approach to business growth recommended in this book. Rather than wasting time in pursuit of cure-all solutions, the most successful business leaders invariably, as a matter of habit, apply strategic principles and practices that dramatically increase the possibility of establishing and retaining a strong market position. These are the principles and practices that, collectively, we call *breakout strategy*. In what follows, we argue that the pursuit of a carefully crafted yet essentially simple strategy provides the best means for a business leader or entrepreneur to maximize corporate value.

If properly implemented, the optimal strategy bestows industry power on a company, enabling it to change or modify the rules of competition and increase its supply-chain authority. A well-defined and clearly communicated strategy facilitates the acquisition of new customers while retaining existing customers. Strategic innovation, practically grounded, confers authority on the business leader, creating a window of opportunity for the introduction of far-reaching transformational change. In the broadest sense, strategic excellence is the proven key to value creation in modern business, and therefore is of vital importance to the well-being of shareholders, employees, customers, and society at large.

Unfortunately, strategic excellence is not the norm. Robust tools and techniques for financial management and control are employed routinely in large corporations, but there is no comparable body of know-how when it comes to strategy. Certainly, planning tools and project management techniques exist in abundance. These, however, are of little use in helping business leaders to engage creatively in the strategy process. A wealth of detail on industry and market trends often serves as a substitute for more fundamental thinking about what makes a product or service appealing or how that product or service can be delivered reliably to customers. As a result, managers down the line all too often are confronted with the task of implementing strategies that they don't understand fully and that are based on strategic thinking that doesn't always appear to make sense. It is a painful truth that confused or misapplied methodologies continue to blight the business landscape and up-end companies. The inherent flaws that were implicated in some of the major business disasters of recent times, which are so apparent in retrospect, could well have been recognized much earlier had corporate leaders approached strategy with the rigor that the subject requires.

What Is Breakout Strategy?

The central idea of this book is that of *breakout*. In a business and management context, *breakout* is a forceful emergence from a restrictive form or position. It is a structured and purposeful approach to corporate change and market or industry transformation, leading to dramatic performance improvements and business success. A deliberate and innovative course of action, breakout is initiated by individuals and teams that are pursuing high growth and market prominence. *Breakout strategy* is an action-oriented framework for delivering accelerated growth and is founded on the concept of strategic excellence from beginning to end. It is a systematic approach to market triumph that leaves rivals floundering in your wake and struggling to respond.

To this you might respond, “Isn’t that what every business wants (more or less) and every strategy is meant to deliver?” Surprisingly, the answer is no. Companies that explicitly set out to excel are remarkably few and far between. Those that do so in a logical and consistent way are even fewer. Breakout strategy is a state of mind as much as a step-by-step process; it reflects both your intent to be the best and a method of getting there.

This book answers a question that is asked by businesspeople the world over: how can a company seemingly come from nowhere to become a formidable competitor—if not a leader—in national and international markets? We have in mind companies that have risen suddenly or unexpectedly from subordinate or recently established positions to dominate markets and industries. In newer fields, such as information and communication technology, companies like Microsoft and Cisco Systems have grown relentlessly from startup minnows to global megacorporations.

But the phenomenon is not confined to newer, high-growth industries and fields. The rollout of the world’s largest airliner—the A380 superjumbo—reminds us that Airbus, once barely a blip on Boeing’s radar screen, now commands half the world market for wide-body airliners. Likewise, in building materials, the Mexican company CEMEX, founded in 1906, rose from a position of relative obscurity to become a leading global cement producer by the end of the 1990s. Similarly, in the 1990s, Starbucks advanced from a modest U.S.-based coffee retailer to an international cultural phenomenon, and U.K. retailer Tesco has risen from relative obscurity as a discount food-store chain to the undisputed leader in U.K. retailing—in terms of both market share and profitability—and an emerging force among international retailing giants. Certainly there are many individual factors that explain the success of these companies, but the companies all have something in common—a track record of strategic excellence and a determination to stand out from the crowd.

In our intensely competitive world, business leaders increasingly must demonstrate the ability to use strategy to create and take control of the future of their companies. Whatever its defects and disadvantages, capitalism remains a dynamic and self-renewing system, populated by companies large and small that are striving to get on the fast track to business growth and sustained profitability. In this world, corporations are at center stage, and change is endemic. New companies are created, and others change in form and purpose as they try to survive and prosper. Those that fail to make the grade are taken over by rivals or driven out of business. Value creation is the reward of success; value destruction is the price of failure.

In this context, breakout may be associated with the rapid growth of a new industry or market arena or the emergence of a formidable new competitor that rises to become dominant in an established industry. Breakouts typically are accompanied by sudden and dramatic increases in output and levels of activity. From a strategy perspective, what matters is the process by which enterprises come from nowhere to achieve prominence, if not preeminence, in their chosen markets, usually in the space of a few years. In some cases, entirely new companies, such as Dyson and jetBlue, experience breakout. In other cases, established companies, such as Apple and Burberry, break out from existing positions to create or conquer new markets at home and abroad. Whatever the company, the evidence points to strategy and strategic leadership as crucial determinants of success or failure in attempted breakouts, and this book provides the road map to capitalize on these opportunities.

For enterprising business leaders who want to raise a company from a subordinate to a more dominant market position by creating double-digit growth, it is crucial both to pursue the optimal strategy and to excel in its execution. Increasingly, shareholders and the financial markets are expecting double-digit growth on a regular, if not constant, basis. As Charles Lucier, senior vice president emeritus at Booz Allen Hamilton, notes:

> *It used to be that CEOs of major corporations were expected to produce very steady returns, albeit average ones. . . . These days companies are expected to provide annual returns of 15 to 20 percent—a much higher standard than just a decade ago.*[1]

Few companies are able to meet this expectation, particularly on a sustainable basis. But breakout companies can and do. In relation to our reference to double-digit growth, the 15 to 20 percent annual return mentioned by Charles Lucier seems appropriate but somewhat arbitrary. We are emphasizing consistent returns that are well above the industry average, as measured in particular by operating revenue and pretax profit. In a sense, though, we are using the term metaphorically and not defining it more specifically simply because when breakout happens, measures may be imprecise, but success is obvious.

Business potential, driven by social and technological change, is inherent in markets, but it is only through strategy that the potential for rapid growth can be unleashed. A compelling strategy—one that is clear, consistent, distinctive, well grounded, straightforward, and deliverable—is essential for rapid business growth. Examples of success abound: Dell, Disney, Google, Nestlé, Samsung, and IKEA have all been proclaimed as products of the strategic imagination. Yet, for every example of strategic success, it is possible to find an equally spectacular example of strategic failure. The fact is that strategy is a double-edged sword: it can be the source of value creation on a massive scale, but equally, it can be the root cause of cataclysmic failure.

Breakout Strategy Perspectives

All practical business strategies depend in both form and substance on the specific circumstances, internal and external, of the individual company. The approaches presented in this book have validity as analytical categories and sources of insight, but they are not prescriptions for action that can be applied routinely or mechanically. There are few business leaders whose first instinct is to rush for a favorite academic treatise when faced with a major business problem. This having been said, to be grounded in the strategic realities of different types of growth-oriented businesses is certainly of value to any business leader, aspiring business leader, or business analyst. This book is based on our research into what successful and unsuccessful leaders do in the actual circumstances that confront them. This has led us to three broad perspectives on the realities of strategy in companies that regularly turn in double-digit growth figures.

First, during the research for this book, we have found that what is amazing about successful breakout companies is not the sophistication of their approaches to strategy but the brilliance with which they execute a *simple strategy*. Consider how the most successful companies lead with a straightforward, easy-to-understand value proposition—but one that is backed up with robust and finely tuned business models.

Successful retailers such as Wal-Mart and Tesco illustrate the point perfectly, as do the best budget airlines, such as Southwest and Ryanair. The same is true of seemingly more complex organizations such as Microsoft and Fidelity, which, despite their global reach, embrace a focused approach to making and implementing strategy. At Tesco, the value proposition put to the customer is one of consistent good quality, excellent choice and product features, attractive facilities, and high service standards at acceptable prices. It is no secret that the company is positioning itself to serve the broad market space at the center of the food and household retailing industry, but its U.K. rivals have found it remarkably difficult to fight back. Starbucks has shown similar resolution in repeating its outwardly simple formula in seemingly very different markets, and in return, the company has been rewarded by exceptional growth and profitability. Rather than being constrained by overly sophisticated yet essentially wrong-headed policies, companies such as these have found that the most successful approaches often are the simplest, adhering to the realistic and comprehensible practices that are at the heart of winning strategies:

- Creating a workable vision by understanding needs and aspirations
- Facing customers with a value proposition that covers all the important bases
- Aligning what you do with what the customer really wants
- Balancing the people and process sides of business to deliver on your promises
- Liberating the energies of any strategy's toughest critics—those who work within the business

Our second broad finding is that companies that break out successfully, whatever their starting point, have well-thought-out and collaborative strategy processes in place. As might be expected, such processes vary considerably in form and substance among organizations; there is no evidence of the use of common methodologies, templates, tools, or techniques. Yet, although high-growth companies favor the application of organizationally distinctive strategy routines, these routines to some extent are similar to those found elsewhere. They involve, for example, strategy reviews, business planning, formalized setting of strategic objectives and performance targets, and the establishment and monitoring of strategic projects and programs. What makes these processes stand out in breakout companies is their careful alignment with the company's mission and their world-class execution.

Integral to strategy development in many high-growth companies are processes for acquisition and assimilation, innovation and new product development, business growth, and knowledge management. At CEMEX, for example, expansion into emerging markets on a global scale has been made possible through the application of comprehensive acquisition and assimilation procedures. The rapid incorporation of acquired businesses into a global framework supported by advanced information systems has enabled tight cost management, correspondingly high returns on investment, and the generation of high levels of free cash flow to fund further acquisitions in emerging markets.

The third broad perspective we put forward is that close familiarity with organizational context and industry dynamics is a prerequisite for effective strategy making. When companies such as Marconi are brought to their knees, it is most often because of a monumental failure on the part of the leadership team to recognize and understand the difficulties of the course they have embarked on—in this case, making a significant play in a market that is already populated by knowledge-rich and dominant enterprises.

In contrast with Marconi's experience, it is noticeable that many of the most brilliant corporate success stories of modern times feature CEOs who are steeped in the realities of their companies, industries, and markets. Strategic leaders such as Terry Leahy of Tesco, Lorenzo Zambrano of CEMEX, John Browne of BP, Pierre Bellon of Sodexho, Lindsay Owen Jones of L'Oréal, and Jim Koch of Boston Beer Company have served their companies for more than two decades and take a deep personal interest in all aspects of their business, particularly in the experiences and changing demands of customers. These CEOs are lauded as strategists and value creators on a grand scale, yet what impresses most people whenever these CEOs are interviewed is their industry knowledge and their supreme command of operational detail and customer preferences. It is their sureness of touch and grasp of market realities that enables them to be confident that their big moves will maintain profitable growth and strengthen their companies still further.

Five Essential Practices

What is it, then, that differentiates successful breakout companies and leaders from those that get stuck and fail? The answer, this book argues, is that the most effective leaders in the most successful breakout companies employ, in their own particular way, five essential strategy practices. These practices are deeply engrained in the behavioral patterns and mind-sets of these leaders, to the point that they seem instinctive. But—and this is critical—what appears instinctive from a distance actually is the product of careful analysis, thoughtful application, and energetic leadership. The specific strategic routines deployed in high-growth companies reflect the capabilities of these companies' leaders, individually and collectively, and are brought to life through the exercise of day-to-day leadership. It is through strategy, from conception to execution, that business leaders have the greatest opportunity to create or destroy value, and it is to strategy that the most accomplished leaders pay the most attention.

This is not to say that operational efficiency and effectiveness are of little concern. They most emphatically are, because no organization can achieve strategic objectives for long without them. In successful breakout companies, strategy is deeply rooted and inseparable from all matters bearing crucially on business performance. The distinction between what is operational and what is strategic is rarely clear-cut.

The five most essential practices identified through our work are as follows:

1. Pursuit of a corporate vision that is both inward- and outward-looking and is grounded in a realistic assessment of current possibilities and capabilities. We hold that successful breakout leaders have the capacity to articulate a vision of what

the company might become a few years down the road with respect to its market position, internal organization, external relationships, and corporate culture. Such visions go beyond the realm of aspirations because they recognize current constraints and difficulties and thereby help to set a realistic agenda for change. Corporate visions that differentiate between winners and losers also need to go beyond old notions and slogans that are more form than substance. Pursuit of a unified corporate vision is both a more encompassing activity and a process that many companies approach ineffectively. Any worthwhile vision helps in answering the question, "What must be our highest priority if our business is to gain significant forward momentum?" Answering this question and demonstrating to internal and external audiences that the company can have a bright future, with substantial value being created for all stakeholders, results in unity of purpose and the drive and commitment that are essential to any breakout.

2. Identification and progressive improvement of an attractive value proposition that serves as a magnet for existing and potential customers. We find that successful breakout leaders are fully in tune with the main drivers and shapers in their company's chosen markets. They recognize the "hot buttons" that differentiate one product offering from another and are skilled in assembling value propositions that target large, growing, and lucrative market segments. In nascent markets, which breakout companies often serve and in which the potentialities of a new product or service are not yet fully apparent, the breakout leader has the challenge of demonstrating the advantages of purchase to wary and possibly skeptical consumers. In these circumstances, the role of the strategic leader is to define and seek to dominate a new or previously ill-formed market space.

3. Development and continuous refinement of a business model capable of routinely delivering the organization's value proposition. Successful breakout leaders have the capacity not only to shape markets but also to build

organizations that are capable of serving those markets. A company may conceive of a winning value proposition, but if it fails to deliver, it will be dubbed a charlatan and punished by the market as a purveyor of false promises. It therefore is essential to breakout that the company's leaders secure the correct inputs in the right quantities and configure them appropriately according to the requirements of the company's business model. These requirements change frequently as markets grow and evolve, and refreshing and extending organizational resources and capabilities is a constant challenge. Structures, systems, and processes all need to keep pace with the market, as do the number and skills of personnel within the business. It is for this reason that strategy cannot be decoupled lightly from operational requirements.

4. Setting and implementing an agenda to ensure that investment resources are targeted precisely to achieve the organization's vision, value proposition, and business model. Successful breakout leaders have consummate change management and business transformation skills. By its very nature, breakout is a dynamic process involving simultaneous and continuous change in many parts of the business. New is the watchword attached to capacity, distribution, products, personnel, policies, procedures, methods, systems, processes, markets, customers, suppliers, and partners—and holding all these elements together is a monumental task. Avoiding serious error when caught up in such a whirlwind of change requires the leader to engage in detailed planning exercises covering all aspects of the business while simultaneously remaining open to unanticipated opportunities (relating, for example, to acquisitions or strategic alliances). What counts most is that leaders keep a level head, channeling the available resources into the projects and programs that are most critical to the achievement of strategic objectives.

5. Building the commitment of all stakeholders to operational excellence and the achievement of strategic objectives. Successful breakout leaders, as individuals or as members of teams, display the full range of leadership capabilities. It is leadership that inspires internal and external stakeholders to keep faith with the organization and to give their best, often in difficult circumstances. However well breakout companies plan and manage the growth process, there are always a multitude of unanticipated difficulties to contend with. Key employees, for example, who are themselves learning something new each day, have the burden of bringing on desperately needed new recruits while delivering beyond the call of duty at the front line. The imperative is to boost morale by building confidence in the company, keeping the big picture at the fore, developing sound relationships internally and externally, remaining flexible enough to alter course when necessary, and avoiding any hint of panic when times are rough.

In recognizing the prevalence of these five practices in successful breakout companies and their relative absence in those that have failed, we were led to think afresh about business strategy. Rather than taking an abstract, theoretical perspective, we have focused on what can be learned from successful and unsuccessful breakout companies and the experiences of breakout leaders. It was on this basis that we set out to develop our own set of strategy constructs, models, and techniques, encapsulating some of the lessons learned from both triumph and disaster by breakout companies and leaders.

Breakout Strategy as Product and Process

The main aim of this book is to provide entrepreneurs, business leaders, aspiring leaders, and business analysts with the insights, concepts, tools, and techniques needed for the effective appraisal of strategies for corporate growth and transformation. We define *strategy* as *the means by which leaders create and take control of the future*. Strategy is not an abstraction; it is born of action, and it has the very real intention of improving the fortunes of an organization by allowing that organization to break free from existing constraints and limitations. The best strategies are simple and easily communicated but not naive or simplistic, and they have buy-in across the business. A good strategy harnesses and directs the energies of all the people in the organization, fostering enthusiasm, forging identity, and building confidence. By contrast, ill-conceived or unrealistic strategies often fail to penetrate downward from senior management to grip the imaginations of those charged with delivery, and in turn, those at the top often fail to recognize the negative reactions that flawed strategies create in those below.

Strategy making is different from business planning. It is a bigger idea. Sound planning is necessary for the effective delivery of a strategy, but it should be seen as part of a process rather than a discrete activity. Likewise, a business plan is not a strategy; it is just one of a series of outputs that may emerge from the strategy process. Planning is valuable for dealing with changes that are relatively discrete and predictable, defined parts of the jigsaw puzzle, whereas strategy deals with the bigger picture, with fundamentals such as the market space the company is seeking to occupy and how customers or clients will be won and retained. In this sense, strategy may be conceived as the mechanism for binding the many parts of an organization together, expressing unity of purpose, establishing direction, and building the momentum needed for growth and beneficial change.

A further defining feature of strategy as a practical endeavor is the ongoing tension that exists between the constant organizational impulses toward continuity and toward change. If a strategy is to serve its purpose as a mechanism for beneficial change, it cannot be subject to significant alteration on a frequent basis. Continuity of purpose is essential to the successful implementation of a strategy, and a strategy that is not implemented is not a strategy at all—it is window dressing. At the same time, however, no organization can control its external environment completely, and for most companies, markets and competitors regularly deliver shocks to the system that demand a series of appropriate responses. Therefore, learning and flexibility are just as essential to strategy as underlying continuity of purpose, and the incorporation of refinements and changes on a regular and systematic basis is a feature of any sound strategy process. Small changes at regular intervals, of course, may have a significant compound effect on business performance.

In our view, the products and processes of strategy are deeply entwined. The breakout strategy cycle presented in Figure 1.1, which captures each of the five essential practices introduced earlier, underscores the fact that strategy making is an intrinsically iterative process. The four main products of the process at the corporate level are an *organizational vision*, an overarching *value proposition*, a customized *business model*, and a set of *projects and programs* aimed at strengthening the organization's business model to better deliver its value proposition.

Each of these products is the outcome of a particular strategic process. *Strategic thinking* involves critical thinking and high-level

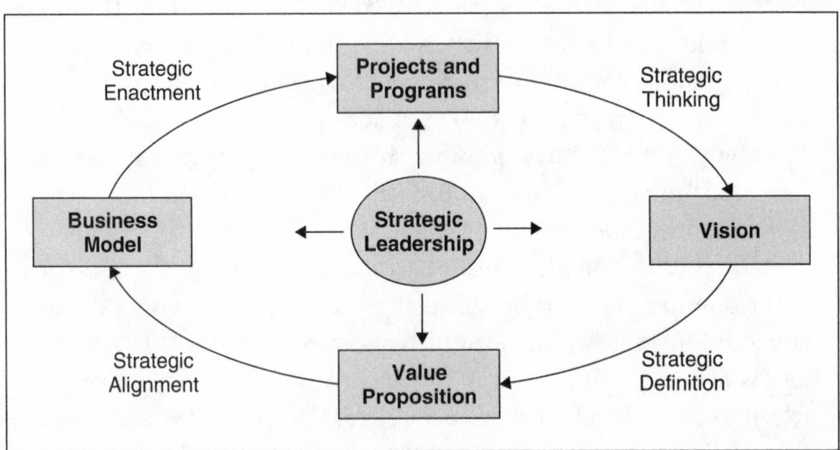

Figure 1.1 The Breakout Strategy Cycle

analysis concerning the market, the industry, and other external developments, as well as the current fitness of the organization to compete successfully from both internal and external standpoints. This is "big picture" thinking that delivers a realistic and grounded assessment of what the organization is now and what it might become in the future.

Strategic definition involves the identification and refinement of an attractive value proposition—the distinctive offering made by the organization to its customers or clients—based on an evaluation of customer behavior and industry dynamics. *Strategic alignment* involves configuring and developing the organization's business model so that the organization can deliver its value proposition effectively and consistently.

Finally, *strategic enactment* involves taking all the actions needed to bring the business model to life, deliver a value proposition, and realize a future vision. It is in this phase of the strategy cycle that strategic and business planning assumes an important role because tradeoffs and choices frequently have to be made, particularly with respect to the allocation of scarce resources.

This book demonstrates repeatedly the importance of viewing strategy holistically. If strategic leaders, whose personal capabilities and qualities are portrayed in Figure 1.1 as illuminating the entire breakout strategy cycle, are inadequate with respect to one or more of the fundamental strategy processes, then the performance of the entire organization will be diminished. However, through the application of good practice, managers can cut through much of the chatter and confusion that surrounds strategy to lay bare what the company really needs to do to hit the fast track to business growth.

A paradox is evident within breakout strategy: rapidly growing or transforming companies may succeed in keeping their strategies simple and consistent, but the changes needed as an organization evolves are numerous and all-embracing. The requirements of breakout invariably are formidable, and if these requirements are not met, then growth will be frustrated.

As a result of overreaching, companies may be forced into unwelcome compromises, possibly diluting or failing to deliver on a value proposition and inflicting severe damage on their reputations as a result.

The case of America Online (AOL) comes to mind. The business grew rapidly from a standing start in 1985 by giving customers at home access to e-mail and the Internet. By 1996, AOL had six million subscribers, but it was beginning to feel the impact of increased competition, as a large proportion of new subscriptions were being offset by defections to flat-rate, unlimited-hours service providers. This led CEO Steven Case to go into marketing overdrive, offering existing and new customers a low-cost flat-rate service with the added benefit of a free trial period, accessed through a widely distributed diskette. Demand for the service skyrocketed; a further two million customers joined AOL between November 1996 and January 1997, and existing users more than doubled the time they spent online. The problem was that AOL had not increased the capacity of its infrastructure in anticipation of the rise in demand, and consequently, the quality of its service deteriorated sharply.

AOL plainly had failed to deliver its value proposition, which led, in turn, to serious legal and reputational challenges that could have been prevented by better strategic management. Effective management of strategic change, as the AOL case confirms, is essential for the execution of those strategies in breakout situations. This is a lesson that is of particular relevance for the modern-day AOL as well, which, after struggling for years with a declining dial-up customer base, has recently positioned itself to benefit from the growth in Internet advertising and again become a prominent player in the industry.

Types of Breakout Strategies

Pursuit of a breakout strategy is not confined to any particular type of company. However, the environmental and local conditions that prevail at the starting point invariably have a major influence on the formation of strategy. In the purest breakout situation, when a new company has been formed to exploit a new product or service, the typical situation is one of capital scarcity. The financial assets that the founder has access to generally are limited, but more positively, there is likely to be some original intellectual property that the company is seeking to exploit, and there may be some supportive business and social relationships arising from the founder's previous activities. There is unlikely to be much realizable brand value or reputational capital unless the founder is blessed with an exceptionally positive personal reputation. Many would-be high-technology firms find themselves at this starting point.

In the case of Cisco Systems, for example, the company was founded with modest financial capital to exploit an original technological breakthrough that enabled two or more computers to talk to one another in a primitive network. The founders had extensive personal relationships in a technology-hungry university environment, and they quickly attracted others to the vision of easy electronic communication, data transfer, and resource sharing through ever-expanding computer networks. What happened next is well known. The new technology found favor in the market. As the market leader, Cisco could charge premium prices for its devices. Cash flow was strong from an early date. The cash was reinvested in more advances in technology, developed in-house, or brought in through acquisitions. As sales grew, prestigious customers were brought on board, and brand and reputational assets accumulated. Likewise, a series of technology partnerships and alliances created new possibilities for growth. A virtuous circle was established, taking the company from a front-room business to a multinational enterprise in the space of a few years.

The breakout of Cisco, like that of Microsoft, was remarkable for its rapidity and the brilliance of its execution. It demonstrates that breakout is a dynamic process in which the asset base of the organization is forever growing and changing, with one form of capital being transformed continuously into others. In this case, the original knowledge and social assets powered the creation of financial, organizational, and brand assets, which, in turn, were transformed through a multitude of resource-allocation decisions into further knowledge, organizational, and reputational assets.

The same principles apply in other forms of breakout. Over the course of its long history, IBM has reinvented itself several times—most recently as a business services company under the banner of "e-business on demand." Each of these reinventions has seen the company break out from one position to create a new position in the business world, with dramatic shifts in the proportions of revenues coming from its main business sectors.

The changes in statistical indicators are just as dramatic as those for start-up breakouts and in some ways are even more impressive. However, the starting point is different. Established businesses generally begin with extensive organizational and reputational assets and ready access to financial resources. Breakout is intended to carry the enterprise into new markets that offer the prospect of higher returns on the capital employed in the business. To make this possible, financial capital has to be transformed into knowledge-based assets in the form of fresh intellectual property and know-how. In its bid to become a highly responsive supplier of business services, IBM acquired the global consulting business of PwC at a cost of $3.5 billion. Armed with this new capability, the company moved forward with an enhanced value proposition and reengineered its business model to deliver that proposition. By any standard, this was a bold move—a classic example of an essentially simple strategy requiring implementation skills of the highest order.

The Cisco and IBM cases illustrate two of the four generic types of breakout discussed in this book. The first of these is that of the high-growth startup, where a recently formed company seemingly comes from nowhere to create an enterprise of significance within the space of a few years. We call this *taking by storm*, and it is exemplified by the rise to prominence of such companies as Cisco, Dyson (the household appliance manufacturer best known for its cyclone vacuum cleaner), the U.S. low-price airline jetBlue, the electronic auction site eBay, and the global catering services company Sodexho.

The second generic form of breakout occurs when an established company that has languished for some years in the doldrums is revived by new leadership and a new strategy and turned from laggard to leader in its field. The *laggard-to-leader* type of breakout is typified by companies such as motorcycle maker Harley-Davidson and clothier Burberry, whose brands have been energized in recent times, with highly beneficial consequences for growth and profitability.

The third type of breakout we call *expanding horizons*, which refers to the rapid expansion of a company from a narrow (local-regional) to a broad (national-international) geographic base. Classic examples are the international spread of the Starbucks coffee chain, cement maker CEMEX, the Best Western hotel group, and the Japanese car maker Toyota.

The fourth and final type of breakout, typified by the most recent reinvention of IBM, we refer to as *shifting shape*. This occurs when an established company makes a radical move away from its existing core business by seizing a transformational new business opportunity and in the process turns itself into a very different kind of company. Illustrating this form of corporate renewal are the transformation of Apple from a maker of personal computer systems to a global leader in multimedia and the radical repositioning of winemaker E.&J. Gallo from a mass producer of low-end wine to a differentiated producer of a distinctive family of higher-quality wines.

There is a deep situational logic inherent in each of these four forms of breakout, and that logic is captured in Figure 1.2. A company's initial scope and industry standing determine the breakout path that company takes. Startup companies almost invariably are small, narrowly focused, and in subordinate positions within their chosen industries and markets. In order to grow strong in any emerging or established industry in which economies of scale and scope are significant, they must change the competitive landscape by offering products or services with value propositions so compelling that they carve out new market spaces or take over parts of markets previously occupied by established suppliers. This is exactly what Google has done in Internet search, for example, by essentially creating a new set of products whose value to customers is immediately apparent.

INITIAL SCOPE	INITIAL INDUSTRY STANDING: Subordinate	INITIAL INDUSTRY STANDING: Dominant
Narrow	Taking by Storm	Expanding Horizons
Broad	Laggard to Leader	Shifting Shape

Figure 1.2 Breakout Types

The challenge for every ambitious new venture is to take the market by storm—to win business quickly at prices that yield margins generous enough to fund expansion though borrowing, attracting fresh equity, or generating significant free cash flow. The strategic objective is to move the business swiftly from a subordinate to a more dominant market position in order to fend off the inevitable competitive challenges from rival companies. In the process, senior management must oversee the creation, in the context of rapid growth and structural change, of a brand-new organization with a business model that is sufficiently robust to deliver the company's advertised value proposition. Any failure in this regard is sure to lead to damage to the company's reputation, stunted growth, and eventual dissolution as competitors take advantage of the company's faltering attempt to break out and overcome the limitations of size and substance. The fact is that in dynamic industries, getting on the fast track to business growth by pursuing a well-executed breakout strategy often may be a matter of organizational survival as well as one of business growth.

The strategic challenges facing leaders of large, established companies that are performing poorly are in some ways similar to those of startup companies, but in other ways very different. Similarities arise from the fact that poor performance is manifested by low returns and modest and sometimes negative free cash flow. Companies such as these are subordinate to industry leaders; they are trend followers rather than pacesetters, and they find it difficult to command or sustain premium prices. They have relatively weak value propositions and creaky business models. The strategic challenge, like that facing start-up companies, is how to get from a modest starting position onto the fast track to business growth before suffering the indignities of takeover or liquidation.

Here the similarities end. These companies have the advantages of an established brand and sufficient organizational capabilities to have continued doing business on an extensive scale. The urgent need is to build on what is good and eliminate the problems that have led to underperformance. Typically, this involves strengthening the company's value proposition and business model. It is here that many senior management teams flounder. Turnaround situations are difficult for many reasons, including lack of resources, weak systems, poor middle management, and an inherent cultural resistance to change. One of the main advantages of start-up companies is their freedom from accumulated corporate problems. To go from being an industry *laggard* to a *leader* demands strategic change management skills of an order that few companies are lucky enough to possess. Certainly such leadership skills were central to the transformation at Harley-Davidson, which went from a poorly performing manufacturing company to a branding juggernaut that not only boasts the best-known brand in its industry but also is involved in restaurants, clothing, and financial services, among other ventures.

Dominant companies are far better placed to break out than those that are lower in the corporate pecking order. A typical situation is for a company that has grown strong at the regional or national level, thereby exhibiting a compelling value proposition and capacity to deliver, to seek to expand its horizons and operate across a broader geographic area. In such cases, the strategic goal is to increase the scale and geographic scope of operations while keeping the business focused on the delivery of a proven value proposition. Value is created through integrating and improving previously geographically separate businesses in established markets, as banking giant HSBC has done, or via the duplication of existing activities and the physical expansion of market space, as in the case of a company like Coca-Cola.

For the low-fare, no-frills airline easyJet, this has meant adding more airport hubs and destinations across Europe, systematically increasing its physical capacity to deliver while rigorously maintaining common systems, standards, and pricing models. The particular challenges of this type of breakout arise from the need to operate across multiple cultures and jurisdictions. However standardized a company may wish to keep its products and operating models, it invariably has to make compromises in order to satisfy local tastes, values, customs, and regulations. This implies considerable learning and increased sophistication in terms of organizational routines and practices.

The best breakout situation of all might be that of dominant companies that are already operating on a truly global basis. Dominance implies the ability to command and shape markets through continuous improvements in products and business processes. Dominant companies already have all-round organizational capabilities and typically are rich in knowledge, network, and reputational assets. They have large revenues, accumulated financial assets, and strong free cash flows. This places them in an enviable position in labor markets, especially in their ability to attract and retain top talent. They have the financial resources needed to innovate and change. Yet, even at the very pinnacle of the corporate world, all is not plain sailing, and seemingly invincible business positions can be undermined quickly if the application of due care and attention is lacking. Rivals with lower costs can copy and improve on products, switching some products from premium price to commodity.

It is for this reason that from time to time, even dominant companies operating on a global basis are driven to move on, to break out into newer, more lucrative markets, and to shift shape in real time. This is precisely the challenge confronting General Motors today. Lessons emerge from a study of shape shifters, such as IBM and Samsung, that have broken out from broad and dominant positions because they feared that these positions were unsustainable. IBM has shifted toward business services and e-solutions, having lost its advantage in its previously core computer hardware and software businesses. Samsung has moved from being an imitator of a disparate range of electronic products to being an innovative, focused developer of high-value, technology-rich, and design-centric products. It has done so in response to both shareholder demands for greater returns and the threat that lower-cost rivals might undercut the company in the commodity sector. The future for Samsung, the company announced, should be to build on its latent potential and become a truly world-class high-technology company.

Research Foundations

The perspective we bring as authors of this book is based on years of studying strategy and leadership in organizations not only in academic settings, but also through active engagement with leaders in private- and public-sector organizations in many parts of the world. Our roles with these leaders have included executive educator, consultant, and trusted advisor. It was from listening carefully to these leaders and exchanging ideas with them that the perspectives and concepts presented in the book began to take shape. In particular, we were alerted to the fact that many business leaders, individually and in team settings, had three important questions at the forefront of their minds. First, how does my company break free from the constraints that threaten to limit its growth, business development, and profitability? Second, how does my company engage more fully and creatively with the strategy process to capture and run with ideas that will bring about a step-change improvement in business performance? Third, how do I, as a business leader, have more impact as a practical strategist?

These three questions resonated with us. We began to trade ideas and stories concerning breakout companies, strategy, and leaders, and it soon became apparent that while they had no easy answers, these questions were an excellent foundation for a research agenda. A compact was formed and a fundamental decision taken—that we would research breakout strategy from the standpoint of what successful and unsuccessful breakout companies and leaders *actually do in practice* rather than approaching the subject with pre-existing theoretical ideas. The decision to work primarily from experience to theory rather than vice versa proved liberating in two ways. First, it led naturally to the decision to develop multiple case studies as the primary means of gathering data. Each of us had already researched a number of cases, and we could update and build on some of these as pilot studies before engaging in more extensive research and analysis. Second, it freed us to test and refine emerging models and techniques with managerial audiences in live settings with real company data. Many of the concepts presented here were forged and developed in this way, and we are grateful to the many workshop participants and interviewees who have contributed to the formation of our ideas.

In total, we compiled more than 100 breakout case studies for this research. The appendix provides the entire list of companies and individuals mentioned in this book. Some cases were explored in much more depth than others and inevitably are referred to more extensively. Some are talked about only briefly here and there, whereas others are used at length in one or more chapters. Data were drawn from a variety of sources, including annual reports and accounts; company Web sites; published interviews with business leaders; newspaper and magazine articles; academic books, articles, and case studies; and company analyses accessed through information services such as Datamonitor, Factiva, Global Business Browser, and MarketLine. In 16 cases, we had privileged access to additional information from business leaders within the case company. In 22 other cases, one of us had conducted extensive research on the company and was well placed to develop the case in question. In selecting cases, we consciously sought to identify breakout companies from a range of business sectors and a variety of countries. The sample frame includes companies from the following sectors: aviation, automobiles, entertainment, education, biotechnology, food and beverages, consumer and industrial electronics, hotels, fashion and design, financial services, cosmetics, information and communication technology, media, retail and restaurants, steel, dot-com, Internet service providers, and energy. The companies have their roots in different countries and in various parts of the world—North America, Europe, and Asia-Pacific—enabling us to avoid problems of cultural bias and to respect the differing business traditions and practices to be found around the globe.

The Book in Brief

In this opening chapter, we have introduced the concept and themes of breakout strategy and explained their relevance to success or failure within the ever-changing world of corporate capitalism. We have argued that successful breakout companies and leaders embrace five essential strategy practices and that these are brought to life in four types of breakout, which we call *taking by storm*, *laggard to leader*, *expanding horizons*, and *shifting shape*.

In Chapters 2 and 3 we build on and illuminate our breakout strategy typology. Chapter 2 examines how subordinate companies—new ventures and laggard enterprises—break out and get on the fast track to business growth. Chapter 3 considers how already dominant companies plan to stay out front, either by expanding geographically or by reinventing themselves from within. The aim of both chapters, in comparing and contrasting successful and unsuccessful companies, is to discern patterns, teasing out the common strategic and leadership characteristics that are the hallmarks of companies with double-digit growth.

The analysis is deepened further in Chapter 4, which explores how the dynamics of breakout can be understood better and managed more effectively by skilled business leaders.

The next four chapters (Chapters 5 through 8) focus one by one on four of the five essential breakout strategy practices outlined earlier. In each chapter, models or frameworks are introduced that encapsulate the thinking and practices of successful breakout companies. Chapter 5 is concerned with the formation, content, and application of an organizational vision. Chapter 6 defines the elements of a value proposition and shows how compelling propositions create magnet companies. Chapter 7 shows that a business model is the counterpart of a value proposition, a unique disposition of organizational assets and routines designed to ensure the consistent delivery of a value proposition. This sets the scene for Chapter 8, which demonstrates how projects and programs can best be designed to effect strategic change and deliver breakout. When taken together, the models and frameworks presented in these chapters constitute a robust and holistic system for strategy development and implementation.

The question of how this approach to breakout strategy might be brought to life through the exercise of strategic leadership is the subject of Chapter 9. Issues relating to transformational change form the context for an exploration of breakout leadership capabilities and how business leaders develop these capabilities. The main objective is to guide existing and aspiring business leaders in the improvement of their strategic leadership skills.

Conclusion

The evidence of far-reaching change in the world of corporate capitalism is all around us. Companies from China, India, Russia, and a plethora of emerging economies that were once held in check by regulation and statism have increased competitive pressures and reshaped the global economic order. In this new order, opportunities abound, but so do the possibilities for strategic error. Increasing interdependence with respect to supply chains, markets, finance, and risk has made for more complexity, not less, as companies have entered into a variety of alliances, partnerships, and joint ventures. In order to break out, survive, and prosper in this challenging environment, companies must become ever more strategically adept. Those that lack first-rate strategic capabilities invariably find it difficult to chart a viable course, are more vulnerable to competitive attacks, and are in danger of making costly, sometimes fatal mistakes.

This book is a research-based work with an emphatically practical purpose. It is predicated on the argument that strategy as a practical pursuit is the core activity of business leaders in growth-oriented breakout companies. Within this context, the research presented highlights the importance of both companies and business leaders choosing a path to breakout (sometimes more than one) and assimilating five essential strategy practices while doing so. These practices are given practical expression in different ways in different companies. By synthesizing, interpreting, and abstracting from both best and worst practices, we have been able to develop a comprehensive set of models, tools, and techniques for strategy development and implementation.

These are presented in what follows not as prescriptions, but as a practical guide to the practices that have taken some of the world's most successful companies from strength to strength.

Endnote

1 Charles Lucier, quoted in Irwin Speizer, "The Best CEOs in America," *Institutional Investor* 40(1):36, January 2006.

CHAPTER 2

GETTING ON THE FAST TRACK

The thrill of capitalism lies in its being simultaneously light and dark, creative and destructive. Companies that seemingly come from nowhere to achieve market dominance may create value, but invariably they damage, if not destroy, other companies in the process. When new products and services find favor with customers and clients, one-time market leaders must respond appropriately or suffer the consequences. We have to think only of the triumphs of such companies as AirAsia, Dyson, and eBay to recognize the radical nature of the process by which new entrants make and remake entire industries.

In this chapter we go behind the scenes to demonstrate that what looks like a company's coming from nowhere and achieving prominence, if not preeminence, in an industry is never as simple as that. What matters most is how companies contain and manage, through strategy, the complex web of transformations required to create new products and capabilities. Our research into such companies as Boston Beer Company, Google, and the Apollo Group and iconic enterprises such as the design company William Morris reveals what companies must do to get on the fast track to business growth—to emerge from the pack to inspire customers and chasten competitors.

Taking by storm is perhaps the purest form of breakout strategy. The company intends to win market share as quickly as possible by launching a value proposition so compelling that sales, revenues, and free cash flow all move upward before existing and potential rivals wake up to the fact that something special is happening. Speed and surprise are of the essence. Before such companies truly register on competitors' radar screens, they have already bonded with first-wave customers, enticing them with new or better value offerings.

If companies taking by storm were noticed and taken seriously before they gained a foothold in the market, their competitive maneuverings might be severely constrained by the responses of established competitors. A brief example is instructive. When Britain's leading employment agency, Reed Executive, started out in 1960, it first located near London's burgeoning Heathrow Airport. This choice of location proved decisive. Business boomed from the beginning, enabling the agency's founder, Alec Reed, to leverage his business and quickly lay the foundations for a national chain. Reed was very canny; he was careful not to celebrate his success, and he was conscious of the need to keep a low profile lest bigger and more powerful competitors such as Alfred Marks move in to challenge him on his own ground. In an interview, Reed was asked to explain why his business had been a near-instant success. He responded:

> *I charged more than anybody else. Honestly, that's the best thing I ever did. I charged 25 percent more than the competition. . . . I grew up in the area, and it was one of the hottest markets around in the country, probably in the world. . . . It gave us tremendous power. . . . We had more money to spend on advertising and more business in turn. And then we had freshness about the place. We had very crude advertising, but it was fresh every week. And people know if you are fresh and have more polish, and they are attracted to you. . . . It was sort of like a gold rush actually. We opened more branches, and we then in fact bought another small agency—the only thing we have ever bought—an agency with ten branches.*[1]

Reed kept it simple. He ploughed his profits back into the firm to build momentum, advertising and opening new branches so that he could become a large player and establish his brand before competitive pressures forced him to reduce his prices. He recognized early that to take the industry by storm, he needed to execute this simple approach with brilliance and conviction: "We had loads and loads of ideas, and we were refreshing things all the time to keep ahead of the game."

It is not only new entrants that make or remake industries. From time to time, a slumbering enterprise awakens, is transformed, and gets on the fast track to business growth. Adidas, Renault-Nissan, and Texas Instruments, for example, are companies that were enlivened through strategic regeneration. Interesting questions abound: What led to the awakening? How was the new vision formed and the new direction set? How did they shed the cultural baggage of the past? What caused stakeholders to get on board and grow in confidence? How were the inevitable credibility gaps overcome?

Once again, the evidence points to clarity, simplicity, and systematic execution of strategy as vital ingredients in the transformation process. A classic example of the *laggard-to-leader* form of breakout strategy is provided by the British fashion house Burberry, where in the late 1990s a new leadership team reinvigorated the brand, creating an explosion of interest among younger consumers in its distinctively styled, authentically British products. Prior to its big surge forward, Burberry had been content to adhere to industry norms and practices; it was safe in its market niche and making positive returns, but it was not realizing its full potential or standing out from the crowd.

The company's complacency was shattered following the appointment of an American, Rose Marie Bravo, as CEO in 1997, lured from Saks Fifth Avenue in New York. Top designers Robert Menichetti and Christopher Bailey were hired to use the signature Burberry camel, red, black, and white plaid in a range of fashionable products to attract better-off, highly aspirational customers. Advertising, promotion, sales outlets, and logistics were all aligned in a strategy of delivering a wide range of distinctive and prestigious fashion items to increasing numbers of high-income consumers in large cities across the globe.

In essence, the transformation of Burberry from laggard to leader has not involved a fundamental change in the company's values or identity; instead, the company's aspirations and performance have been lifted dramatically through the adoption of a simple yet compelling breakout strategy.

Four Ways of Getting on the Fast Track

The magic of any type of breakout strategy lies not in the strategy itself but in its fine details and implementation, as the Reed and Burberry cases suggest. It is not possible to develop a universally applicable formula for growth because every business situation depends on a myriad of circumstances relating to markets, competitors, and organizational capabilities. We can, however, learn to *read strategic situations* and *manage strategic processes.*

It is important to recognize, for instance, that companies that are endeavoring to get on the fast track to business growth are doing so from very different starting positions. Our research has led us to the conclusion, given expression in Figure 2.1, that there are in fact two main types associated with each breakout strategy. These types depend, in turn, on the nature of the growth opportunities that the company perceives. All major growth opportunities ultimately require a superior value proposition, but there is a clear division between a proposition targeted to an emergent market and one targeted to an established market.

Companies that pursue a taking-by-storm strategy in an emergent-market context are *true originals.* These companies typically are first or near first to market with a product or service whose features strongly resonate with the latent demands of potential customers. They tap into a previously unmet or

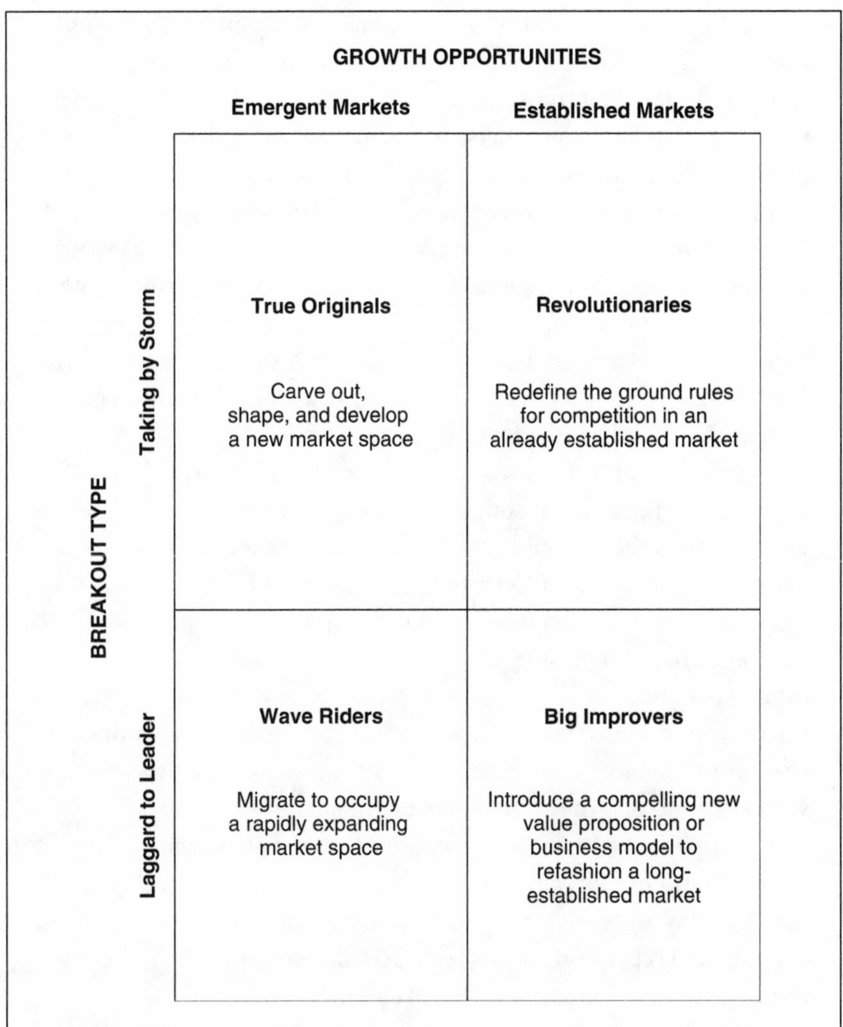

Figure 2.1 Companies Getting on the Fast Track

unperceived reservoir of demand, and when that reservoir is large, the effect is akin to an oil exploration company's "hitting a gusher." Rapid growth ensues. If the company is able to keep pace with the market, it becomes established as a market leader and is able to reap exceptional first-mover advantages, including the ability to command premium prices and generate internally the financial resources needed for double-digit growth.

In exceptional circumstances, consumer fealty to the company is so strong that the brand becomes identified with the name of the product; outstanding examples are Hoover and the vacuum cleaner in the past and, more recently, Google and the Internet search engine. Other notable technological true originals identified through our research include Bell Telephone (AT&T since 1899), Edison General Electric (General Electric after a merger with Thomson-Houston in 1892), Research in Motion (famed for the Blackberry), Cisco Systems, and eBay. Outside the technological arena, we have researched true originals as different in nature as the iconic British design company William Morris (founded in 1862) and the high school nostalgia company Friends Reunited. Each demonstrates the crucial importance for business growth of recognizing the previously unseen potential for markets to emerge, take shape, and gain critical mass within the space of just a few years.

Companies that pursue a taking-by-storm breakout in an established-market context are *revolutionaries*. These companies pursue rapid growth by changing the competitive rules of their chosen markets in a fundamental way. They may be just as innovative as true originals, but their brilliance takes the form of radically improving an existing product or service rather than of creating an entirely new market. They aim to win market share very quickly by giving customers a much better deal than those that are currently on offer from existing suppliers—by delivering a superior product, a lower price, or both.

The already-cited case of Reed Executive is a good example. Before Reed appeared on the scene, recruitment services paid little attention to adding value through enhanced service features such as providing detailed skills testing for temporary personnel. Other examples abound. The Boston Beer Company, founded by Jim Koch in 1984, triggered the microbrewery revolution in the United States by producing high-quality beers such as Sam Adams Boston Lager for more discerning upper-income consumers. In the world of education, the Apollo Group—through its University of Phoenix subsidiary—successfully challenged traditional universities' domination of higher education by creating flexible, career-related learning opportunities for working people, first in the United States and later in other parts of the world. In personal, home, and auto insurance, revolutionary start-up companies such as the United Kingdom's Direct Line, which cut out brokers and other sales intermediaries, have enjoyed rapid growth by simultaneously offering lower prices, improved product features, and better service.

The breakout phenomenon is not confined to start-up companies such as Google, eBay, the Apollo Group, and Dyson. Laggards may be turned into leaders through successful pursuit of a transformational, growth-oriented breakout strategy, and in these cases, too, the basic distinction between emergent and established markets applies. Companies that pursue a laggard-to-leader strategy in an emergent-market context are *wave riders*. These companies have not previously displayed much potential for growth or transformation, but are trying to move from a subordinate to a dominant competitive position. At some point, and for reasons not always easily discerned by outsiders, they recognize the potential of an emerging market trend and make the decision to enter the competitive fray.

History affords many examples. The French company Michelin was founded in 1832 and for 50 years confined its activities to manufacturing industrial pumps and agricultural machinery on a small scale. Its breakout dates from 1891, when the company began to manufacture detachable pneumatic tires that made bicycling more comfortable and enjoyable. Michelin went on to ride successive waves of new modes of transportation from bicycles to automobiles and airplanes, becoming in time a technological leader and a first-rank global enterprise.

In a similar fashion, Glaxo, founded in New Zealand in 1873 to manufacture dried-milk products, was transformed after 1935 into a leading British pharmaceutical company; it is now part of the global giant GlaxoSmithKline. Equally dramatic is the taking-by-storm breakout of the French-based international catering-services group Sodexho under the leadership of Pierre Bellon, its chairman and CEO. Bellon's family had run a modest maritime catering business for cruise ships for over 60 years before Bellon recognized the growth potential of the onshore contract catering business. He founded Sodexho in 1966 and embarked on a sustained quest for expansion, transforming the company into a global leader in food services and facilities management.[2]

Companies that pursue a laggard-to-leader strategy in an established-market context are *big improvers.* These companies stand out by suddenly coming to market with a radically improved value proposition. Customers quickly become aware that the company has changed dramatically for the better; as a consequence, its revenues, reputation, and profits all move upward in a benign spiral of growth.

This is what happened at both Best Buy and Burberry, and it is mirrored in many other case companies. Harley-Davidson, for example, was on the verge of bankruptcy in 1983, having suffered badly from competition with more technologically sophisticated Japanese rivals that could offer better motorcycles at lower prices. Only by reducing prices while simultaneously improving reliability, product features, and customer support could the company hope to survive. It has done this to a spectacular degree, with the rewards being soaring sales, a bulging order book, high customer satisfaction rates, premium prices, and high profit margins. Comparable success stories include the revival of Home Depot and Texas Instruments over the past decade and the spectacular rise of Tesco to become the United Kingdom's number-one retailer, far ahead of its nearest rivals.

Our research into each of the four types of fast-track companies confirms that breakout invariably involves the formation and pursuit of a guiding vision and the putting together and delivery of a truly compelling value proposition. What is more difficult to discern, however, is what sets these companies apart from their lesser competitors, allowing them to go so far in such a short period of time. It is this search for more elusive qualities that we now turn to by looking in more depth at the breakout experiences of selected true originals, revolutionaries, wave riders, and big improvers.

True Originals

As a musical artist, Bob Dylan indisputably is a true original. In the early 1960s, he carved out, shaped, and developed an entirely new market space within the contemporary music firmament. When Dylan left Minneapolis for New York in 1960, at age 19, he was an aspiring folk musician who could sing and play the guitar and harmonica. He played other people's songs in his own distinctive style, and, like many others, he began his career by playing the folk music clubs and bars in and around Greenwich Village. Here, folk artists of all types and varying degrees of competence vied for attention. There was little money to be earned, and Dylan lived cheaply, relying on the goodwill of friends and acquaintances for somewhere to sleep. He was acutely aware of the gulf between his aspirations and his present status.

How, then, did Dylan move from being an unknown to being an international superstar within just a few years? What led to his being signed by a major record label, Columbia Records, and the release of his debut album in 1962? How did he succeed in taking the market by storm over the next few years? The trite but frequently cited explanation for his spectacular breakout is that the youth of America were quick to recognize Dylan's genius; his words and music tapped into, reflected, and expressed the changing spirit of the times.

There is undoubtedly some truth in this, but exceptional creativity and happenstance alone are not sufficient to explain why Dylan emerged from the pack to capture the imagination of a generation. What Dylan had, and the majority of his fellow musicians did not have, was an instinctive understanding of how the game was played in the music business. He was able to take stock of his position, to set himself goals for improvement, and to take the practical steps necessary for breakout. Dylan was a clever analyst, tactician, and strategist.

Dylan's brilliance as a practical strategist who made the most of his creative talents and originality can be seen in the way he spent his time and the choices he made immediately prior to his breakout. Most obviously, he was a prodigious and accomplished social networker. He took the time and trouble to get to know and learn from the top folk artists of the day, such as Dave Van Ronk and Woody Guthrie, and he used his connections to get on the bill at top folk music venues such as the Gaslight and Gerde's Folk City, giving him much wider exposure than otherwise would have been possible. It was following a performance at Gerde's in the autumn of 1961, which got a rave review in the *New York Times*, that Dylan was signed to Columbia by the legendary record producer John Hammond.

Less obviously, but equally crucial to his breakout, during his early years in New York, Dylan worked very hard and deliberately to find his distinctive voice. He cultivated a unique and arresting performance style, reworking old songs and playing them very fast. He read widely—literature, history, poetry, the classics, biography, psychology, and social theory—acquiring images and allusions that he would use in his later work. By degrees, he gained the confidence, skill, and knowledge needed to compose original songs. In a telling passage in his 2005 autobiography, *Chronicles*, he explained

> *You want to write songs that are bigger than life. You want to say something about the strange things that have happened to you, strange things that you have seen. You have to know and understand something and then go past the vernacular. . . . What I did to break away was to take simple folk changes and put new imagery and attitude to them, use catchphrases and metaphor combined with a new set of ordinances that evolved into something different that had not been heard before. . . . One thing for sure, if I wanted to write folk songs, I would need some kind of new template, some philosophical entity that wouldn't burn out.*[3]

When Dylan signed with Columbia in 1961, the company had seen enough to believe that he was a star in the making, but he had not yet completely formulated his "new template." This came with the album "The Freewheelin' Bob Dylan," which contained nine original songs and marked his breakout as an original artist. By creating the new template, Dylan had created a new and compelling value proposition, carefully crafted to meet the needs of the market space he was seeking to occupy. The songs were original, elliptical, melodic, and beautifully performed. They were perfectly in tune with the sentiments of the generation that filled the university and college campuses across North America and Europe.

The decision to sign with Columbia, a behemoth of the establishment, may seem strange for a musician who is popularly seen as "the voice of protest." But Dylan always was more than this. He was ambitious and hungry for commercial success. Columbia was best placed to exploit his talent. It had global capabilities in production, distribution, marketing, and publicity, and, as Dylan was well aware, it knew how to make him a star.

In 1861, almost exactly a century before Bob Dylan launched his recording career, the British craftsman-designer William Morris founded Morris & Co., one of the most original and influential design houses of the modern age.[4] "The firm," as it was known prior to its dissolution in 1940, is best remembered for its stained glass, furniture, wallpapers, fabrics, carpets, and tapestries, as well as for major interior design commissions for public buildings and private houses. Many Morris flat-pattern designs for wallpapers, fabrics, and carpets are still in production today, having a vital living quality—a timelessness—that the work of lesser designers almost invariably lacks.

The characteristic flowing lines, intricate patterns, and bold coloring of Morris designs are suggestive, rather than imitative, of nature and are so familiar that the appellation *Morrisian* sometimes is used as a shorthand term for the output of the entire arts and crafts movement of the later nineteenth century. Breakout, it may be concluded, is a root cause of change, of discontinuity and disruption in markets and in society more generally. It is identified by a "sudden dash," the breaking onto the scene of a new product, brand, person, or company. At its most extreme, in the cultural sphere, you may have little or no awareness of a creative talent one day, but by the next day there is seemingly no escaping that artist's presence.

True originals such as Morris and Dylan are iconic cultural figures precisely because of the effect they have on the cultural landscape. However, we should not lose sight of the fact that their celebrity stems ultimately from their commercial success, which, in turn, was the product of practical strategy and deliberate action. Breakout is rarely, if ever, accidental. In the case of Morris, the firm was launched with the circulation of a prospectus announcing that its owners, which included the Pre-Raphaelite artists Rossetti, Madox Brown, and Burne-Jones, felt the "want of some one place, where they could either obtain or get produced work of a genuine or beautiful character." By combining their talents, they intended to rectify the situation, offering customers "good decoration, involving *the luxury of taste rather than the luxury of costliness*." This went to the heart of the firm's value proposition.

However, only by taking full advantage of its extensive social network, which spanned all sections of the ruling elite, could the firm break out so spiritedly. As with Dylan, immediate traction in the market inspired a positive creative response while stimulating demand for more and better designs and products. The firm's reputation for value, originality, and quality went from strength to strength; its products and services were eagerly sought after by the burgeoning middle and upper middle classes of the English-speaking world.

True originals such as Dylan and Morris have an enduring and transformational impact on society. They introduce to the world products that satisfy a widely felt, if previously unarticulated, need, and in the process they shape the way in which large numbers of people think, feel, and live their lives.

The breakout of the Internet search and indexing company Google since 1998 is a cultural phenomenon of similar magnitude. Google was the brainchild of two Stanford University computer science graduates, Larry Page and Sergey Brin, who as graduate students in the mid-1990s developed algorithms and software systems for ultrarapid Internet search and indexing. Search engines already existed, but none of them had the technological sophistication of Google, which returns answers to queries with lightning speed and ranks them by their likely importance and accuracy. Google surely has a long way to go before it satisfies Larry Page's definition of the perfect search engine as one that "understands exactly what you mean and gives you back exactly what you want." Even so, Google has improved the lives of countless millions of people by making valuable information routinely accessible at no cost.

For the user, Google's service is fast, reliable, easy to use, and free of charge because the company's business model calls for Google to generate revenues through contextually relevant advertising and by making its technology available to other service providers. This, indeed, is a compelling value proposition to both end users and advertisers, and it accounts for the remarkable expansion of the service across the world.

Google is a classic case of breakout strategy in action. The company has the straightforward but supremely ambitious goal of organizing the world's information and making it universally accessible. Its aim is to improve the user experience, to make the service available to as many people as possible, and to develop new search technologies and products. Investment resources are ploughed into infrastructure development, search-technology research, and operational improvements. From all this has sprung wireless search technology, different language versions, the capacity to handle documents in numerous formats, and customized search tools and services. It is a story of exceptional growth and organizational transformation from a small company to a global corporation within a few dramatic years.

To achieve this, Google put together an experienced senior management team under the leadership of CEO Eric Schmidt, and it created robust financial and commercial systems to complement its technological capabilities. Management leveraged the company's knowledge assets though partnerships with market-leading companies while cultivating the contacts and relationships that were needed to gain access to rapidly emerging markets. In this, Google has been greatly assisted by publicly putting social purpose ahead of making money as the ultimate goal of the organization. At the time of Google's first public stock offering in 2004, the founders made their position clear to potential investors[5]:

> *When Sergey and I founded Google, we hoped, but did not expect, it would reach its current size and influence. Our intense and enduring interest was to objectively help people find information efficiently. We also believed that searching and organizing all of the world's information was an unusually important task that should be carried out by a company that is trustworthy and interested in the public good. We believe that a well-functioning society should have abundant, free and unbiased access to high quality information. Google therefore has a responsibility to the world.*[6]

Google's founders did not see having a higher social purpose as being incompatible with business growth and profitability—echoing the sentiments of William Morris long before, when he remarked perspicaciously that "beauty is a marketable commodity." True originals, we may conclude, have their finger on the pulse of their time, showing an ability to rise above the immediate and focus on the satisfaction of important social needs, capturing the *Zeitgeist* of the moment, and tapping into the fact that, in Dylan's immortal words, "the times they are a-changin." In doing so, they help to form and forge the future. They also have the discipline, perseverance, and capabilities needed to deliver what they promise.

Revolutionaries

Revolutionary companies invariably are intensely market-facing. They perceive that customers could and should get a much better deal than any that are presently being offered. They may identify quality or performance problems with existing products, or they may see ways of delivering products of similar quality at much lower prices. In essence, they believe that incumbent suppliers have become inward-facing and self-serving, comfortably complacent rather than dedicated to improving the lot of the customer. Upon entering the market, they almost invariably position themselves as "champions of the people," as luminaries striving for a much better deal for customers.

Jim Koch of the Boston Beer Company, for example, championed the cause of flavorful, high-quality beers brewed in the United States using traditional methods, with no artificial additives and only the finest ingredients. His starting position was to characterize the U.S. beer market of the early 1980s as having settled down into dull uniformity, dominated by mass-market brewers such as Miller and Anheuser-Busch, with the only real alternative to blandness being provided by imported foreign beers. The launch of Sam Adams in 1984 as a top-quality "independent" U.S.-brewed lager not only put Boston Beer on the corporate map, but also triggered the microbrewery revolution that transformed the image of beer drinking in the United States. The company's success demonstrated that there was a ready market for premium domestic brands—offering top quality at high prices—and in the process it extended the social reach of beer drinking. There are now hundreds of microbreweries in the United States, inspiring the big brewers—domestic and foreign alike—to respond creatively to the challenge of rising customer expectations.

Revolutions occur regularly in consumer markets. The introduction of the bagless vacuum cleaner by James Dyson is a prime example. Dyson was already a successful product innovator, having invented a barrow transported by a heavy-duty plastic ball rather than a conventional wheel, when he turned his attention to the vacuum cleaner. His criticism of existing cleaners, born of practical experience and observation, was that they lost suction rapidly because the dirt bag quickly became clogged, preventing the air that was sucked in from flowing outward. He reasoned that if he could produce a bagless cleaner, the suction could be improved and made constant, thus radically improving functionality. The solution lay in sucking up dirt by creating cyclones within two tubes arranged one inside the other, with the air spinning at high speeds. With this arrangement, it became possible to filter out both very large and very small particles and deposit them inside the machine without the need for a bag. It took the production of more than 5,000 prototypes before Dyson perfected the dual-cyclone system.

The launch of the first dual-cyclone machine in the United Kingdom in 1993 began a bagless revolution. This was heralded by the machine's bold colors and see-through dirt collector, which combined functionality with distinctive styling. Competitors that once had spurned Dyson's offers of collaboration began to wake up to the threat confronting them. The new technology was demonstrably superior, and in its promotional activities the company could point to genuine advantages of purchase. Cleaner homes, consistent high performance, bagless operation, and exceptional customer support were set alongside the intangible advantages of modern styling and state-of-the-art technology.

These advantages enabled Dyson to sweep the market in the United Kingdom, claiming more than 50 percent of sales by value in 1997. Ownership of a Dyson became a status symbol. Prices were high, yet sales remained strong, enabling the company to launch a range of new models, each with trademark features and styling. In less than a decade, Dyson had repeated its U.K. success in markets around the world and was established as a prestigious global brand.

The founders of most great enterprises have humble beginnings but big dreams. In his teens, Ingvar Kamprad launched a mail-order business from a tiny shed in his hometown of Älmhult in southern Sweden. He sold nylon stockings, matches, and cigarette lighters to people across the region of Småland. Lacking the resources to deliver the packages to his customers, Kamprad came up with a dependable, low-cost option: he arranged for his goods to be delivered by local milk trucks. This was the first of many creative approaches that he adopted to reduce costs and deliver what his customer wanted. Today, Ingvar Kamprad's company remains based in the small town of Älmhult, but it has long since outgrown using milk trucks for distribution. It also has moved on from its original limited product range and now offers the widest range of home furnishings to the greatest number of people around the world. In the process, its founder became one of the richest men in the world. Just as Dyson did in the home appliances business, Kamprad, through his company IKEA, revolutionized home furnishings.

So what are the revolutionary foundations of IKEA's breakout? Like Direct Line in the insurance business and Southwest Airlines in air travel, IKEA changed the ground rules for competition in a dull, traditional market. When IKEA entered the fray, the home furnishings industry was conservative and uninspiring. It was characterized by large stores selling cheap, usually poor-quality goods and small stores selling high-end, expensive pieces. The two types of stores had two things in common: poor value for money and a lack of customer orientation.

IKEA changed all this. Its flat-pack, self-assembly products, warehouse layout, and mass-production techniques deliver cost savings that benefit the customer through low prices. Also, Kamprad emphasized cost-conscious design, giving his designers the task of being creative—but on a budget. The company's convenient out-of-town locations, large free parking lots, in-store playroom facilities, long opening hours, and pleasant restaurant facilities (serving dishes such as IKEA's much-loved Swedish meatballs) all appealed to a long-suffering and underserved market of time-strapped young professionals and first-time parents.

These features, combined with low prices and eye-catching designs, made for a winning formula; IKEA had caught the competition off guard, making it difficult for competitors to respond. The Swedish innovator catapulted ahead of the pack, capturing new and existing customers and dominating the young and aspirational market segments. As with all successful breakout revolutionaries, customers' expectations increasingly were shaped by their experience with IKEA, and competitors had to respond through imitation or differentiation.

As IKEA's business and brand grew and expanded geographically, it took on another dimension. IKEA was fast becoming more than just a store; it was being transformed into a lifestyle choice. Some people[7] describe this as a state of mind that revolves around contemporary design, low prices, wacky promotions, and an unrivaled enthusiasm. Just like Virgin, Harley-Davidson, and Starbucks, IKEA has come to reflect an individual's personality and has even become a guardian of people's lifestyles. At a time when consumers face so many choices, IKEA provides a one-stop sanctuary for coolness. It has become far more than a purveyor of furniture and soft furnishings. It sells a lifestyle that customers around the world embrace as a signal that they have good taste and recognize value. "If it wasn't for IKEA," wrote the British design magazine *Icon*, "most people would have no access to affordable contemporary design."[8]

The result is that today IKEA is globally unrivaled. Wal-Mart may be a colossus in the United States, but its international forays have been much less spectacular. France's Carrefour is massive in many countries, but it has never made it in the United States. IKEA has not always gotten it right—its initial entry into the U.S. and Japanese markets suffered setbacks—but it learned from its mistakes, responded quickly, and moved forward relentlessly.

By 2006, the company had close to 250 stores and 420 million shoppers across Asia, Europe, Australia, and North America. Its annual revenue growth was in double digits, and its pretax operating profit was over $1.7 billion. The company's 2005 operating margin of 10 percent was double that of U.S. rival Pier 1 Imports and well ahead of another strong competitor, Target. Challenges persist, and competitors such as Target and Kmart are piling on the pressure, but IKEA remains in the pole position.

The most important thing about revolutionaries is that these companies ultimately have a major impact on their business realm, altering the perception of value in the eyes of consumers and redefining norms in the minds of competitors. Dyson and IKEA achieved this beyond their founders' wildest imaginations, unleashing extraordinary growth and creating exceptional value for shareholders.

Wave Riders

Wave riders pursue a particular type of laggard-to-leader strategy. These companies have trailed their chief rivals for some time before *reviving* and *refocusing* their product offering to gain fresh impetus and a new sense of direction. They come to the fore in relatively untested and emergent markets. Unlike revolutionaries, which reconfigure the rules and norms of competition, wave riders piggyback on existing methods and models, adapting and delivering on them to gain first-mover advantages, or at least a competitive edge over rival companies. The emergence of companies that were once perceived as being of little consequence from obscurity to become dominant players in their chosen markets is one of the most remarkable features of the business world. In certain cases, the opportunities inherent in emergent markets, where products, processes, and technologies are evolving rapidly, encourage laggard companies to make a dash for growth. New vistas open up and more expansive visions are formed, and companies that make the right strategic choices break out to enjoy the fruits of growth in buoyant markets.

There are few better illustrations than that of the Japanese electronics companies, which in the 1960s and 1970s rose seemingly from nowhere to take the lion's share of the burgeoning global market for consumer electronics. Prior to that time, companies that are now household names, such as Matsushita, Toshiba, Hitachi, NEC, and Sony, assembled low-technology household electrical goods for sale inside Japan. In the 1950s, however, the United States, intent on preventing Japan from falling under Communist control, was instrumental in giving the country extensive practical assistance in developing its industrial capacity. The future giants of the electronics industry were well placed to take advantage of this assistance. U.S. management specialists such as W. Edwards Deming championed the quality movement in Japan, and giant corporations such as General Electric were encouraged to license their technology to Japanese companies on favorable terms. It was through a licensing agreement with Western Electric, for example, that Sony first gained access to transistor technology. Other companies followed suit, and within the space of a few years, Japan had the know-how and the facilities to manufacture high-quality radios and television sets on a large scale.

The spectacular growth of the Japanese electronics industry after 1960 is unusual in that several companies were able to break out simultaneously. These wave riders migrated as one to occupy a rapidly expanding market space. Japanese companies were content to follow the lead of their initially more formidable U.S. counterparts. The markets for transistor radios and televisions were growing rapidly all around the world, and Japanese companies were uniquely well placed to respond. They had access to solid-state technologies and manufacturing processes. They had a large, disciplined, and low-cost workforce. They had access to international markets, yet they were able to protect their home market from foreign competition. With these advantages, they could offer a compelling value proposition—low price, advanced features, and high quality—to customers in the expanding consumer markets of North America and Europe.

Sales and revenues skyrocketed, generating the financial resources needed to support further rounds of investment in technology, plant, marketing, and global logistics. Before the consumer electronics companies of the United States and Europe had woken up to what was happening, many of them were at the point of being eliminated; Japan's corporate laggards had been transformed into industry leaders. Within a decade, they had entered a virtuous circle of growth and were investing heavily to develop future winning products, from color televisions to video recorders and computer games.

The wave-rider breakout strategy is a remarkably effective way to get on the fast track to business growth. The strategy is a feasible one for both powerhouse brands and lesser-known brands. Consider the Dublin-based low-cost airline Ryanair. At present, Ryanair is Europe's most profitable low-fare airline, operating more than 300 routes within and between 21 European countries. With its relentless cost-reduction methods, operational efficiency, and rapid route and fleet expansion, Ryanair has grabbed the pole position in a highly competitive industry, establishing itself as the world's most profitable and fastest-growing airline.

When people look at Ryanair, they assume that its success was based on a taking-by-storm revolutionary approach. This is not the true story, however; Ryanair adopted a budget airline model only after six failed years as a regional carrier. Established in 1985, Ryanair began by providing daily service between Waterford on the south coast of Ireland and London's Gatwick Airport, using small turboprop aircraft. The company was courageously attempting to challenge the Aer Lingus/British Airways duopoly on routes between Ireland and the United Kingdom. But a regulated business environment (unchanged until the mid-1990s) and a lackluster business model meant that Ryanair never got off the ground in a commercial sense. By 1990, Ryanair was serving 26 city pairs and carrying 700,000 passengers but had financial difficulties. The airline was hemorrhaging cash, and a new strategy was needed urgently.

When 29-year-old accountant Michael O'Leary was made deputy chief executive in 1991 (becoming CEO two years later), his first instinct was to close down the ailing airline. When he looked across the Atlantic for inspiration, however, his pessimism soon passed.

O'Leary is renowned for his tenacity and resourcefulness, and he resolved to turn the company around and take it from industry laggard to industry leader. His approach was clear and decisive: looking at the United States, he saw the potential for a Southwest Airlines–type business model in Europe. This market space was not yet fully viable in Europe, but the ongoing market-deregulation process, driven by the European Commission, soon would allow every European-based airline full and free access to all European Union air traffic routes. O'Leary was determined to ride the waves of change by being the first to offer customers a low-price alternative to existing suppliers.

The market entry of this independent, privately owned airline was the first real threat to the near monopoly that the state-owned carrier Aer Lingus and the larger, recently privatized British Airways had on routes between Ireland and the United Kingdom. Ryanair's strategy was simple: offer a no-frills, low-fare service to all. In essence, Ryanair's recipe for success is captured in a simple formulation: lower fares → more passengers → lower unit costs → lower fares. This formula proved hugely attractive to an increasingly cost-conscious traveling public. Ryanair made no attempt to distinguish between different passenger groups. Price-conscious businesspeople, students seeking summer work, emigrants visiting their families—all were part of Ryanair's target market, and all shared the same nonassigned seating arrangement.

This egalitarian offering was in stark contrast to the more opulent, differentiated, and expensive service offered by Ryanair's main rival, Aer Lingus. The state carrier had grown lax and was genuinely shaken by the competitive threat posed by the newly energized and aggressive Ryanair. Ryanair's authentic and innovative cost-reduction strategy enabled the company to achieve operational efficiencies never before seen in Europe. This allowed the airline to offer its customers consistently low prices and simultaneously to ensure sustainable and radically improved profit margins.

Within a decade of its turnaround, the airline was carrying over nine million passengers annually and operating at annual net profits of 72.5 million euro (up 24 percent from the previous year). By 2001, Ryanair had become the ninth largest airline in Europe, measured in terms of passengers carried. Within two decades of its launch, Ryanair had grown from an initial staff of 25 to over 2,700 people across 12 European bases. Despite periodic setbacks, its profits have remained strong, growing by 19 percent in the 2004–2005 period—a remarkable performance in an industry plagued by massive losses.

By 2006, Ryanair was operating more than 100 aircraft and carrying over 35 million passengers on more than 300 routes across Europe. O'Leary's wave-rider breakout clearly had worked and delivered to an extent that even he could not have envisioned back in the airline's dark days of unprofitable growth. The key to success: a strategy of piggybacking on an emerging trend—in this case, the marriage of business process and value proposition—to deliver low-cost, low-price air travel before competitors were able (or willing) to do so.

Ryanair, as we can see, had little choice but to change direction if it was not to go under. Not all cases are so clear-cut. Migrating to occupy a position in a rapidly expanding market space also can be controversial, especially when it raises questions about brand image and reputation. The entry of Porsche, the German car manufacturer famed for its high-performance sports cars, into the sport utility vehicle (SUV) market through the launch of the Cayenne is one such example. Porsche migrated into the rapidly expanding SUV market space, and its subsequent success—particularly in the United States—turned the company around. The long-established prestige sports car manufacturer was operating in the red in the early 1990s, but a decade later it was the most profitable car manufacturer in the world. Porsche already was on the move, but it was the Cayenne that projected the company into the high-growth breakout league.

Porsche entered the SUV market in late 2002. At this point, the market already was crowded, but the potential of the SUV had not yet been fully realized—particularly at the upper end of the market. Despite this, few experts believed that Porsche was right to develop an SUV. The argument against doing so was simple: the SUV business and the high-performance sports car business were polar opposites, and combining them risked dilution of brand equity. But Porsche had little choice. Sports car sales were sliding and revenues shrinking: "It was mandatory for Porsche to build a third leg to be able to balance that kind of volatility . . . and put the company on a solid growth basis, because we have to grow to stay independent," noted Porsche's marketing chief, Hans Riedel.[9]

Porsche pressed ahead regardless and proved its critics wrong. The company had spotted the opportunity to sell its product to high-income people who, because of family and lifestyle commitments, required the space and sturdiness of an SUV but also the performance and image of a sports car. The Cayenne retains the core features of a Porsche—pace, handling, quality, and "muscular" styling—while being practical for family use.

The market responded with enthusiasm to the new Porsche value proposition. In 2002, prior to the Cayenne's launch, the company's sales dipped for the first time in six years. In the Cayenne's first year, Porsche sold 20,000 SUVs, and it sold double that number in the following year. The subsequent three years witnessed strong double-digit growth, fueled by sales of the Cayenne. This has led Porsche down a new path, extending its product range and leveraging the power of its brand.

In 2007, for example, it will launch a four-door coupe to rival saloon cars such as Jaguar's XJR, BMW's M5, and the Mercedes E55. The strategy of Porsche's visionary chief executive, Wendelin Wiedeking, is to take Porsche from being a niche player to being a top-end car company with a range of models, achieving significant economies of scale and scope in the process. By increasing sales to over 100,000 vehicles per year—from less than 50,000 cars before the Cayenne—the car maker intends to further improve its already lofty profit figures. Profit aside, Porsche's size makes it vulnerable to takeover in an industry dominated by global giants. Its rivals are all backed by large parents—Ferrari has Fiat, Aston Martin has Ford, and Lamborghini has Volkswagen—so Porsche's wave-rider breakout is as much about survival as about making money.

The Japanese electronics companies, Ryanair, and Porsche are excellent examples of the benefits for laggard companies of identifying "the next big thing" and migrating to occupy a new position in the market. Wave riding is not without its risks and difficulties, though, and if these are not managed properly, then a period of rapid growth might well be followed by an equally spectacular collapse. This is what happened at Bankers Trust, which in the early 1990s, under the leadership of Chairman and CEO Charles Sanford, entered the world of derivatives trading and won a reputation as a high-flying quasi-investment bank. Derivatives were new financial instruments that had created big opportunities for investment bankers who could master their arcane mathematics. Into this rapidly expanding market space came Bankers Trust, seeking to establish itself as a classic wave rider.

What made Bankers Trust so successful on the upside (while sowing the seeds of its ultimate demise) was its boldness as a risk taker and aggressive trader. The company hired extremely smart, innovative, and pushy traders who were lavishly compensated through the payment of commissions. A competitive culture developed within the company, and sales boomed as traders vied with one another for recognition and financial rewards. This led to an explosion of risk-taking on a grand scale that ended in conflicts with major clients, the most dramatic being a lawsuit by Procter & Gamble (P&G). Early in 1994, Bankers Trust and P&G entered into multiple derivatives contracts. One particular contract was based on interest rates and was highly leveraged, or the possibilities for both gains and losses magnified. In February 1994, interest rates rose unexpectedly, resulting in significant losses for P&G. According to Edwin Artzt, P&G's chairman, "the issue here is Bankers Trust's selling practices."[10] Mr. Artzt continued, "There is a notion that end users of derivatives must be held accountable for what they buy. . . . we agree completely, but only if the terms and risks are fully and accurately disclosed." In October 1994, P&G sued Bankers Trust to recover the $102 million loss it had incurred.

The P&G lawsuit effectively brought the breakout of Bankers Trust to a spectacular end. In a cover story in *BusinessWeek* in October 1995, it was revealed that the company had been accused of fraud, misrepresentation, lies about valuations, and causing significant and repeated losses for clients. In addition, P&G filed racketeering charges, claiming that Bankers Trust maintained a "culture of greed and duplicity."[11] The tapes used to verify trading activity were used as evidence, with one trader being heard to say, "Funny business, you know? Lure people into the calm and just totally f—- 'em."[12] Bankers Trust had some strong lines of defense, not least that such evidence had been taken out of context and that the company was being pilloried for mistakes made by naive corporate executives. But the damage had been done. In December 1994, the Federal Reserve Board and Bankers Trust reached an agreement that required increased disclosure to customers of the risks of derivatives sold by Bankers Trust, and a $10 million fine was levied. Other settlements were made with the Securities and Exchange Commission, the Commodity Futures Exchange Commission, and the New York State Banking Commission.

The P&G suit could have been prevented and could have been handled to better effect. To innovate in the financial services business, employees need to be given the freedom to explore new products. In Bankers Trust's case, however, they were given too much freedom, and there was too little oversight. The financial derivatives sold to P&G should not have been sold without full and explicit disclosure of the risk, clearly stating their speculative nature. If Bankers Trust had been able to make a case that P&G had full and explicit information, the company's troubles might never have escalated to the level of scandal. Furthermore, Bankers Trust should have had controls in place to limit what types of products could be sold. A leveraged interest-rate bet must not be pushed to a consumer products company—it was inappropriate behavior that, when it became generally known by the outside world, harmed Bankers Trust's reputation.

Bankers Trust's reputation was its most valuable asset and should have been treated as such. Explicit disclosure and increased oversight could have prevented the public relations nightmare caused by P&G's suit. In addition, once the derivatives had been sold and huge losses were apparent, Bankers Trust could have handled the situation better. Although Bankers Trust made a strong legal case, the company clearly lost in the public arena and in the offices of chief financial officers around corporate America.

A less antagonistic approach, clearer corporate communication, and earlier settlement could have lessened the suffering. In fact, Bankers Trust absorbed massive losses for years until Deutsche Bank acquired the firm in 1999. By refusing to institute appropriate controls and adopting a "cowboy" stance in this new market, Bankers Trust self-destructed. Wave riding, perhaps even more than the other breakout strategies, requires courage and the willingness and ability to break out of your comfort zone, but doing so does not grant you a waiver from following world-class business process and execution.

In sum, we can see that wave riders can come from surprising places. Even a company as steeped in tradition and mystique as Porsche can take advantage of a new wave in its industry. The Porsche story, along with those of Ryanair and the Japanese electronics companies, shows the power of the wave-rider strategy.

As we have seen, a wave-rider company gets on the fast track by latching onto a good product or a great process before its market potential or reach is fully realized—or, in some cases, before rivals even see it. The wave rider proceeds to add value through brand extension (Porsche), process adaptation (Ryanair), or a compelling blend of low-price, high-quality, and leading-edge design (the Japanese electronics giants). When the strategy is controlled and managed properly, as it was at Porsche and Ryanair (but not at Bankers Trust, where cavalier attitudes compromised the business), breakout lifts the entire business to a new and higher plane.

Big Improvers

The second type of laggard company that seeks to become a market leader we refer to as big improvers. These companies remain in the markets that they have served traditionally, but they manage to cast off the shackles of the past, putting before customers an attractive new value proposition that rapidly finds favor, triggering breakout and entry into a virtuous cycle of growth and development.

A classic example is Tesco, the British food and household retailing giant. The company was founded in 1924 by the entrepreneur Jack Cohen, who used the gratuity he received for his army service in World War I to invest in a small grocery business in London's East End. Cohen opened the first self-service store in the United Kingdom in 1948, borrowing the idea from the United States. By the early 1960s, Tesco had become a familiar name in British retailing and could be found on Main Street in many towns. Yet, for all its initial success and early innovations, Tesco found it very difficult to keep pace with archrival J Sainsbury, which had long been the most progressive force in British food retailing.

All this changed when Terry Leahy took over as CEO in 1997. His strategy was brilliant in its simplicity: understand what the customer wants and deliver on it time and time again. He captured this in a short but insightful vision statement: "Creating value for customers, to earn their lifetime loyalty." Leahy put the customer at the heart of the business. He was the first British retailer to introduce loyalty cards (Clubcard), and he followed this with home shopping (now Tesco.com), Tesco Babyclub for parents, and Tesco Personal Finance, a joint venture with the Royal Bank of Scotland that offered customers good deals on insurance and personal loans. Leahy also pioneered "One in Front," or opening new checkout lanes at times of increased business, and "Would I Buy It," which focused on ensuring that each product is always of the highest quality for the customer.

By the close of the 1990s, Tesco had overtaken J Sainsbury—and all other contenders—to become the largest and most profitable British retail food company. Its online shopping unit, Tesco.com, had become the largest grocery home-shopping business in the world. Tesco moved from being the number three domestic retailer to being one of the top three international retailers in the world, with 2,318 stores and 326,000 employees.

Notwithstanding this success, Sir Terry Leahy, knighted in 2002 for his contribution to British business and society, is anything but complacent. Tesco's more recent innovations include the launch of its own Fairtrade brand of 15 products, susch as orange juice, coffee, tea, chocolate, South African wine, and fresh fruit and flowers, including luxury roses from Kenya. Tesco has developed a new shopping cart called "Trim Trolley" that is designed to allow consumers to exercise while they shop by offering differing resistances when pushing and allowing the counting of calories. This seems like an outlandish idea, but it reflects modern life trends and Tesco's forward thinking.[13]

Innovation that leads to improved value propositions and business models is at the heart of any big-improver strategy. This can be seen at play at Triumph, which has a long and proud history as a manufacturer of motorcycles. Who can forget images such as Steve McQueen's daredevil jump over a barbed wire fence on a 1961 Triumph TR6 Trophy Bird in the movie *The Great Escape*?[14] Yet, despite its proud history and strong brand, Triumph went out of business in the 1980s, paying the ultimate price for failing to keep up with the times. What went wrong, and how was Triumph revived and relaunched in the 1990s?

Triumph was founded in the United Kingdom in the 1880s by a German entrepreneur, Siegfried Bettmann, who started manufacturing bicycles under the name Triumph.[15] After the invention of the motorcycle at the turn of the twentieth century, his business became an early pioneer of this new mode of transport. The company was credited with many novel technological advances, such as the kick-starter. The company supplied the British military during both world wars, earning the nickname "Trusty" during World War I. The company became part of the Birmingham Small Arms (BSA) Group in 1951 and prospered during the 1950s and 1960s, the so-called golden age of motorcycling. With success came celebrity endorsements, with cult Hollywood actors such as Steve McQueen, James Dean, Marlon Brando, and Clint Eastwood being seen on Triumph bikes.

As often happens, however, management at Triumph began to take its success for granted, and by the 1970s, the company was in a constant state of flux, with little or no attention being paid to strategic direction or product innovation. When reports of a

750-cc Japanese bike surfaced, they were shrugged off by a management team that was sure of Triumph's market dominance and confident that such a machine could never be produced. Then it was. Fortunately, some of Triumph's executives had been working, without BSA approval, on their own 750-cc bike. This was rushed out, but it was too little, too late. It could not challenge the superior quality and lower price of Japanese models. The company collapsed, finally closing its doors in 1983.

The residual rights in Triumph—to its designs and brands—were purchased in the mid-1980s by the property developer John Bloor for a modest sum. It is Bloor, who had little technical knowledge but great vision, who deserves credit for restoring an extreme (virtually defunct) laggard to a position of industry leadership. Initially, the marque was kept alive by the expedient of working with parts manufacturers to produce a small number of motorcycles each year. Meanwhile, Bloor assembled a cutting-edge design team made up of former Triumph employees and other experts. The team visited the Japanese factories of Kawasaki, Suzuki, and Yamaha. Inspired by their methods, Bloor imported Japanese equipment into the United Kingdom for a new state-of-the-art factory.

The new Triumph range of bikes appeared in the 1990s. They were widely accepted by the motorcycling cognoscenti, who recognized the authenticity and integrity of the brand and its historical associations. The machines generally are large (750 to 1,200 cc), although there are two outliers (a smaller 600-cc model and an enormous 2,290-cc model). They are stylish, and most have an *American-retro* design (which shows off the engine and places emphasis on a chrome finish (many other bikes are encased in plastic). Triumph has a distinctive calling card in the form of three-cylinder engines—all other manufacturers make two- or four-cylinder engines.

The company also has a wide range of parts and accessories. The bikes are more customizable than other brands, with the exception of Harley-Davidson. As with Harley-Davidson, a large range of branded merchandise, such as Zippo lighters, pens, and clothing, also has emerged.

By the early 2000s, the company was spending $15 million a year and employing 90 people in research and development (almost 10 percent of the total number of Triumph employees). The results are impressive. Double-digit sales growth has become the norm, with an average growth rate of 25 percent between 2003 and 2006. Triumph is most definitely back. Its focused leadership, technologically advanced facilities, classic designs, and revived brand have proved a winning formula, bringing its big-improver breakout strategy to fruition.

Big improvers come in many different guises and can be found in a wide variety of contexts. You might think, for example, of the successful breakout in recent years of perpetual sporting underdogs. None is bigger or better known than the Boston Red Sox. The Red Sox were the epitome of hard luck and failed endeavor for sports fans for almost a century. A perpetual laggard, one of the oldest teams in baseball couldn't seem to shake off the so-called curse of the Babe that had dogged it ever since Harry Frazee sold the legendary Babe Ruth to the New York Yankees after the 1919 season.

For so long the bridesmaid and not the bride, the Red Sox ended 86 years of hurt by beating the St. Louis Cardinals to win the 2004 Baseball World Series. The Red Sox completed an unprecedented 11-day turnaround when the team defeated the Cardinals 3-0 to win its first World Series since 1918. While many sports franchises have endured years of losing, no team has tantalized its faithful by coming so close and continually falling short. Most famously, the Red Sox came within one strike of winning the 1986 World Series, only to collapse as a ground ball went between first baseman Bill Buckner's legs.[16]

What made 2004 so different, and how did it prove to be the year that the curse was lifted and the Red Sox broke out to become one of the biggest improvers in recent baseball history? A lot of it comes down to the new era heralded by the 2002 sale of the Red Sox to a business consortium. In particular, the subsequent appointment of Theo Epstein as general manager proved decisive. Epstein, who at age 28 became the youngest general manager in the history of the major leagues at that time, grew up in nearby Brookline, Massachusetts, rooting for the Red Sox. He understood the team's history, and he felt passionate about its future. He understood the importance of building a team based as much on a desire to win as on talent and ability. But perhaps most important of all, Epstein and the rest of the Red Sox top brass understood that the old business models for crafting a winning baseball team were not working.

One of their approaches was to turn for advice to long-time baseball writer and statistician Bill James, whose approach placed a much higher premium on actual rather than potential performance. This approach had not worked that well for the Oakland Angels, but the Red Sox had more than this in the team's arsenal. Management fielded a team that combined twenty-first-century thinking with old-fashioned grit. Success came especially from the combination of Epstein's vision of renewed greatness, a business model emphasizing reliability and relationships, and an implementation process founded on hard work, improved technique, and, above all, the passion and determination to win. This was the breakout strategy. The result was that within two years the Red Sox achieved an epic comeback unprecedented in baseball history.

As with any type of breakout, there is no guarantee of success for those that set out to become big improvers. The breakout and subsequent trials and tribulation of doughnut maker Krispy Kreme are instructive. Krispy Kreme began in a small rented North Carolina store in 1937 and for its first 50 or more years was a resolute laggard. Only in the mid-1990s did the company seek to break out beyond the narrow confines of the Carolinas. A remarkable spate of growth ensued, and by 2004, Krispy Kreme had 4,400 stores in 45 U.S. states, Australia, Canada, Mexico, and the United Kingdom.

Krispy Kreme seemed to have a winning formula that was destined to take it from industry laggard to leader, a big-improver breakout that had taken competitors—chiefly Dunkin' Donuts—by surprise. Its doughnuts had attracted a devoted, even fanatical customer base—especially for the best-selling hot-glazed, yeast-raised doughnut known as the Krispy Kreme Original Glazed. *Fortune* magazine was calling Krispy Kreme the "hottest brand in the land." And its sales figures and profit margins seemed to prove the magazine right.

By the close of 2004, though, less than a decade after Krispy Kreme's first tentative steps beyond its home region, the company was on the brink of disaster. Sales were falling by 20 percent a quarter, and several of its franchises were filing for bankruptcy and were forced to sell off stores across large parts of the United States. By the end of 2005, Krispy Kreme had lost close to 90 percent of the market value it had had during the heady days of 2003. What could possibly have gone so horribly wrong? How could a company with an almost legendary product and a loyal customer base fall so far so fast?

The answer brings to mind the parallel experience of Bankers Trust. Krispy Kreme fell victim to overambition, overreach, and loss of integrity. At the heart of the company's problems was an expansion strategy that was overly ambitious and that stretched the company too thin. As marketing consultant and author Bill McConnell has noted, "Growth became its mantra, and growth as a mantra is like dancing with the devil."

To continue to meet Wall Street's earnings expectations, the corporation kept expanding rather than finding ways to make more money from its existing stores. Herein lay the fatal flaw: Krispy Kreme began to lose its cachet. In the rush to sell to as many people as possible in as many places as possible, Krispy Kreme's management team sanctioned the selling of doughnuts in supermarkets, drugstores, and gas stations. The company also opened smaller "satellite" stores that didn't make their own doughnuts—an act of heresy in the eyes of many Krispy Kreme doughnut aficionados.

Ubiquity became a curse. Loyal customers resented how "common" Krispy Kreme doughnuts had become and questioned the quality and freshness of the products sold in these new outlets. Just as companies such as Burberry realized in the late 1990s, you cannot position yourself at the premium end of the market if your products can be bought at any local store. Krispy Kreme was pricing its products at a premium, and as a consequence, when customers made a purchase, they wanted not just great taste but also a product that said something about them as consumers. This high-value brand equity was frittered away when Krispy Kreme glazed doughnuts could be purchased at most branches of the drugstore chain Walgreens.

Related problems emerged subsequently. Financial mismanagement and possible improprieties were uncovered as Krispy Kreme became the subject of an accounting probe by securities regulators. It received a formal Securities and Exchange Commission inquiry in July 2004 concerning its accounting related to the buyback of several franchises. As the stock price plummeted, a raft of lawsuits from various shareholders followed.

Krispy Kreme successfully introduced an attractive value proposition based on high quality, great taste, and a cool image, allowing the company to refashion the long-established doughnut market. But the rush to be a big improver saw the company shoot from laggard to leader—and back to laggard again. Krispy Kreme ran into problems not because of awkward shareholders, fickle customers, or predatory competitors. Changes happened and challenges emerged, sometimes unexpectedly and unforeseen. But if the company had stuck to its strategy and followed its big-improver breakout clearly and consistently, listening to its customers and expanding selectively, we doubt that it would have fallen on such tough times.

The Krispy Kreme story contains many useful lessons for other big improvers. The key takeaways are, first, never listen to market analysts and investors ahead of your customers, and second, beware of undermining the source of your improvement simply to make short-term gains. As we have just seen, big-improver breakouts come in all shapes and sizes. Successfully introducing new value propositions or business models in established—sometimes saturated—markets is no easy task. Turning this into consistent double-digit growth is a far greater challenge. Where

Krispy Kreme stumbled, Triumph and Tesco succeeded by sticking unfailingly to a customer-centered breakout predicated on a clear and appealing product offering that was delivered consistently.

Conclusion

Taking-by-storm companies—whether they are true originals or revolutionaries—are united in their clarity of purpose and determination to succeed. Getting on the fast track to business growth is uppermost in everything they do, surpassed only by a desire to be number one. Bill Gates at Microsoft and Larry Page at Google created new markets and never-before-seen products, whereas Ingvar Kamprad at IKEA and John Sperling at the Apollo Group saw an opportunity to redefine the way in which business is done and made it their own. These entrepreneurs have a good deal in common. They understand how a compelling value proposition should be crafted and how it might be delivered. They have the tenacity and leadership capabilities needed to hold a business together as it grows and changes during breakout.

Laggard companies come in all shapes and sizes; some are prominent, whereas others are less well known. None of them intended to be laggards—particularly those that had experienced the glory of market leadership in the past. All those that have turned themselves around and risen to the top—for either the first or the second time—have followed the essential practices of a breakout strategy. Both wave riders such as Ryanair and big improvers such as Tesco have understood that nothing within markets remains fixed forever and that their customers will respond with alacrity and enthusiasm to the offer of something new or better. The requirement in these cases, as we will see in later chapters, is to get everyone in the business to rise to the challenges of breakout without loss of integrity or erosion of ethical standards.

Inspired by the lessons of taking-by-storm and laggard-to-leader breakouts—and chastened by the examples of failure for each—we can move forward to the third and fourth breakout types and their twin expressions. We have seen already that the specifics of any breakout strategy stem from where you are starting. In looking at companies that pursue expanding-horizons and shifting-shape strategies, the same observation applies. There is a big advantage in recognizing this from the start. Our research shows that the most successful breakout leaders are those that understand but succeed in overcoming the constraints of immediate and inherited circumstances. They do this through application of the principles of breakout strategy. As this book unfolds, we provide you with the route options and maps needed to get to your destination.

Endnotes

1 Interview with Alec Reed, May 29, 2001.
2 Robert C. Ford, "Pierre Bellon, Founder and President-Director General of Sodexho Alliance," *Academy of Management Executive* 17:1, 2003.
3 Bob Dylan, *Chronicles*, Vol. 1.London: Simon & Schuster, 2004. This quote is an amalgam of several extracts from the book, most notably on pages 51 and 73.
4 For further details on William Morris, see Charles Harvey and Jon Press, *Art, Enterprise and Ethics: The Life and Work of William Morris*. London: Cass, 1996.
5 This is taken from Larry Page and Sergey Brin's letter from the founders, "An 'Owner's Manual' for Google's Shareholders," a document inspired by Warren Buffett's "An Owner's Manual" to Berkshire Hathaway shareholders.
6 The last part of this statement met with some incredulity and criticism (from media watchdogs such as Reporters without Borders) after Google's compliance with Chinese government demand that it launch a self-censored search engine in China. Google responded by arguing that it

could play a more useful role in China by participating than by boycotting it, despite the compromises involved.

7 Kerry Capell et al., "IKEA: How the Swedish Retailer Became a Global Cult Brand," *BusinessWeek Online*, November 14, 2005, http://www.businessweek.com/magazine/content/05_46/b3959001.htm.

8 Ibid.

9 These comments were made in an interview with BBC reporter John Madslien, "Porsche's Daring Expansion Plan," BBC News, June 1, 2004.

10 Saul Hansell, "P&G Sues Bankers Trust over Swap Deal," *New York Times*, October 28, 1994, Sec. D, p. 1.

11 Ibid.

12 2 Ibid.

13 Datamonitor, *Tesco PLC: Company Profile*, July 2004, p. 26.

14 The Triumph actually was disguised to look like a BMW because it was meant to be a stolen German Army bike.

15 Thanks are due to Daniel Field, James Hawes, Camilla Lovelle-Hoare, Elsa Perira Luk, and David Shalom for their input into this case study.

16 Mike Dodd, "Finally! Red Sox Win World Series," *USA Today*, October 27, 2004.

CHAPTER 3

STAYING OUT IN FRONT

One of the most remarkable features of the turbulent world of business is the ability of a select band of companies to maintain their dominant position for many decades, the illustrious survivors of numerous challenges, wars, and financial crises. In Germany, for example, despite the numerous trials and tribulations of the twentieth century, companies founded under Imperial rule remain pillars of the economy today.

Siemens (founded in 1847), Bayer (1863), BASF (1865), AEG (1883), Bosch (1886), Mercedes (1886), and BMW (1913) not only have remained in business, but also continue to be among the global leaders in their respective fields. Likewise, in France, the great names of Saint-Gobain (1665), Michelin (1832), Schneider (1838), Renault (1898), Air Liquide (1902), and L'Oréal (1909) bear witness to the ability of historic enterprises to adapt and stay out in front decade after decade. The same observation applies equally to British-headquartered global companies such as Barclays (1690), Rio Tinto (1873), HSBC (1865), and BP (1909) and to the Japanese industrial giants Mitsubishi (1871), NEC (1899), Toshiba (1904), and Hitachi (1920).

In the United States, meanwhile, many of the most managerially sophisticated companies of the present day, including DuPont (1802), Procter & Gamble (1837), Otis Elevator (1867), General Electric (1892), Goodyear (1898), and IBM (1911), have their roots in the great industrial surge of the nineteenth and early twentieth centuries.

The histories of these and other long-lived giant enterprises are instructive. Many of them achieved a leading position in their national markets at an early date through their control of critical technologies, know-how, or industrial assets.

Procter & Gamble (P&G), for instance, began making its high-quality Ivory brand soap for the mass market in the 1880s, using high-volume mechanical crushers that enabled the company to achieve significant economies of scale. General Electric's original competitive advantage stemmed from its control of the Edison patents for electricity generation and illumination and the heavy investments needed to commercialize these inventions. These developments were mirrored in Germany by AEG, which used Edison's patents and know-how to manufacture and install power and lighting systems. In building an industrial position based on technological excellence, AEG was following the earlier example of Siemens in telegraph and cable equipment.

Companies such as these were first movers in their fields. They commanded high prices, earned above-normal profits, and reinvested heavily in manufacturing, distribution, marketing, and product development to establish positions of industrial dominance. International expansion followed, with subsidiary companies being formed to shape and occupy emergent markets in other countries. Both AEG and Siemens created extensive international power-generation and traction operations during the later nineteenth and early twentieth centuries. U.S. brand leaders Quaker Oats, Heinz, and Coca-Cola had manufacturing plants in Europe before World War I. Ford, General Motors, P&G, and many others followed in the 1920s and 1930s, each exploiting its possession of technologies and know-how that were lacking elsewhere in the world. In effect, such dominant companies entered a virtuous circle of growth, with fresh rounds of investment bolstering their organizational capabilities and the resulting capacity to shape and dominate markets.

This, needless to say, is a highly simplified account of how long-lived companies adapt and stay out in front in their chosen markets. It fails to recognize the magnitude of the changes that companies need to make from time to time if they are to survive and prosper. If corporate growth were self-sustaining, then the survival rate of once-dominant companies would be far higher than it actually is. In fact, the historical record is not one that should lead any company, however dominant it may be at present, to be complacent. The number of companies that actually manage to stay out in front over long periods is dwarfed by the number that disappear.

Since 1955, *Fortune* magazine has been ranking U.S. companies in terms of total revenues. When the first list appeared, Europe and Japan were still rebuilding after World War II, and there was no talk of "Asian tigers" or emerging economies, and certainly not of the business strength of India and China. The top 100 U.S. companies were at the very pinnacle of global business. Yet, when we compare the rankings for 1955 and 2005, we find that just 20 of the top 100 companies in 1955 are still in the upper echelons of corporate America. What happened to the others? Some were merged out of independent existence, many went out of business entirely, and still others continue to exist but have been replaced at the top by newer companies that capitalized on changes that the old guard did not, such as Microsoft, Intel, Cisco, Wal-Mart, Home Depot, and Best Buy.

The history of the once-celebrated British motor vehicle industry sounds a warning. In 1960, it was second only to that of the United States in terms of output and exports, boasting numerous famous marques. Within a decade, despite the runaway success of the Mini Cooper, the industry was in crisis. Two decades later, after many desperate reorganizations, the production capacity of indigenous British automakers was a fraction of what it had been at its peak, and the future of motor vehicle manufacturing in the United Kingdom lay almost entirely in the hands of foreign companies.

There are parallels with the present situation of U.S. automakers. General Motors (GM) has been a colossus of the world automotive industry, and the 1950s claim that "What's good for General Motors is good for America" has held true over the intervening decades. Yet this once seemingly invincible company is now confronted with a complex set of problems that threatens its very existence. Some of these relate to the immediate appeal of its products, but others are structural and endemic. In more prosperous times, workers were given generous health care and pension benefits that now have created liabilities many times greater than the funds available to meet them. The challenge for GM's present leaders is to leverage the company's capabilities and brand assets sufficiently to generate the cash needed to cover its inherited obligations.

There are three often-related reasons why once-dominant companies fail to stay in front and eventually face elimination. The first is that the competitive landscape can change for the worse so quickly and so fundamentally that viable strategic options are limited. As international trade has been liberalized, for example, manufacturing companies with plants in high-wage economies have found it increasingly difficult to compete with those based in low-wage economies. In industries as diverse as textiles, consumer electronics, shipbuilding, plastics, and steel making, companies that within living memory employed hundreds of thousands of people have been swept away.

The second factor at work is the one that is currently in evidence at GM. Long periods of stability, when times are good and revenues flow easily, may have the insidious effect of breeding tolerance of deficient management and cultural practices. In these circumstances, potential productivity gains are missed, and the pressure to improve product quality, design, and functionality is reduced. "Cultural sclerosis" makes the search for solutions all the more difficult when competitive pressures intensify and problems accumulate.

The third main cause of organizational failure is strategic ineptitude. While companies that stay out in front recognize and respond appropriately to fundamental challenges, those that fall behind invariably misconstrue the nature and magnitude of external threats and as a result pursue wrong-headed approaches.

The changing landscape of the motor vehicle industry again is a good example. The threat that British automakers faced in the 1960s came from trade liberalization, which exposed indigenous companies to heightened competition from continental European and Japanese rivals. As competition intensified, margins tightened and internal sources of funds for reinvestment began to dry up. The industry's response was to pursue wave after wave of mergers in an attempt to achieve economies of scale, which were seen as a cure-all for the industry's problems. Eventually, by 1968, just one national champion remained, the ill-fated British Leyland (BL), which owned 40 different plants and an incoherent product line that included cars, vans, trucks, buses, and road-surfacing equipment. BL was the epitome of a culturally sclerotic enterprise, riddled from top to bottom with labor disputes and under the control of a poorly trained and ineffectual management. The company went bankrupt in 1975. Its government-backed successor went the same way in 1982.

In this case, the main strategic error made by senior management was focusing on mergers and rationalization at the expense of new-product development, quality, and productivity. Management embraced complexity when the solution lay in pursuing a simple strategy of improvement focused on producing better-designed and higher-quality vehicles. The contrast with the strategic response of the German car maker Volkswagen, which faced challenges very similar to those faced by BL, could not be more marked.

At Volkswagen, beginning in the late 1960s, management concentrated its resources on finding a replacement for the outdated Beetle that would have strong appeal for motorists. The elegant, superbly engineered, and fully featured Golf line was introduced in 1974. It has remained, through five generations, the backbone of Volkswagen's product line until the present. The success of the new line laid the foundation for a strategy of international expansion that has seen Volkswagen expand production in low-wage economies and take full advantage of growth in emerging markets.

Four Ways of Staying Out in Front

The contrasting fortunes of Volkswagen and BL emphasize the importance of strategic regeneration for staying out in front. If the mining company Rio Tinto, after more than 50 years at the top, had not responded appropriately to the dangers of rising nationalist sentiments in Spain in the late 1920s, it would have faced extinction when General Franco came to power in 1939. In fact, the company staved off the threat by using its resources, expertise, and networks to secure a large stake in the emerging, and ultimately very lucrative, copper industry of northern Rhodesia (Zambia). Staying out in front for long periods almost invariably requires companies to make bold strategic moves of this kind.

The rationale is simple: it is much easier to break out and renew from a position of strength than from one of weakness. At P&G, the company's elevation into the corporate superleague came with the launching and wildfire success of Tide, the first synthetic detergent.[1] There are few better examples of corporate regeneration by seizing the strategic moment. Tide, code-named "product X," was developed in 1945 through in-house experimentation with the cleansing properties of synthetic compounds. The test results were so compelling that P&G abandoned its exhaustive product- and market-testing procedures in order to steal a march on its competitors, Colgate and Unilever. Resources were quickly ploughed into developing new manufacturing facilities and processes and into refining and communicating the Tide value proposition. When the product was launched in 1946, it caused a sensation. The product worked superbly, and the advertising caught perfectly the postwar feeling that there was a brighter, more optimistic, technologically enabled future ahead. In time, the financial resources generated through massive sales transformed P&G from a U.S. soap company into a global provider of household products.

Figure 3.1 describes the four main ways in which established companies can break out to stay ahead of the competition. It identifies four breakout types, the product of two breakout strategies at play in two types of market, emergent and established. Companies

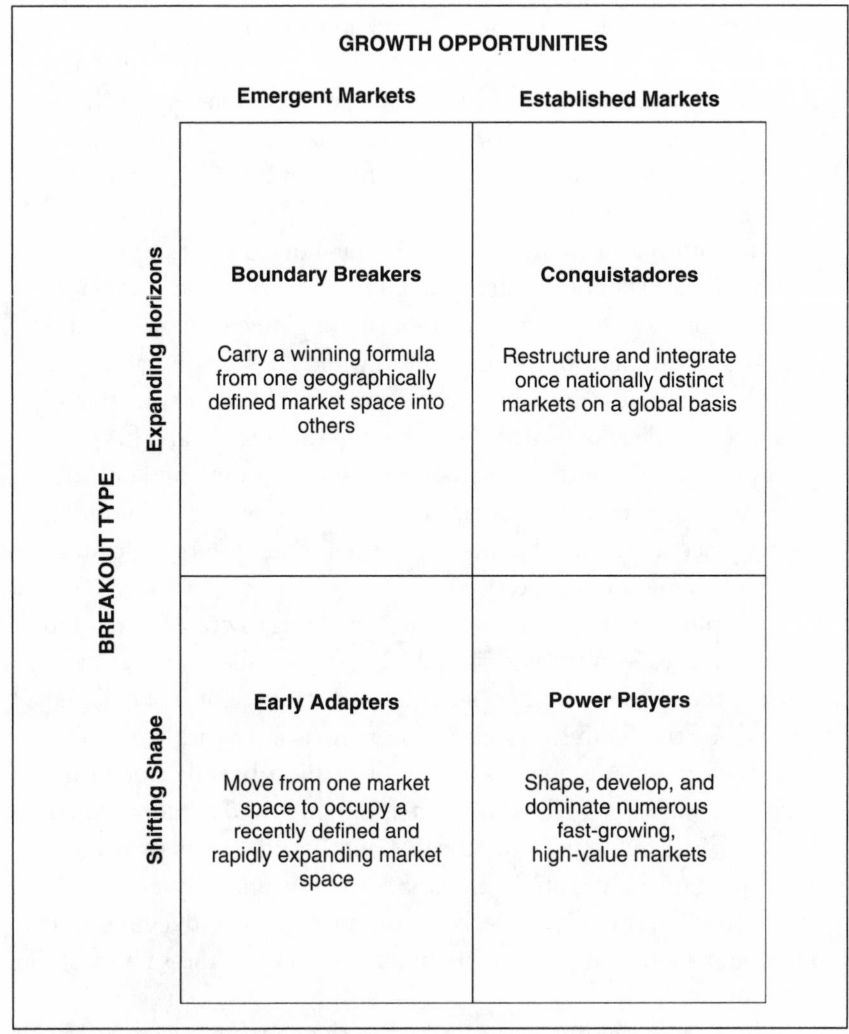

Figure 3.1 Companies Staying Out in Front

that pursue an *expanding-horizons* strategy have in common the intention to grow rapidly through the application in fresh geographic markets of business ideas or products that have already been proven elsewhere. However, the implementation of geographically expansive strategies differs fundamentally in form and content between emergent and established markets. Companies whose intention is to *shift shape* are focused on product rather than geography; often they have become international businesses at an early stage of development. Their common aim is to migrate into new markets to take advantage of high-value opportunities. Again, however, the expression of strategy differs fundamentally depending on whether the opportunities for growth are in emergent or more-established markets.

Companies that pursue an expanding-horizons strategy in an emergent-market context are *boundary breakers*. These companies tap into some of the most basic impulses of global capitalism: aspiration and emulation. When a brand becomes fashionable in a wealthy country, woven into its cultural fabric and expressive of its success, it develops kudos elsewhere in the world. The first pull is toward other wealthy countries with similar values and cultural dispositions; the second is toward rapidly growing economies, where price levels may be lower, but the market is large and standards of living are on the rise.

This phenomenon is most evident in the growth of fast-food outlets such as McDonalds and KFC, coffee retailers such as Starbucks, and fashion houses such as Benetton. The spectacular growth of the Spanish group Inditex in recent years is illustrative. The company owns a family of fashion brands (including Zara, Pull and Bear, Massimo Dutti, Bershka, and Stradivarious), each with its own chain of stores. Each brand has its own identity and expressly stated values. Segmentation is by consumer group, not nationality; the Zara brand expressly declares that "boundaries do not prevent anyone from sharing the same fashion culture."

Boundary breaking is not limited to the consumer sector. The same forces can be seen at work across a whole range of business, financial, and professional-service markets. Swift Trade, Canada's direct-access electronic trading center, began to internationalize once it had established itself coast to coast at home. Its strategy has been to open offices on a joint-venture basis in rapidly developing economies from Brazil to China. The innovative U.S. design company IDEO, founded in 1990 and based in Palo Alto, California, likewise has extended its range and influence by opening new offices, first in the United States and more recently in the United Kingdom, Germany, and China. What IDEO promises clients is enhanced brand value by improving the functionality and aesthetic appeal of new products. In effect, the company's design methodology is to identify human needs and design products to meet them, directly strengthening the value propositions of client companies.

Companies that pursue an expanding-horizons strategy in an established-market context are *conquistadores*. The logic underpinning the breakout strategies of these companies is very different from that of boundary breakers. Conquistadores aim for global domination of well-defined product or service markets. Their belief is that they can reap significant economies of scale and scope by merging the assets of national or regionally based companies to form giant supranational organizations. Their vision is one of a global industry served by a handful of global companies, each dominant with respect to its supply chain and product markets. Consolidation, driven by the most efficient companies, which have the best systems and technologies, is proclaimed to be in the best interests of all concerned—investors, consumers, employees, and governments.

The efficiency gains resulting from economies of scale, improved plant utilization rates, and the coordination of production and distribution on a global basis certainly lead to improved financial returns for the company's owners, but they also lead to improved product quality, assured supplies, and continuity of employment. In other words, cross-border mergers and takeovers, while understandably threatening to many of those involved, ultimately work to the benefit of all stakeholders. This argument, so seductive in its general appeal, can be found running as a common thread through the public statements of all companies with a voracious appetite for global restructuring.

When BP launched its successful bids for AMOCO (1998) and ARCO (2000), for example, restructuring, consolidation, and operational synergies were featured heavily as the standard bearers of change. These megamergers propelled BP to the forefront of the world energy industry, presaging further bold moves in Russia and other parts of the world by CEO Lord John Browne, whose motto is "No risk—no gain."

Companies that pursue a strategy of shifting shape within an emergent-market context are *early adapters*. These are companies that recognize the limitations and dangers of remaining wedded to their current markets and business models and resolve to shift their position to take advantage of emergent-market developments. There is an element of "jumping on the bandwagon" in these cases, but by shifting shape sooner rather than later, early adapters can, in the most favorable circumstances, establish themselves as market leaders.

There is no better example than the Finnish company Nokia. Founded in 1865 to produce wood pulp, the company gradually diversified its activities into chemicals, rubber, and telecommunications equipment. Breakout came in the late 1980s and 1990s when the company recognized the potential of digital communications technology and focused on the development, manufacture, and marketing of cellular telephones. This required Nokia to expand at lightning speed, greatly extending its organizational capabilities, while learning to discern, fashion, and take advantage of consumer trends.

Likewise, it is through recognition of emergent-market trends that Apple Computer has been able to revive its fortunes in recent years. By 2001, when it entered the market for mass-storage digital music players, Apple had been reduced to the status of bit-part player in the personal and business computer markets. The iPod was a superbly conceived strategic response to the company's commercial difficulties. Apple created a device that had all the characteristics of its brand—it was highly functional, yet stylish and easy to use. The company has been able to charge premium prices and still claim the lion's share of the market. Its music download service was launched in 2003, and by piggybacking on the iPod has proved to be another runaway success.

Companies that pursue a strategy of shifting shape within an established-market context are *power players*. These companies are the titans of the global economy. Many of them have long histories, and they invariably have accumulated formidable organizational, knowledge, network, and reputational assets. They have many products, and their operations span many countries. They have access, internally and externally, to very large financial resources, and they acquire other companies whenever it is strategically necessary to do so. They devote massive amounts of resources to research and development, generating intellectual property, which is translated into products and is heavily protected by law. For these superleague companies, such as GE, IBM, P&G, Sony, L'Oréal, Nestlé, Siemens, Bayer, and Phillips, staying out in front requires constant vigilance and a willingness to shift shape, to break out periodically in order to lead and dominate dynamic, high-growth markets. Transformation—of products, markets, and ways of doing things—is the watchword of these companies.

Yet, despite all the evident advantages that power players have, they are susceptible to serious competitive challenges on a regular basis, with the result that even the mightiest, should it fail strategically, can be brought low. The dangers inherent in success are illustrated by the recent history of the Japanese electrical giant Matsushita.[2] For many decades, up until the early 1970s, the company was led by its inspirational founder, Konosuke Matsushita. The company was at the forefront of the global breakout of the Japanese consumer electronics industry, with brands such as National, Panasonic, JVC, and Technics. It took full advantage of the expansion of the domestic and international markets, driving down costs through mass production and introducing a stream of hit products such as the VHS-format video recorder.

In the 1990s, though, after decades of profitable growth, Matsushita ran into serious trouble. Like other Japanese producers, it had to confront the problems of the rising value of the yen, which made its products more expensive abroad, and increasing competition from low-cost producers elsewhere in east Asia. The company was caught off guard. Its long-established divisional structure, decentralized processes and decision making, supply-chain relationships, and lifetime employment policies all stood in the way of a coherent response to the crisis. Panic measures such as the purchase of the Hollywood entertainment company MCA merely made matters worse.

Only in recent years has the company faced up to the need for root and branch reform. Matsushita has begun its revival by eliminating redundant plants; streamlining operations; restructuring its sales, marketing, and distribution operations; focusing outside Japan on the Panasonic brand; and bringing to market a raft of higher-value products with features that it knows customers want.

Our research into the four types of companies that are striving to stay out in front highlights the different strategic rationales that are at play in different markets. Strategies are never pure. They are conditioned by the particular circumstances of companies and markets. What matters in all circumstances, however, is that the strategy pursued is suitable for the purpose and is executed to good effect. In what follows, by looking in more depth at the breakout experiences of selected boundary breakers, conquistadores, early adapters, and power players, we identify what differentiates companies that succeed in staying out in front from those that fall by the wayside.

Boundary Breakers

If a company is to break out by expanding rapidly across geographic boundaries, it must be able to satisfy seven critical conditions. The first is market readiness. In emergent markets, demand is latent rather than expressed, and the genius of first-wave entrepreneurs lies in recognizing potential through indirect market signals. Shifts in purchasing power, lifestyle, tastes, social ideas, and aspirations are all homologous indicators of presently unexpressed demands. It is through reading the symbols and forming a vision of what might be that a company can move swiftly from local to global. Second, the company's value proposition must be both compelling and readily transportable, appealing equally to potential customers in many parts of the world. This suggests that mechanisms for consumer learning, including the media and direct experience through travel, must be in place. Third, it is necessary to have a business model that is readily scalable, capable of delivering the company's value proposition without dilution as growth occurs. Fourth, robust mechanisms must be put in place to deliver growth physically, duplicating the company's formula in one place after another. Fifth, business relationships of various kinds must be formed to facilitate growth in different legal jurisdictions. Sixth, the company must engage in organization building, putting in place the formal structures, systems, and processes that are needed to control and coordinate its operations. Finally, it is through capturing economies of scale, widening margins, increasing free cash flow, and developing the brand that boundary breakers are able to create the momentum they need to expand their horizons rapidly.

It is by satisfying these conditions that companies such as Starbucks, Inditex, and Best Western have established themselves as global leaders in their respective fields. In the case of Starbucks, the potential for breakout, first recognized by Howard Schultz when he took over the company in 1987, was that large numbers of increasingly affluent consumers might embrace specialty coffee as one part of a more discerning lifestyle. He had already begun to experiment and test his ideas a year earlier when he opened his own Italian-style café in Seattle. But Starbucks, which already roasted its own coffee, represented a much bigger opportunity. It was an established regional brand that, if allied with the right value proposition, had the potential to go national and then international. His big idea was to offer customers first-class products served by dedicated staff in culturally distinctive settings—comfortable and visually interesting, with sophisticated background music and the arresting aroma of freshly ground coffee. This formula, he reasoned, would be readily transportable, enabling Starbucks to establish itself as a premium brand commanding high prices.

He was right. Customers responded with enthusiasm. Starbucks went national in 1987 and international when the company opened in Japan in 1996. Within 15 years, the company had 5,700 outlets spanning 28 countries and revenues of $3.3 billion. Growth on this scale was made possible by setting up specialist teams for property acquisition, store design, and application of standard store formats. In order to build the brand and ensure consistent delivery, Schultz eschewed franchising as a vehicle for expansion, preferring instead to keep direct control of its stores through ownership or long-term agreements with overseas partners.

Meanwhile, the company made large investments in roasting facilities, infrastructure, logistics, quality control, and employee training. Economies of scale have been reaped, and new products have been introduced to leverage the power of the Starbucks brand.

Similar growth dynamics can be seen at Inditex. Here, the story dates from 1975, when Amancio Ortega opened his first Zara store.[3] The original concept for Zara, which remains at the heart of the brand's value proposition, was to offer highly fashionable clothes, inspired by the latest international designs, at relatively modest prices. Ortega's idea was perfectly in tune with the spirit of the times. In Spain, the repression of the Franco era had been recently consigned to history, and the country was beginning to enjoy the fruits of its newfound economic prosperity. Younger people were relishing the opportunity for self-expression, and, as elsewhere in the world, the demand for fashionable clothes at affordable prices was on the rise.

By having in-house designers who visited all the major international fashion shows and fairs, Zara was able to emulate breaking styles quickly. By manufacturing in-house, the company could have the latest designs in stock in retail outlets within weeks. These outlets were located in the most prestigious districts of major towns and cities to reinforce the brand image of contemporary sophistication. Zara took off very quickly, and in 1985, Ortega established Inditex as a vehicle for future growth.

Its fast-fashion model has been refined and extended continuously in the two decades since. By 2006, the company had 2,700 retail outlets in 62 countries supporting a family of brands, neatly segmenting the market while taking advantage of a common corporate infrastructure. Inditex has the further advantage of ultra-rapid feedback on customer choices allied with just-in-time manufacturing and advanced logistics, reducing waste and shortening the time between design concept and in-store display. New facilities in lower-wage economies have enhanced the company's manufacturing capabilities. In short, Inditex, like Starbucks, has invested heavily in its corporate vision to emerge as a powerhouse of world fashion.

Not all boundary-breaker breakouts have been as successful as Zara. Carrying a winning formula from one geographically defined market space to others is easier said than done. Despite the globalization of taste, design, and service, big differences among countries persist. Zara's emphasis on the winning combination of international design, fashionable products, and affordability enabled it to appeal to an image-conscious, upwardly mobile market across a wide range of countries. This was not the case for British retailer Marks and Spencer (M&S), which ran into difficulties when it pursued a boundary-breaking strategy during the 1980s and 1990s. At its zenith, M&S had stores in 28 countries across the globe, but since then it has retrenched and is present today mainly in former British colonies. Attempts to expand into mainland Western Europe and the United States failed owing to the lack of appeal of the M&S value proposition: high prices allied with high quality and service standards.

M&S entered the United States in the late 1980s in a blaze of glory with the purchase of clothier Brooks Brothers for $750 million and the up-market food retailer Kings Supermarkets for $108 million. The Kings acquisition proved difficult from the start. Boundary breaking is based on taking your tried and tested formula for success into a host of different markets. M&S had built up a niche reputation for food retailing in the United Kingdom based on offering a limited range of products that were different and exciting and that genuinely met consumer needs. At the forefront of its approach were single-portion "complete meal" dishes. The meals were not frozen (such products existed in other supermarket chains) but chilled. Chilled food is prepared fresh and needs to be heated or lightly cooked before serving. There is no defrosting process. The range of dishes chosen was semi-exotic rather than everyday (Szechwan chicken and aromatic crispy duck were among the most popular selections). These products were not cheap, nor were they designed for family eating. Instead, the typical customer was a busy professional who, after a hard day at work, might enjoy a "special" meal without the bother of preparation. Very few consumers were expected to shop exclusively at M&S for food. Instead, they would use the store to augment the purchase of everyday items.[4]

Could this strategy work abroad, particularly in the sophisticated and crowded U.S. market? In fact, transporting this value proposition to Kings Supermarkets proved very difficult. First, U.S. consumers had very different expectations. Paying premium prices did not come naturally, and if they did, it was for food with an emphasis on low fat and high fiber. Thus, the dishes that were attractive to British customers did not work in the United States. Second, competing supermarkets in the United States already stocked a wide variety of take-home and premium easy-to-cook meals. The American deli and in-store salad bars offered a range of fresh products that made the M&S chilled-food concept less appealing. Third, chilled food requires carefully controlled supplier and distribution networks. The cost and complexity associated with this are manageable in a country the size of the United Kingdom but much more difficult in a country the size of the United States.

The translation of the M&S clothing value proposition also ran into problems. In acquiring Brooks Brothers, M&S was buying the oldest retailer in the United States, founded 175 years earlier in New York. The retailer was best known for selling suits and button-down shirts. It operated over 150 stores across the United States and also had outlets in Japan. But Brooks Brothers never managed to live up to its potential, and M&S failed to integrate it with its clothing operations elsewhere in the world.

What went wrong? The main difficulty was that Brooks Brothers was a business that was already sliding, suffering from an increasingly dowdy and out-of-date image. M&S, which was itself rather staid and conservative, did not have the management or the creative talent to turn this situation around. In late 2001, M&S sold Brooks Brothers for $225 million, less than a third of the $750 million it had paid for it 13 years earlier. Its boundary-breaking strategy lay in tatters, and it was plain that the time had come for it to rein in its international expansion, particularly in those markets where there was no preexisting demand for the M&S brand and value proposition.

The power of any brand, as this story of international expansion and retreat confirms, lies in its ability to inspire positive feelings in consumers, inclining them toward purchase. These feelings, in turn, are related to confidence that the product or service will deliver what it promises and the prestige associated with ownership or consumption. Only when a company routinely delivers on its value proposition can brand value be accumulated.

The global spread of the Best Western group is a good example. Best Western makes its money by collecting fees from privately owned member hotels around the world. The hotels receive various services from Best Western, such as booking referrals, access to a reservation center, management of a loyalty scheme, tie-ups with airlines and travel groups, and consortium advertising. However, perhaps the greatest benefit of membership is identification with the Best Western brand, which says to customers that the hotel they are checking into is guaranteed to have high standards. Customers can expect the hotel to have its own special features and country-specific service differentiators, but they can be confident because they know that Best Western hotels, as a condition of membership, regularly must pass stringent quality checks. In effect, the Best Western value proposition is predicated on the idea that its brand enhances those of its individual members. This effect has been so powerful that from a modest start in 1946, the organization has grown to become the world's biggest hotel brand, with more than 4,000 member hotels in 80 countries around the world.

Boundary breaking by its nature is liberating. Customers' lives are enriched through the availability of desirable new products and services, and for such companies as Starbucks, Inditex, and Best Western, there is the excitement of pushing the limits of possibility. Those that succeed in their quest to stay out in front do so by shaping the business and cultural practices of people the world over. In some cases, as at Starbucks, the brand and its associated value proposition are inextricably linked to the values and identity of the company. In other cases, as at Inditex, where multiple brands are promoted according to the logic of segmentation, the fortunes of the company and the brand are more loosely coupled. In all cases, however, staying out in front demands that brand loyalty be cultivated through the relentless pursuit of customer satisfaction.

Conquistadores

There is nothing new about industrial restructuring on a grand scale. In the United States, the late nineteenth and early twentieth centuries witnessed a battle royal for industrial control, led by all-conquering companies such as Standard Oil and Carnegie Steel and by all-powerful individuals such as John D. Rockefeller and Andrew Carnegie. Indeed, the breakout strategies of Rockefeller and Carnegie remain prescient. It was Rockefeller who gathered 40 companies into the Standard Oil Trust in 1882 to control 90 percent of refining capacity in the United States. The master plan was to invest massively in a network of pipelines connecting oil fields with refineries and to concentrate production in a small number of highly efficient refineries. This bold move was driven by the potential to cut the costs of production dramatically through the realization of economies of scale. It paid off handsomely. Standard Oil became highly cash generative and applied its enormous financial resources to integrate backwards into crude oil production and forward into distribution.

Carnegie likewise was driven by the logic of economic efficiency. He was the first steel magnate to build an integrated Bessemer steel rail mill, the Edgar Thompson Works in Pittsburgh, which began production in 1879 and was for decades the world's largest steel plant. He moved quickly to take control of other steelworks and make major technological improvements. Carnegie had a passion for measuring costs and experimenting to reduce them, and, like Rockefeller at Standard Oil, he pursued vertical integration, investing backward to secure supplies of coal and iron ore and forward into fabrication. At every turn, he instilled the need to produce goods of the very highest quality. The upshot was that Carnegie created, by dint of first-class strategy and brilliant implementation, the best-managed and most profitable steel company in the world.

The enduring logic of industrial consolidation, given full expression by the likes of Rockefeller and Carnegie, is manifest today in the global restructuring strategies of conquistador companies such as Mittal Steel, cement maker CEMEX, and EADS, the European Aeronautical Defense and Space Company. The parallels between Carnegie Steel and Mittal, which by 2005 was the largest steel company in the world by volume, with a production capacity of 70 million metric tons, are striking. Mittal has its own Andrew Carnegie in the form of Lakshmi Mittal, who has led the company in its transformation from Indian minnow to global giant over three decades. His conviction, stated and restated, is that the global steel industry simply has too many players to be truly efficient and profitable. In a highly cyclical business, he reasons, the stability needed to think long term can be attained only by progressively eliminating small and inefficient producers. By concentrating production, massive economies of scale can be achieved through the employment of state-of-the-art technologies and world-class management practices and through greater control over the supply chain.

Mittal, like Carnegie, has mastered the arts of cost management, technological innovation, and quality improvement. It is this mastery that enabled the company, beginning in the late 1980s, to take over and revitalize failing companies in Trinidad, Canada, Germany, Kazakhstan, France, Romania, Czechoslovakia, Poland, Bosnia, and the United States. At the same time, the company has integrated by centralizing trading operations, implementing a global enterprise management system, opening research and development centers, and securing control of raw material suppliers.

Another conquistador breakout occurred in the cement industry at around the same time. The moving spirit behind Mexico's global cement company CEMEX is Lorenzo Zambrano, grandson of the founder, who was appointed CEO in 1985, having studied engineering at Monterrey Tech and business at Stanford. By the late 1980s, the logic of global consolidation in the cement industry already was apparent and was being actively pursued by companies such as Lafarge of France. The parallels with the steel industry are all too apparent. Bigger companies, operating a network of large plants, might increase plant utilization rates and drive down costs by increasing operational efficiency. Cyclicality might be combated by diversifying geographically. By integrating forward into ready-mixed concrete, companies might attain greater control over the supply chain. They might gain further advantages through more effective management of distribution channels.

Zambrano read the situation correctly, and rather than having his company taken over, he resolved that CEMEX should become an industry consolidator. The process began at home in Mexico. Noncore businesses were sold, operational efficiency was increased, and other Mexican firms were taken over. A number of big moves followed in the 1990s. The first was to acquire and merge the two largest cement companies in Spain, a country with which CEMEX felt a strong cultural affinity. Other acquisitions followed to extend the company's reach across Central and South America and the Caribbean. Asian acquisitions followed, beginning in the late 1990s.

In 2000, CEMEX's profile was raised in a dramatic fashion through its acquisition of South Down, the largest cement manufacturer in the United States. This was followed by further takeovers in Asia and a foray into France. In 2004, the United Kingdom's largest ready-mix cement company, RMC, became part of the CEMEX global empire of 50 cement works and 475 ready-mix plants spread across 30 countries.

Growth on this scale was the result of the remorseless pursuit of a simple three-pronged strategy. First, all new acquisitions are brought into the fold swiftly by postacquisition teams focused on driving down costs. Second, CEMEX makes sophisticated use of its global information technology assets to manage capacity, overhead, and all aspects of the supply chain, improving efficiency and driving up free cash flow. Third, much of the resources needed for growth are generated from the reinvestment of free cash into the business, relieving the company of the massive burdens of debt that have caused other acquisitive firms to lose their independence. By executing the acquisition process more skillfully than most, CEMEX is well positioned to continue along the road to global domination.

Conquistadores are found not only in basic industries like steel and cement. In aerospace, for example, the costs of developing new aircraft have multiplied decade after decade. Ever larger companies, born of multiple mergers, have emerged in response to the need for access to very large financial and technological resources. The European Aeronautical Defense and Space Company (EADS), like Boeing in the United States, is the product of a long process of consolidation and capacity building. Formed in 2000, the company brought together the core resources of the French, German, and Spanish aerospace industries, including those of Airbus. It is the world's second-largest aerospace company and has 70 production sites in Britain, France, Germany, and Spain.

Airbus is the jewel in the crown. Its success in rivaling Boeing has stemmed from the commitment of all stakeholders to think long term in developing a complete family of aircraft that in terms of design, operational efficiency, advanced features, and technological sophistication could claim to be among the best in the world. The ultimate expression of this ambition was the launch in 2006 of the A380 superjumbo, the largest and most advanced passenger aircraft in the world at that point. Under joint French and German leadership, EADS has formed alliances and established production facilities in important national markets to curb resistance to its tendering for high-value defense and civil contracts. This is especially true in the United States, where EADS North America manufactures helicopters and other products and has acquired the specialist testing and services company Racal Instruments.

Common to all conquistador companies is the conviction that size matters. Dominant companies such as Mittal Steel, CEMEX, and EADS have accumulated the resources needed to progressively restructure entire industries and reap significant economies of scale and scope. In breaking out while others languished, they have created a platform for future growth. These companies, like Carnegie Steel and Standard Oil before them, know the importance of developing and maintaining leading-edge organizational, managerial, and technological capabilities. This is the true basis of their power and global reach.

The validity of this point is evident when one considers the strategic failure of a would-be conquistador, the retailer W.T. Grant. This case is interesting because it highlights the fact that size—in the absence of organizational, managerial, and technological capabilities—is not enough to support a successful breakout. What Grant set out to do in the late 1960s and early 1970s was to control the U.S. nonfood retail sector by creating outlets that could satisfy all customer needs under one roof. CEO William Staley decided that W.T. Grant would become a combination of all its successful rivals—discount, department, and variety stores all in one. The move created confusion in customers' minds by complicating the W.T. Grant image, brand, and value proposition. The situation was made worse by Grant's having stores of very different sizes and the company's practice of giving local managers a high degree of freedom with respect to stock selection. The stores operated essentially as autonomous units, with the manager of each being compensated based on his or her own store's profitability. This system encouraged abuses and competition between Grant stores, even those in the same markets. Because each store manager was responsible for his or her own inventory, the corporate center was unable to track companywide inventories effectively. Store managers began ordering goods and delaying passing the invoices to the head office, which, in turn, increased purchasing budgets and understated the cost of sales.

W.T. Grant was an exceptionally badly managed business. It positioned itself in the middle between the discounters and the quality service merchandisers and was able to compete effectively against neither. Moreover, Grant lacked a sales classification system that would have given the head office a better picture of market trends; instead, the corporate office was given only total store performance figures, without information on specific item performance. This, in turn, wrecked havoc on corporate buyers, who had no idea what to promote. To make matters worse, the company launched a credit strategy aimed at attracting consumers and capturing market share.

Essentially, Grant became "a finance company with a retail appendage."[5] It offered all its customers very easy credit for literally any purchase. The only terms were a minimum payment of $1 each month, with 36 months to pay the full balance. Credit approval and records were the responsibility of individual store managers, another recipe for disaster. Many customers were unreliable and did not pay their bills. However, since clerks at the Grant stores were paid an extra dollar for every creditor they signed up, more and more customers were enrolled in the failing credit program. The consequences of strategic failure and management incompetence eventually hit home in 1974, when the company posted a loss of $177 million. With massive debts, falling sales, and suppliers that were unwilling to extend further credit, Grant spiraled swiftly downward. In 1975, Grant lost a further $111 million and filed for Chapter 11 bankruptcy protection, declaring total liabilities of more than $1 billion.

The mistakes made at W.T. Grant are not difficult to discern. The company embarked on a harebrained breakout strategy without proper controls. Corporate management simply did not establish a means of achieving accurate oversight of store managers, whose compensation system encouraged only self-interest. On top of all this, corporate governance broke down, and the board failed in its responsibilities.

This is in stark contrast with the breakout of Kmart. The first Kmart opened in 1962, and by 1970, the company was the third-largest retailer in the United States, behind Sears and JC Penney. Kmart had embarked on a growth strategy at the same time as Grant and was the largest builder of retail space in the early 1970s. The keys to its success that escaped Grant are fairly clear. Kmart's growth strategy involved detailed planning of operations and simplicity and standardization across the company. Added to this was high-quality management with the best training and development programs in the industry.

The reason that Grant failed to follow similar implementation strategies inevitably comes down to its lack of a focused approach and weak management that did not have the proper tools to understand what was happening. The lack of simplicity in the organization's structure and systems only exacerbated the problems. The burgeoning inventories, management abuses, and easy credit terms are all symptoms of this more fundamental strategic failure. The outcome was that Kmart became a conquistador breakout company, overcoming competitors such as W.T. Grant and becoming a dominant retail player across the United States. W.T. Grant failed to become one of the nation's leading retailers and disappeared into the annals of business history as a result of its dash for greatness.

Early Adapters

Expanding horizons neatly expresses the purpose and logic of corporate goals for geographically expanding businesses, both boundary breakers and conquistadores. The same is not quite true of the label *shifting shape*, which captures the essence of certain types of strategy but suggests the ambiguity and even the complexity of the strategy process. Shifting shape, whether in the context of emergent or established markets, is the most difficult of the four types of breakout strategy to conceive and execute. It applies to companies that are entrenched in particular markets, identified with particular brands and value propositions, and supported by established and finely tuned business models.

The perceived need to shift shape—to set a new strategic course and engineer radical change—often stems from sudden changes in the competitive landscape. When serious threats to profitability and survival arise, they must be dealt with, but doing so is never straightforward. There is often ambiguity concerning the nature and magnitude of nascent competitive threats, and any reaction that smacks of panic may precipitate a damaging crisis of confidence. Good timing and fine judgment are at a premium. It is necessary to respond proportionately and in a timely fashion, turning the organization to face the future without damaging its existing operations. Shape shifting demands that strategic leaders take their customers, suppliers, employees, and shareholders on a journey into the unknown, and to do so, they must overcome powerful cultural and systemic resistances to change. The need is for a compelling strategy, confidently communicated and superbly executed.

These qualities can be seen at work at the Irish air carrier Aer Lingus, where (now former) CEO Willie Walsh responded swiftly to the extreme competitive threat posed by the emergence of low-cost airlines such as Ryanair and easyJet.[6] As we saw in Chapter 2, years of government protection and subsidy had resulted in the state-owned company's becoming inefficient and complacent. It was genuinely shaken by the competitive threat posed by the newly energized and aggressive Ryanair in particular. Walsh was appointed CEO in October 2001. He inherited command of an airline that was plagued by high costs, low operating margins, and a severely negative bottom line. He had the advantage, however, of knowing the airline inside and out, having risen through the ranks since 1979, when he was appointed a cadet pilot.

It was apparent to Walsh that low-cost competitors were here to stay and that they would continue to win market share at the expense of Aer Lingus if he did not do something about it. The strategic solution, he reasoned, was to adapt early by migrating Aer Lingus toward the rapidly expanding value-for-money sector of the market. This did not mean throwing the baby out with the bathwater. Aer Lingus had a reputation for excellent customer service and was well liked by business travelers. It made sense, therefore, to maintain the airline as a differentiated service provider, offering business class and economy cabins (on most routes), and to retain the features that customers truly valued: friendly service, assigned seating, direct flights to major airports, and the promise never to leave passengers stranded. The value proposition that would work best for Aer Lingus, therefore, was one of competitive prices pitched across market segments in tandem with good service standards. This would win new customers and bring others back, increasing seat occupancy rates and creating the potential for sustained growth.

Soon after Walsh's appointment, Aer Lingus showed its resolve and commitment by halving business fares and sharply reducing others. Customers' response was predictably positive. However, the real test lay not just in customer acceptance of such a radically improved value proposition but also in whether the company could reengineer its business model sufficiently to sustain its delivery.

It was here that Walsh's inside knowledge paid off. He was able to win acceptance for change with no half measures from all stakeholder groups. He knew where the fat was in the business and how to slim down the workforce by 40 percent without damaging operations, safety, or service quality. He seized the opportunity to embrace online booking as the main vehicle for customer access, driving down booking costs by 40 percent. He closed down historic loss-making routes and opened many others across the European network, taking full advantage of the good relations that Aer Lingus enjoyed with the regulatory authorities. The effect was to make the airline leaner, more flexible, and more competitive. Within six months, a significant loss had been turned into a respectable profit, and, still more positively, revenue growth was rising steeply—a remarkable turnaround by any standard.

The rise to international prominence since the 1990s of the Californian winemaker E.&J. Gallo bears elegant testimony to the advantages of early adaptation. The company has grown from small beginnings in 1933 to a global giant with more than 45 wine brands and sales in 95 countries. In its first incarnation, Gallo was famed as the "Campbell's soup of the wine industry," offering fair-quality wines at modest prices. The brand was trusted, but its products were considered "jug wines," acceptable for everyday drinking but not good enough for special occasions. The company's value proposition was based on its low price, and its wines were to be found on most supermarket shelves in the United States.

Sales continued to grow, but by the early 1980s, Ernest Gallo, a cofounder and the strategic brain behind the company, had realized that market trends were working against the company. As standards of living continued to rise, the wine market was becoming more segmented, with customers in the rapidly growing midsection of the market becoming more discerning with respect to quality. Margins were under increasing pressure at the low end of the market and were many times higher for wines perceived to be of superior quality. This analysis led Gallo to adapt early and shift shape.

The strategy underpinning Gallo's second incarnation has been to segment the market and offer branded wines that are respected for their quality and consistency in all segments except the lowest and the very highest. In short, the Gallo family of wines has moved up-market and has increased in size, with each member of the family having something different to offer wine drinkers in terms of taste, quality, and price.

Realization of this vision has been a long-term project for Gallo. No quick fix was needed, as at Aer Lingus; instead, the company needed long-term policies for production, distribution, and marketing. Vineyards have been acquired regularly over the past two decades in the best grape-growing districts in California, such as Napa Valley and Sonoma Valley, and the company has positioned its brands around the locator "Gallo of Sonoma," intended as a mark of assured good quality. The company now has access to each of the prime grape-growing districts in California and produces wine in every category.

Leading brands include Ernest & Julio Gallo, Turning Leaf, Ecco Domani, Walkabout, Anapamu, and Rancho Zabaco. As at the Spanish fashion company Inditex, each brand is seen as having its own personality and devotees. Yet this diversity of product is brought to market through a very savvy business organization operating on centralized lines. Gallo is a leader in automated production, bottling, and logistics. It invests heavily in research on soils, growing methods, grape varieties, and winemaking techniques and in market research to evaluate changing tastes and consumer lifestyles. No company has done more through its promotional activities to elevate the standing of the Californian wine industry, which now generates revenues of $45 billion globally.

Aer Lingus and Gallo had been around a long time when they decided to shift shape. At HIT Entertainment, the decision came much sooner, when the business was still at a formative stage. The company was formed in 1989 by Peter Orton, who had worked for many years for Jim Henson, the puppeteer famous for creating *The Muppet Show*, *Fraggle Rock*, and *Sesame Street*. Orton had been responsible for international distribution, and when Henson sold out to Disney, Orton successfully laid claim to the HIT (Henson International Television) name. Acquiring the HIT brand enabled Orton to branch out on his own as an independent distributor specializing in the sale of children's programs and associated merchandising rights. The company soon came to specialize in preschool entertainment and natural history programs, reasoning that such properties have a long shelf life and ready international appeal.

Orton was a well-known figure in the broadcasting world and had little trouble signing new properties, but gradually things began to change. U.S. broadcasters, following regulatory changes, increasingly favored originating their own content, and channels such as Discovery began doing deals directly with the production companies. HIT felt the intermediation space being squeezed. Its response was to become an early adapter, radically shifting shape to originate and exploit its own properties.

This change in strategy heralded the breakout of HIT, which within a few years went from being second fiddle to international impresario. Orton set out to make HIT the world's leading independent owner of preschool television rights and, ultimately, content. His confidence stemmed from his belief that HIT knew how to identify strong preschool concepts, fully exploit properties, and make deals in all parts of the world. The company went public in 1996. Important projects followed that saw the launch of *Bob the Builder*, *Angelina Ballerina*, and *Percy the Park Keeper*, among others.

The runaway success, in terms of both television sales and merchandising, was *Bob the Builder*. Its success raised HIT's profile and paved the way for its acquisition of other production companies, notably Lyrick Studios, the owner of *Barney*, and Gullane, the owner of *Thomas the Tank Engine*. This combination of organic and inorganic growth resulted in the market value of the company rising from $24 million when it went public to $583 million in June 2003 and $917 million when it was acquired by the private equity firm Apax in April 2005. The company since has gone on to play a leading part in the formation of the first dedicated preschool channel in the world, PBS Sprout.

HIT Entertainment was among the first companies to see the value of owning the rights to endearing children's characters and bringing them to life across many different media—television, books, video, toys, and consumer products.[7] But just because you are one of the first into a new or rapidly expanding market space does not mean that you will endure for long as a serious competitor—or even be remembered as an early adapter. The story of Psion, the pioneer of the handheld personal digital assistant (PDA), is a case in point of a breakout company that failed to stay the course.[8] How many people even know that Psion was in that market before Palm? What caused Psion to lose its early-adapter advantage and cede breakout to its rivals?

Psion was founded in 1980 as one of the first British software technology companies, and it rapidly became one of the country's best-known high-technology enterprises. The initial market that Psion exploited was software publishing, which involved repackaging, marketing, and distributing selected third-party software for the Sinclair microcomputers in the very early days of the microcomputer industry. Psion also sold Sinclair computers to consumers in South Africa, where it had the sole distributorship. Profits from software publishing propelled Psion into the next stage of its growth as a software development house. Psion's founder, David Potter, built a core team of very bright, academically accomplished, and highly skilled software engineers that was focused on developing and selling both application and gaming software for Sinclair computers.

As a software development company, Psion rapidly gained a reputation for high-quality and innovative software for first-generation microcomputers. But competition was already knocking at the door. It was this challenge that prompted Potter and his team to shift into the emerging handheld computer business. Despite the early success of the software business, Psion recognized early on that it would be difficult to keep the competition out. It decided to invest the capital base created by the early returns from the software business into an ambitious new project to build the first portable handheld computer. As David Potter later commented, this was a virgin market—with both high risk and potentially high reward.[9] The new device—the Psion Organiser 1—was brought to market in 1984. Psion became the world's first volume manufacturer of a handheld computing product, the global pioneer of an important new sector.

By the end of 1987, handheld computers and associated peripherals and software accounted for 90 percent of Psion's revenues, which had reached 11 million pounds sterling, with a profit of 1.9 million pounds and 80 employees. By the end of 1988, the company was seen as the dominant player occupying a new market space, with the Organiser being featuring on billboards at that year's Seoul Olympic Games.

However, things began to heat up in the early 1990s, when major competitors such as Hewlett-Packard, Amstrad, and Casio appeared on the horizon. Apple's chairman and CEO at the time, John Sculley, in fact introduced the term *personal digital assistant* (PDA). These new competitors entered the market either with "me-too" products or with similar products targeted at different geographic markets where Psion was not particularly strong, such as Asia. Yet the logic of first-mover advantage once more asserted itself. Apart from the Sharp Zaurus, which became dominant in the Japanese market, and Hewlett-Packard's LX series, whose entry price point was more than three times the price of the entry level of the Psion Series 3, none of the other entrants survived long enough to make any serious impact on Psion's overall market leadership in the portable handheld/PDA mobile sector. Psion was still on top in 1996, with an estimated 30 percent of the world palmtop sales by volume at 1.5 million units.

Enter Palm. The failed Casio Zoomer was brought to market by a loose coalition of players in the United States who had combined some new and innovative technologies in a unique way in an attempt to redefine the value proposition of the handheld computer for the consumer. The Zoomer contained a competitive (though not as sophisticated) operating system similar to Psion's from a company called Geoworks and an innovative handwriting-recognition facility from a company called Palmcomputing. In 1994, Psion had the opportunity of partnering with or even acquiring Palmcomputing when it was seeking additional development funding.

Palmcomputing eventually was bought in 1995 by U.S. Robotics, an American communications company, which funded the completion of the new Palm PDA. Palm launched its new product, with its much-improved handwriting-recognition technology, touch-sensitive screens, and portrait design form factor, in April 1996. It had much less functionality than the Psion Series 3 devices, but it was simple, easy to use, and excellent at synchronizing information with personal computers. Palm was an instant and massive success when it was launched in America. By the end of that year, it had 60 percent of the U.S. market, and by 1998 it was shipping 100,000 units per month, compared with 20,000 units per month for Psion's Series 5. By 1998, Palm, using Microsoft's operating system, had expanded its distribution to Europe and very quickly started to eat into Psion's home turf. By 1999, Palm was the market leader in Europe and around the world.

Following a major drop in its stock price, Psion announced the formation of Symbian, a joint venture of Psion, Ericsson, Nokia, and Motorola with the purpose of establishing the industry-standard operating system for the next generation of integrated mobile communication and computing devices. In early 2001, though, Motorola pulled out of the partnership, and a few months later the stock market collapsed, signaling the end of the technology boom. In July of that same year, with its PDA market share in Europe already eroded and the project with Motorola canceled, Psion exited the handheld market, citing the prevalence of already ultrathin margins in a business that was increasingly attracting the attention of established mass-market consumer electronics manufacturers against which Psion was too small to compete. The early adapter had been forced out of the market that it had forged.

So what went wrong? There are two main reasons why Psion's initial breakout and its leadership in the handheld PDA market were not sustainable despite its having been an initially successful early adapter. First, although Psion managed to dominate the market for handheld PDAs in Europe, it failed to make any real inroads into the larger U.S. market. In retrospect, Psion's management team realized that it should have invested more aggressively to win the loyalty of American technology buffs. Second, although the design of Psion's PDA was more advanced technically in terms of the functionality it offered, the Palm Pilot design had greater and wider consumer appeal because of its simplicity and functionality. The combination of these two factors allowed Palm to dominate the U.S. market quickly. Once Palm had done this, it moved into Europe, Psion's stronghold, and rapidly eroded Psion's market share.

Early adaptation to imminent competitive threats or market trends was instrumental in the breakout of Aer Lingus, Gallo, and HIT Entertainment, relieving each of these companies from the threat of being overtaken by more vigorous competitors. What stands out is the perspicacity of their leaders in reading emergent-market trends and the spiritedness of their response. Each company rallied to new and inspiring visions of the future, leading it to refresh its value propositions and organizational capabilities. The early adapter pursues a higher-risk strategy than our next and final form of breakout—the power player. The early adapter stakes its reputation, its client base, and often its entire future by moving into an emergent market that is not yet fully formed or proven. It does so because it sees the writing on the wall for its existing market arena or business model.

Aer Lingus recognized earlier than other state-owned airlines that cost reduction and price competition were defining features of the emergent air passenger market. E.&J. Gallo saw that tastes were evolving and consumers were becoming more discerning as the U.S. wine market grew and matured. HIT Entertainment recognized that being limited to distribution meant that it had little room for growth and that the future lay in emergent markets, integrating production, distribution, licensing, and merchandising across a variety of media. Power players are under no similar restrictions. They shift shape at will and often inorganically (through acquisition), with the explicit aim of developing and dominating high-growth, high-yield markets.

Power Players

In all fields of human endeavor, power comes from having command over resources, and the more extensive the resources commanded, the greater is an organization's capacity to make strategic investments and shape its own destiny. The aura of invincibility radiating from the giant corporations at the pinnacle of the global economic order is expressive of their power and permanence. Many of these corporations generate more wealth, measured in terms of value added per annum, than the entire economies of the world's smallest countries. They have awe-inspiring amounts of money, physical infrastructure, management expertise, technological knowledge, connections, and brand equity that are applied routinely to the business of staying out in front. They have the resources needed to develop and launch new products on a grand scale, mobilizing their businesses to make power plays in selected markets. Invariably, these markets have the potential to be very large and profitable, with margins well in excess of those in more commoditized sectors. Thus, shifting shape is a natural consequence of breaking out to establish dominant positions in higher-value markets.

Power plays often are signaled by arresting statements of strategic intent, followed swiftly by the announcement of important acquisitions, investments, and alliances. There are few better illustrations than IBM's declaration, following the appointment of Sam Palmisano as CEO in 2002, of its strategy to deliver to customers "e-business on demand." The phrase was intended to encapsulate a new way of thinking about the provision and purchase of information technology (IT) services. Instead of buying hardware, software, and services separately and integrating them in-house, potential clients were invited to consider the advantages of outsourcing their IT capacity and requirements to IBM.

In the proposed new world, a client organization would purchase, on a flexible basis, access to exactly the amount of resources it needed to run its business, scaling its requirements up and down as its needs dictated. The worries of technology would be taken away by IBM, which might help further by reengineering the client organization's systems and processes to take full advantage of the latest technological advances. Under this model of service provision, IBM could run the core systems of large numbers of client organizations, sharing resources on a truly global basis and securing significant economies of scale. This would mean a better deal for customers and increased revenues for IBM.

In order to win customers over to this vision of the future, Palmisano decided to bolster the company's consulting capabilities by purchasing PwC Consulting[10] in 2002 for $3.5 billion. This was part of a $10 billion investment in "e-business on demand," featuring, among other things, a futuristic advertising campaign to inspire clients across the world to explore business solutions with the company. In effect, Palmisano had decided to build on the work of his illustrious predecessor, Lou Gerstner, in shifting the primary source of IBM's revenues from computer hardware and software to business solutions. By 2005, the greatest part of IBM's revenues came from the provision of business services, replacing hardware as the primary driver of the business.

It is the sheer financial muscle of companies like IBM, with annual profits and near-cash reserves typically measured in billions of dollars, that enables them to make power plays of shape-shifting proportions. This can be seen most clearly at General Electric (GE), the U.S. industrial conglomerate that for many decades has been among the largest and most admired companies in the world. GE's portfolio includes power generation, electrical distribution, consumer electronics, jet engines, transportation engineering, health care equipment, plastics, television broadcasting, and financial services. Under Jack Welch, the company's CEO from 1981 to 2001, GE became famous for its relentless drive to reduce bureaucracy and improve financial performance. Numerous programs and initiatives were devised to improve quality, manage the supply chain, and cut costs.

Welch's successor, Jeffrey Immelt, took GE in a different direction, emphasizing innovation in products, markets, and technology as the key to sustained prosperity. This change led to a series of disposals and acquisitions worth $15 billion and $60 billion, respectively, between 2001 and 2004 alone. GE has identified biosciences, media content, security, water treatment, and renewable energy as growth areas for the future, and the company has been divided into 11 operating segments to better reflect its core capabilities. The thrust of GE's approach is to recognize the formative importance of key economic, social, cultural, and political problems and to respond by developing products and services that can be sold globally. The acquisition of biosciences and medical diagnostics company Amersham for $9.5 billion in 2003, for example, accelerated GE's advance in the health care field. As GE shifts shape, what now are small parts of the business will be scaled up and driven ever harder to deliver growth in revenues and the bottom line.

The same disciplined approach to business growth can be seen at the Swiss company Nestlé, owner of many of the world's leading food and beverage brands, including Nescafé, Carnation, Buitoni, Perrier, and KitKat. Nestlé's history is one of growth through acquisition and brand building. Its origins are in coffee, cocoa, and dairy-based products, but in the course of its pursuit of geographic and product expansion, it has shifted shape progressively to become a diversified provider of food, drink, confectionary, pet care, and pharmaceutical products.

Acquisitions totaled $26 billion between 1985 and 2000, accelerating to $25 billion in the first three years of the twenty-first century alone. By rapidly integrating and streamlining the operations of the companies it has acquired, Nestlé has been able to squeeze more from its assets, emphasizing low cost and efficiency as its primary driving theme. A second theme is to increase revenues by exploiting the full range of distribution channels in all parts of the world to ensure that the company's products are always readily available. A third theme is to renovate and innovate to develop brand presence. Families of related products, each with its own personality, are presented to the public rather than individual items. Individual brands then are tailored to meet the needs of particular markets. The final theme is to communicate the qualities and values of all Nestlé brands through conventional advertising and other less conventional methods of developing market presence.

This combination of cost containment and revenue generation has meant that Nestlé has been able to withstand the challenge of "own branding" by major retailers, maintaining healthy trading margins and high levels of free cash flow, which, in turn, have provided the financial muscle needed to pursue shape-shifting acquisitions.

Power players such as IBM, GE, and Nestlé have been in business a long time. The lesson they have learned so well is that of "go forward or perish." Yet even they are vulnerable to complacency and strategic error. In the early 1990s, IBM was caught flat-footed by profound market changes. New hardware and software competitors that could produce similar or better products at lower prices had sprung up in many segments of its core markets. Revenues fell while costs remained high, and huge losses were recorded, peaking at $7.6 billion in 1993. It is a tribute to the underlying strength of the organization and its brand that Lou Gerstner was able to turn the company around by rapidly reducing costs, increasing efficiency, and shifting shape. Thereafter, IBM was restored to the historically more normal position of generating massive revenues globally from a wide range of products and services and earning significant profits.

These are the fruits of domination enjoyed by power players. The essence of their position is that they must invest heavily in new lines of business, organically or through acquisition, in order to stay out in front. GE and Nestlé are proven masters of the art. The strategies of both companies are simple and readily understood. It is the brilliance and conviction shown in execution that set them apart.

Conclusion

Regardless of the reasons for and the pace of expansion or transformation, all the success stories discussed in this chapter had one thing in common—a clear and consistent breakout strategy that combined caution with enterprise. All of the companies involved had lucid visions of what their businesses were about and where they wanted to take them. None failed to realize the importance of having a unique offering to the customer. Each had carefully constructed its enterprise to ensure that it could deliver what it promised and, ideally, surpass expectations. All were led by people with foresight, creativity, and business acumen who succeeded in capturing the imaginations of customers beyond the narrow confines of their own national borders.

Chapter 4 looks at what lies beneath rapid transformation and business breakout at both an operational and a strategic level. Subsequent chapters will explore each of the essential features of breakout in turn, showing how together they provide a road map for successful strategic breakout.

Endnotes

1 For further details, see David Dyer, Frederick Dalzell, and Rowena Olegario, *Rising Tide: Lessons from 165 Years of Brand Building at Procter & Gamble*. Cambridge, MA: Harvard Business School Press, 2004.

2 See Charles Harvey, Mairi Maclean, and Anthony Hayward, "Good Luck or Fine Judgement? The Growth and Development of the Japanese Electronics Industry, 1945–1995," *Asia Pacific Business Review* 8(1):102–126, 2001; and Charles Harvey, Mairi Maclean, and Anthony Hayward, "From Knowledge Dependence to Knowledge Creation: Industrial Growth and the Technological Advance of the Japanese Electronics Industry," *Journal of Industrial History* 4(2):1–23, 2001.

3 Zara is by far the largest and best known of the brands in Inditex's portfolio, accounting for close to 70 percent of Zara's total revenues.

4 Isobel Doole and Robin Lowe, "Kings Supermarket, Inc.," in *International Marketing Strategy*. Stamford, CT: Thomson Learning, 2003.

5 L. J. Davis, "Grant's Tomb," in *Bad Money*. New York: St Martin's Press, 1982, p. 57.

6 See Denis G. Harrington, Thomas C. Lawton, and Tazeeb Rajwani, "Embracing and Exploiting Industry Turbulence: The Strategic Transformation of Aer Lingus," *European Management Journal* 23(4):450–457, 2005.

7 Anna Carugati, interview with former HIT chairman and founder Peter Orton, http://www.worldscreen.com, April 2005.

8 This section is based on research conducted by Akin Oyesola under the supervision of Thomas Lawton.

9 David Potter, "Entrepreneurship: Psion and Europe," *Business Strategy Review* 9(1):15–20, 1998.

10 Formerly a division of the global accounting giant PricewaterhouseCoopers.

CHAPTER 4

BREAKOUT DYNAMICS

At the heart of any breakout is a fast-moving cycle of transformational change. Let's face it: moving from a weak or subordinate position to one of market strength and power requires big changes throughout an organization. The shift to double-digit growth carries with it a requirement for sustained innovation and a clear focus on the marketplaces and opportunities you have chosen to go after. Internally, tired systems and work practices must give way to more robust organizational routines. Week after week, new people are hired to occupy newly created roles. In response to customer feedback, products are improved, modified, and restyled. Complementary products are introduced as one opportunity gives rise to others, and, importantly, you are in this game only because you have fully engaged with customers in a way that you probably never did before.

Working with the inevitable problems and emerging opportunities generates fresh knowledge and know-how concerning products, processes, and technologies. Employees are fired up by the prospects for personal development, promotion, and reward, and they embrace learning and opportunity seeking. Externally, opportunities often translate into new alliances and allegiances as the ever-present tensions of tight deadlines sharpen recognition of mutual dependencies. Where you were once playing on the margins of change, you are now connected to what is happening in your markets and with your customers. In sum, breakout is as much about the sheer pace of adjustment, change, and even re-creation as it is about the new strategic direction.

Consider the breakout of daily disposable contact lens maker Award Technology, founded in the United Kingdom in 1992 by Ron Hamilton and Bill Seden. It was Hamilton, a visionary engineer-businessman, who in 1988 conceived a new process for molding soft contact lenses that lowered the costs of production dramatically. His unique insight was to recognize that one of the two molds used to shape the lens also could serve as the container in which the lens would be packaged. At the time, Hamilton was U.K. managing director of the U.S. contact lens specialist CooperVision, but the company showed little interest in running with his idea.

As a result, Hamilton chose to break out on his own, establishing an experimental contact lens production facility with his colleague Bill Seden. Their research suggested the possibility of a remarkable value proposition: custom-made contact lenses at a price so low that they could be disposed of on a daily basis, guaranteeing sterility and eliminating the hassle and expense of overnight cleaning. They patented the manufacturing process and set about putting their ideas into practice.

However, it was not all easy sailing. The resistance and skepticism of existing manufacturers proved hard to overcome, and as time went by, rival processes began to emerge, potentially limiting the value of the partners' intellectual property. This drove them into a rights agreement with the medical technology group BTG, which had the knowledge and experience needed to defend their intellectual property on a global basis.

The lessons of the early years were hard won. In particular, it had become obvious that ownership of an innovative manufacturing process was not enough by itself to ensure commercial success. Already dominant companies had no immediate incentive to modify their existing processes, value propositions, and business models, which in terms of the bottom line were serving them well. In other words, Hamilton and Seden had to look elsewhere for allies that were interested in breaking the stranglehold of existing business practices.

It was at this point, in the early 1990s, that the two got their lucky break. An old friend of Hamilton's was so impressed by a demonstration of their process that he used his personal contacts to broker a meeting with the managing director of the largest chain of opticians in the United Kingdom, Boots Opticians. The company was easily convonced of the commercial potential of daily disposable lenses and, in return for being first in line for supplies, issued a letter of support containing upbeat sales projections. With this letter and a ringing endorsement of the health benefits of disposable lenses from the highly regarded Department of Ophthalmology of the University of Manchester Institute of Science and Technology (UMIST), the partners finally had the endorsements they needed to persuade potential investors to support the launch of a full-fledged disposable lens business. Scottish Enterprise, the development agency for Scotland, joined forces with Hamilton and Seden in 1992 to establish a manufacturing base in the town of Livingston.

Over the next three years, Award's breakout as a major new force in the market for disposable contact lenses was characterized by incredibly intense activity familiar to entrepreneurs the world over who have been at the helm when their companies made the move from "nothing" to "something." Acquiring equipment, laying out the factory, training operators, and perfecting the production process took precedence during the early months. Meanwhile, Boots, which was striving to gain a first-mover advantage over its rivals, began to train its staff and prepare the market for the launch of daily disposable lenses.

All went according to plan, and as Hamilton recalled when we interviewed him, "When the blue touch paper was finally lit, the daily experience of management went from being like pushing at a piece of string to being pulled along by a heavy rope." Customers of Boots, and later of other opticians at home and abroad, responded with enthusiasm to the daily disposable lens value proposition. Demand continuously ran ahead of supply, enabling Award to charge premium prices and generate significant free cash flow. Its factory geared up to work around the clock, and fresh capacity was added periodically. Hamilton remembers the breakout years as simultaneously being the most demanding and the most satisfying of his business career:

> *We had to scale up from cottage enterprise to international business in very short order. It wasn't all that simple. We had to deal with situations as they came up and find solutions. There was no choice but to be very close to the process—lens design, plastics and fast optical molding, hydro gel manufacture, optical machine tooling, sterile packaging. It all took complete and utter persistence. . . . And at the same time, there were all the normal business problems like creating effective operating, HR and finance systems and getting the right senior management team to take things forward. . . . It was an extreme situation requiring all hands to the pump all of the time.*[1]

Award grew swiftly from a start-up to manufacturing tens of millions of pairs of disposable lenses annually by 1995. Inevitably, the giants of the industry, hit by declining market shares and loss of revenue from sales of cleaning solutions, woke up to the threat posed by the rapid emergence of a vigorous new competitor. The daily disposable lens concept had arrived and could not be ignored. Rival products were soon under development, and Award, having accumulated considerable know-how and intellectual property, became a prime candidate for takeover. In 1996, Hamilton and Seden, together with BTG and Scottish Enterprise, agreed to sell the business to the U.S. eye care company Bausch & Lomb for $33 million, with an additional $15 million for intellectual property payable four years down the line.[2] Hamilton remained with the company until 1997 to oversee the building of a new factory with 15 highly automated production lines. The company's growth didn't stop there, and by 2001,

Award, with 1,200 employees in Scotland, was firmly established under the Bausch & Lomb banner as one of the world's biggest manufacturers of daily disposable lenses.

The sense of excitement and frenzied activity that are so apparent at Award are part and parcel of any major breakout, to a greater or lesser extent. Change and turbulence are the norm in rapidly growing companies, and it is clear that there are underlying commonalities between them. Yet there are equally big differences. True originals, revolutionaries, wave riders, big improvers, boundary breakers, conquistadores, early adapters, and power players break out from very different starting positions. Is it possible, therefore, to compare the dynamics of breakout at a long-established industrial giant such as General Electric (GE) and a fledgling enterprise such as Google in the mid-1990s?

The answer is a qualified yes. All breakouts, whether from a big or a small base, require a compelling value proposition and a sustainable business model. And, as we emphasize in this chapter, the cycles of change at all sorts of companies have remarkable commonalities. The qualification arises because there are big differences between the constraints and opportunities facing dominant companies with a wealth of capital and those facing subordinate companies with little to call their own.

This is not to say that it's always going to be "game, set, and match" for those that are already at the top. Indeed, history tells us that this is rarely the case. What it does mean, however, is that any strategy based on imitation is very likely to fail—and certainly is not likely to create breakout opportunities. Subordinate companies, in particular, need to operate differently from others. To overcome their limitations, they must think subversively, outwitting their competitors rather than copying them. Dominant companies, equally, should recognize that their present size in and of itself provides no guarantee that they have the resources and capabilities that they need if they are to stay out in front.

The Dynamics of Breakout

Before examining specific types and situations, let's take a closer look at the fundamental forces underlying breakout. It is important to really understand these *breakout dynamics* before going on to consider the breakout strategy cycle in the next four chapters. The model presented in Figure 4.1 shows that all companies, however large or small, can be viewed as bundles of four types of capital: organizational, human, social, and symbolic.[3] All of these forms of capital can be made dynamic in a way that unleashes a company's breakout potential. For instance, an enterprise may have cash or ideas, but it is the conversion of these into investments or inventions that enables it to engage with rivals in the battle for customers. Therefore, breakout begins when a business possesses or has access to one or more forms of capital and leverages this capital to create market opportunity or gain market advantage.[4] As we will see, and in contrast to what most people focus on, there actually are multiple forms of capital that have tremendous value for breakout leaders. Each is critical, and each holds opportunities that smart strategists pay attention to.

Organizational capital is the most conventional type of capital and the most easily understood. It consists of financial assets; nonfinancial assets such as patents; tangible assets in the form of facilities, plant, and equipment; and the systems, processes, and organizational routines that facilitate production, distribution, and control. Human capital, in contrast, is what an individual or team, rather than an organization, brings to the breakout table. Individuals make their personal capital available in exchange for financial and other rewards. We are thinking in particular here of the knowledge, know-how, skills, and capabilities of the breakout leader and the people that he or she attracts to the opportunity.

Social capital is partly a function of the connections that exist in all companies to a lesser or greater extent, along with the relationships that key employees "own" and can create that are beneficial to the company. Social capital takes the form of networks,

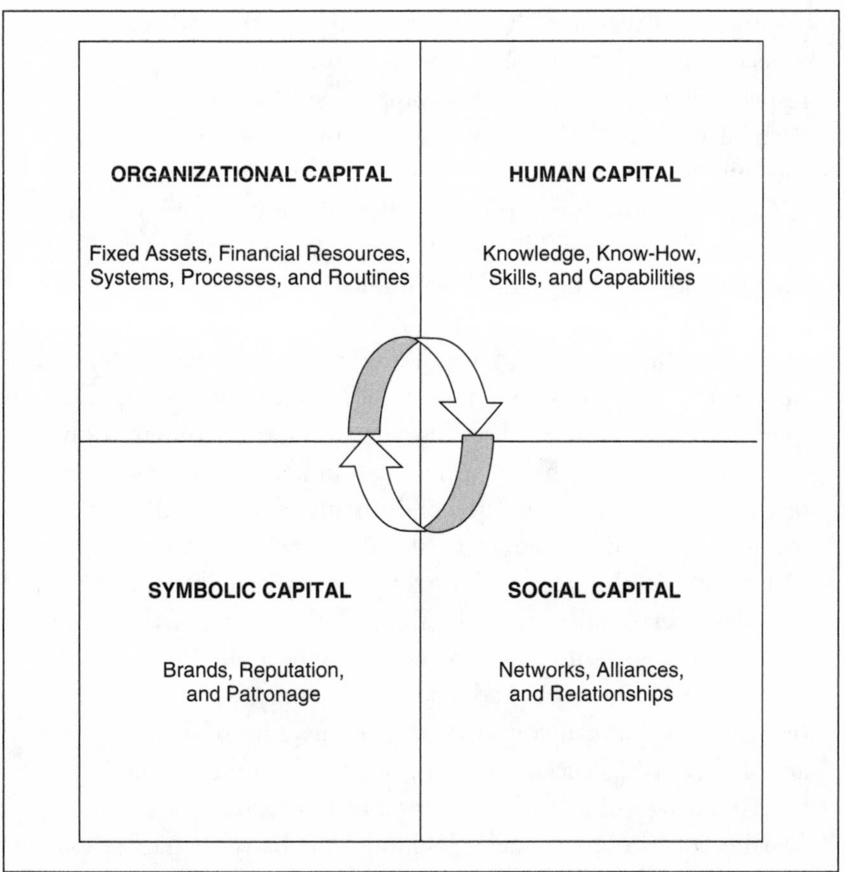

Figure 4.1 Types of Capital and the Capital-Accumulation Process

relationships, and alliances that enable the company to establish and maintain the connections needed to gather timely information and exert leverage within markets and supply chains. Finally, symbolic capital, like organizational capital, is mainly a corporate asset. It is intangible but indispensable, and it is expressed in the belief of customers and other stakeholders (such as supply-chain partners) that the company can deliver what it has promised. When Boots decided to back Award, it conferred on the new company the power of "patronage," the endorsement of a big and prestigious player, which told others that Award had something special to offer. Symbolic capital is the source of power for respected brands and reputable companies, which, by virtue of the faith placed in them, can bring new products to market with the confident expectation of a positive customer response.

Consider how these four bundles of capital were rendered dynamic in a way that liberated the breakout potential of the Irish rock legend U2. The capital-accumulation idea explains a lot of the dynamic behind U2's initial taking-by-storm and subsequent expanding-horizons breakout. The process began with human capital: the four band members (Paul Hewson, or "Bono," Dave Evans, or "The Edge," Adam Clayton, and Larry Mullen, Jr.) had real talent and personality. The profound, almost poetic nature of their lyrics and the unique and distinct sound of their music made them stand out from the crowd. The charisma and passion of lead singer Bono gave the group a further edge over bands with less personality. Closely allied with this were the band's musical "system" and the style and routines it employed.

From the outset, U2 had a sound that was radically different from that of punk-inspired rivals such as The Boomtown Rats and The Clash. Precise, military-style drumming, a repetitive, reverberating guitar riff, a memorable and relaxed bass line, and soaring vocals defined the U2 sound—the band's organizational capital, if you will. The group wasted no time in acquiring social and symbolic capital. Not long after its formation, it won a talent contest on St. Patrick's Day 1978, and one of the judges secured a demo recording for the band with CBS Records. The band subsequently released a three-track EP that did well in Ireland.

One important fan of the U2 style from the outset was Bill Graham, a journalist with the influential music paper *Hot Press*. Graham was an early champion of the band and also introduced its members to their influential manager, Paul McGuinness (often referred to as the fifth member of U2). Breaking out of Ireland and into the United States in particular can be traced directly to the social and symbolic capital that U2 was able to generate. In particular, leveraging its music-industry contacts in Ireland and the United Kingdom, U2 secured a deal with Frank Barsalona, the founder of Premier Talent, based in New York City.

Barsalona had set up Premier Talent in 1964 as the first booking agency to work exclusively with rock artists. He had worked with the likes of Bruce Springsteen and The Who, and his stamp of approval and patronage (symbolic capital), combined with his access to prime music venues and festivals (social capital), were decisive in getting U2 into and noticed in the United States. The rest was up to the band. Performances such as the 13-minute show-stealing rendition of the antiheroin song "Bad" at the 1984 Live Aid concert proved decisive. When Bono entered the crowd to dance with fans, U2 cemented its reputation as the band of the moment, the one that was best able to capture the raw emotion and human connectivity of the global antifamine event. Its breakout was well underway, and the band went on to capture and retain a leading position in the world music industry.

Three main insights result from viewing companies in this way. The first is that a breakout cannot take place unless an organization is prepared to engage in continuous transformation and capital accumulation. In fact, one of the best ways to think about this is to consider the role of free cash flow in the process, represented by the arrows at the center of Figure 4.1. In breakout situations, one form of capital is regularly transformed into others in a beneficial upward spiral of accumulation. At the start of the process, breakout companies experience a surge in demand as customers respond enthusiastically to the compelling features of their value propositions (the ease of use and health benefits of disposable contact lenses, for example).

At this stage, demand typically outstrips supply; the company charges premium prices, and profit margins are high. As a result, free cash flow starts to boom, providing the resources needed for ongoing investments in organizational, human, social, and symbolic capital. Investments in organizational capital lead to economies of scale and scope. Investments in human capital lead to better management, increasing efficiency and effectiveness, and growing levels of knowledge and expertise throughout the business. Investments in social capital lead to a tighter, better-managed supply chain and to relationships that open up fresh lines of business. Think, for example, of the advantages gained by Japanese car companies such as Toyota through the cultivation of close personal relationships between company executives.

Investments in symbolic capital lead to increased brand awareness and give the company a sense of permanence and authority, such as when sporting goods company adidas identifies itself with sporting success by placing its famous three stripes across the clothing of sponsored superstars. The four types of investment are mutually reinforcing, driving up sales, boosting revenues, and generating the free cash flow needed to support further rounds of investment. It is through capital accumulation that fresh organizational capabilities and sustainable business models are created. It is through capital accumulation that the industry minnows of today become the dominant enterprises of tomorrow.

The second main insight stemming from Figure 4.1 is the necessity of all four types of capital—organizational, human, social, and symbolic—to the breakout process. It is not possible to devise a compelling new value proposition without the knowledge and know-how that stem from human capital. Sufficient organizational capital likewise is required to implement a sustainable business model. Without adequate social capital, the essential support of suppliers, partners, and financiers will not be forthcoming. If there is no symbolic capital, it is difficult to convince potential customers of the benefits of purchase, and sales will fail to take off.

Let's go back to the early days at Cisco Systems to see how this all plays out. The company was founded in 1983 by Leonard Bosack and Sandy Lerner, computer services professionals at Stanford University who later became husband and wife. Their shared interest in connecting local-area networks across the university led them to develop and refine a data router that had been invented by a colleague, Bill Yeager. The future industry giant was at first a do-it-yourself, at-home business that depended on word of mouth to generate sales. Yet, small as it was, Cisco was a true original with significant human capital, and through the social capital of its university networks, it was able to generate a promising number of sales. It also had symbolic capital through the personal reputations of Bosack and Lerner and the legitimacy conferred by their association with Stanford.

The company's main weakness was a lack of organizational capital. This problem was solved by the sale of 30 percent of the company to venture capitalist Sequoia Associates in 1986 for $2.5 million and the subsequent appointment of a professional management team, headed by John Morgridge, that had the experience needed to build a big business. The company went public in 1990. Bosack and Lerner left the business, and John Chambers was hired by Morgridge to spearhead Cisco's breakout onto the world stage.

As the Cisco example illustrates, breakouts require all four types of capital, and companies that are lacking any one of these find it very difficult to get the traction they need to move forward. If Bosack and Lerner hadn't had the personal insight to see and the capability to execute on this crazy idea of routers, would there have been the human capital in place to generate a business in the first place? Unlikely. If Bosack and Lerner had been at "No Name University" rather than Stanford, would they have had the symbolic capital they needed if they were to be taken seriously? Unlikely. If Bosack and Lerner had not been interacting with other departments at Stanford already, with easy access to a much larger network of academics in other places dealing with the same challenges, would they have had the social capital to exploit their idea? Unlikely. And if these three forms of capital hadn't already been in place, not to mention if they hadn't been located in Silicon Valley, with access to the Sequoias of the world, would they have had the organizational capital to fund the enterprise? Unlikely. Each form of capital is essential, each depends on the others, and each can build on the others.

The third main insight to stem from Figure 4.1 is that different types of breakout are closely associated with variations in initial capital positions, which, in turn, affect how breakout can develop and pose particular challenges for breakout leaders. The most common starting point for true originals and revolutionaries, for example, is the possession of significant human capital in the form of industrial, technological, and market knowledge, which, in turn, creates the potential to launch attractive new value propositions and business models.

The Boston Beer Company and Dyson are classic examples. In each case, it was the boldness needed to challenge the status quo, along with extensive research and technical knowledge, that lay behind the formation of the new venture. Likewise, as revolutionaries, both of these companies faced similar obstacles in breaking out. In established markets—whether for beer or for vacuum cleaners—an upstart company is painfully aware of being a dwarf in a land of giants, with very little organizational, social, or symbolic capital at its disposal. Investments in such things as plant, equipment, and patents that are small by the standards of big companies are big commitments for start-up companies, as are the softer but equally pressing investments needed in systems, processes, marketing, distribution, and brand building.

Laggard companies, like start-ups, must overcome serious capital constraints if they are to break out. They already possess significant organizational, human, and social capital, but the value in use of each type is much lower than for market-leading companies. Prior to breakout, U.K. retailer Tesco suffered from deficient business systems, lackluster management, and a fragile supply chain. As a result, its brand was weak, and customers increasingly were turned off by its variable quality, poor service, limited choice, and hence even its low prices.

A similar, if less dramatic, picture might be painted of U.S. department store chain JC Penney, which prior to its recent revival seemed incapable of shaking off its reputation as a staid and waning brand. In effect, laggard companies fail to accumulate capital or, in the most extreme cases, destroy it by entering a downward spiral of failure. The once-prosperous U.K. electric motor maker Horace Green & Co. for years failed to invest in its human and organizational capital, refusing to adopt metric standards against customers' wishes, and it paid the price in years of negative growth.[5] Its backward-looking owner-managers continued trading into the new millennium, servicing old motors while selling financial assets to cover mounting losses, until a family feud eventually forced the business to close. The lesson is clear: without an improved value proposition and supporting capital investments, a laggard business ultimately will enter a spiral of decline from which there is no recovery.

It goes without saying that companies that are seeking to break out by expanding their horizons, whether they are boundary breakers or conquistadores, do so from a better starting point than their laggard-to-leader counterparts. Such companies typically have already enjoyed considerable success within their home nation or region. They have proven value propositions and business models, and they have accumulated considerable organizational, human, social, and symbolic capital. They face two main challenges. The first is to introduce a value proposition forged in one culture into countries and regions with different tastes, traditions, and expectations. The second is to scale up their operations across a much wider front without damaging the existing business.

Neither of these tasks is trivial. Business systems and facilities have to be created in different legal jurisdictions, and managers and employees from different cultural backgrounds must be introduced to the company and its ways of doing business. If a company is to expand its horizons, there is a need for extensive new networks and business relationships to establish the company in a variety of local settings. An important factor in the success of boundary breakers such as Best Western is the wealth of social capital within the business; similarly, without investing heavily in social capital, conquistadores such as BP and Mittal Steel could not have extended their global operations on such a massive scale.

Superficially at least, shape-shifting companies, especially the power players at the apex of the global economy, would appear to be well placed to break out into new markets. Companies such as GE, IBM, Procter & Gamble (P&G), Unilever, L'Oréal, Nestlé,

Siemens, and Bayer command entire industries and technologies. They have supreme organizational capabilities, a wealth of human talent, extensive social capital, powerful brands, and formidable reputations. In short, they seem invincible. It is not difficult to see, for example, how massive investments in organizational capital, by producing economies of scale and scope, can generate the funds needed for investments in research, new-product development, joint ventures, and brand building. Each of these forward-looking investments, in turn, creates the potential for fresh growth in the future, and so the cycle of growth and capital accumulation goes on. What is surprising is not that dominant companies remain dominant for long periods but that even given such advantages, they fall prey to the vicissitudes of change. Of all the susceptibilities of dominance—witness IBM before Gerstner—blindness to the revolutionary potential of emergent technologies and markets is probably at the top of the list. Strong cultures can limit the ability to see and think about the future in fresh ways, preventing, in extreme cases, recognition of the need to shift shape—to develop in new directions—until it is too late, and the capital accumulation cycle goes into reverse.

The Dynamics of Taking by Storm

What, then, is the secret to the breakout of companies that succeed in taking markets by storm? The Award story told earlier is in many ways typical of high-growth start-up enterprises. It was animated by a bright idea (molding soft contact lenses within the packaging), and its founders had the resilience needed to bring their idea to fruition. This was not easy. When they left the security of corporate life behind them, they had come up with a new production technology, but they had yet to articulate what this might mean ultimately for contact lens wearers. They had not, in the language of breakout strategy, crafted a complete and compelling value proposition.

It was only after they had solved a myriad of technical problems that the extent to which this production technology might slash unit costs became fully evident. It was then that the revolutionary value proposition intrinsic to the concept of daily disposable lenses crystallized in terms of cost, quality, convenience, and health benefits. Yet, even with the concept proved, Hamilton and Seden found it difficult to launch the product and carve out a new space within the contact lens market. They had limited financial resources, no brand credibility, and none of the organizational advantages enjoyed by established rivals.

Award's experience is instructive in demonstrating how the capital-accumulation model depicted in Figure 4.1 operates in practice. The business was predicated on the human capital of its founders, but without the social capital of Hamilton—which delivered the crucial association with Boots and support from UMIST—the nascent business would have been stillborn. Indeed, the Boots relationship was doubly advantageous, providing both a distribution channel and the reputational benefits of patronage and symbolic association. As soon as Boots had put its weight behind Award, the problem of securing the organizational capital needed to establish a viable business model was solved. Scottish Enterprise accepted Boots' sales projections as proving the business plan and, in exchange for a share of the equity, provided the funds needed to acquire plant and equipment and create a senior management team. Immediately upon entering production, Award became highly cash generative and entered the upward spiral of growth and capital accumulation characteristic of breakout companies.

In practice, of course, the process of transformation and capital accumulation presents taking-by-storm companies with several challenges. The first of these relates to the company's lack of a track record and market presence. When we asked various breakout leaders to explain how they set about overcoming this problem, there was general agreement on tactics. Several reflected on the need to "big up," to project a "substantial image," to "think and act cutting edge," and to "create a sense of excitement about the place." Building reputation by association with well-known customers, partners, and suppliers is a routinely employed tactic, as was the case at Award.

In a most audacious example, the founder of HIT Entertainment, Peter Orton, snatched his company name, a major brand in its own right, from under the nose of the mighty Walt Disney Company. Orton had worked for Jim Henson at HIT for many years, and when Henson sold his creative properties to Disney, Orton was told that he could have the name if Disney agreed. It did so (by verbal contract), little realizing at the time that it was blessing what would turn out to be a major new creative force in the preschool children's entertainment industry. This remarkable coup enabled HIT Entertainment to play in the big leagues from the start, winning access to media boardrooms around the world.

A second major challenge for taking-by-storm companies is to win the hearts and minds of managers and employees from the beginning. A conspicuous feature of the most successful companies is that breakout leaders emerge early and hold things together for many years, imparting something of their own style and values to the business. Bill Gates at Microsoft, John Chambers at Cisco, Jim Koch at Boston Beer, Howard Schultz at Starbucks, and Amancio Ortega at Inditex are outstanding examples, but they are not atypical. Such leaders, around whom the business seems to rotate, display high levels of loyalty to their close colleagues, and when they speak of breakout, they often reflect on the "energy and buzz" that had led people to go the extra mile to complete projects, deliver on contracts, and win new business. The camaraderie and sense of belonging that exist at Google, for example, have helped to release the power of human capital within the business.

In this way, breakout companies make the most of what they have, often stretching and leveraging their resources to a degree that would be inconceivable elsewhere. This requires a willingness to improvise, to "think outside the box," and to find unconventional solutions to pressing problems. The fact that the leadership team displays extraordinary resolve, keeping faith with colleagues and nurturing the "something special" in the business, inspires others to do their utmost to achieve the collective good.

A third big challenge when taking a market by storm is to learn and to change direction at lightning speed. Start-up companies lack many things. Ron Hamilton remembers Award as being "full of holes that had to be filled very quickly." There was, for instance, no pay and grading system for the rapidly expanding workforce, a problem that was solved by adopting the terms and conditions of a local engineering company with similar skills requirements. More fundamentally, the company had to learn how to apply mass-production manufacturing and quality-control techniques to contact lens making, which previously had used a customized batch-production system with high wastage rates. Award had to improve its business processes and systems in real time, pragmatically and creatively, without the extended (and expensive) pilot projects common in larger companies.

What repeatedly impresses—whether it's Ron Hamilton at Award, Steve Jobs at Apple, or Howard Schultz at Starbucks—is the creativity these leaders show in borrowing and adapting ideas from many places to fit their situation. They are remarkably open minded, welcoming suggestions from people both inside and outside the business, yet they are very discerning with respect to what they adopt. As Hamilton reminded us, "Invention, yes; innovation, yes; but you can afford to run with only those things that will improve your product or reduce your costs. Don't waste your time or money on the frivolous—keep focused."

The fourth challenge that all taking-by-storm companies face is the need to achieve critical mass before being overwhelmed by big-league competitors. The driving logic is that of economies of scale. In the early phases of breakout, when the market is buoyant and the competition is slight, the ability to charge premium prices means that free cash flow is strong. By immediately reinvesting their profits and raising additional capital through the markets when necessary, breakout companies have the opportunity to steal a march on the competition. Prices may soften in the future, but if unit costs have been driven down by economies of scale, then margins will remain healthy for much longer. Operating on a larger scale enables the systematic accumulation of organizational, human, social, and symbolic capital.

We can observe this logic in action at the low-cost airline easyJet. From a standing start in 1995, the U.K.-based company now has 109 planes serving 212 routes from 16 hubs across Europe, carrying over 30 million passengers a year. The airline plans to grow its passenger numbers to 55 million by 2008, with new routes and hubs opening on a regular basis and many more planes on order. Revenues consistently have grown by more than 25 percent a year, with profits growing commensurately. These impressive results in a notoriously fickle industry reflect a robust business model sustained by economies of scale and capital accumulation. Steady and constant fleet enlargement has increased the airline's bargaining power and reduced aircraft acquisition and servicing costs. Expanded operations at hub airports have meant that ground crews have been used more intensively, sharply reducing unit costs. Privileged social and business relations at hub airports have resulted in special treatment and low charges, with numerous advantages for the airline and its passengers. Advertising and other brand-building costs have been spread ever more thinly, having been held constant at $40 million while passenger numbers have soared.

By staying ahead of the competition, easyJet has managed to avoid the fate of the majority of taking-by-storm companies: takeover by a larger rival with deep pockets. It has passed through what Ron Hamilton sees as "the barrier that separates those that are fodder for the heavyweights of the corporate system and those that go all the way to the top." He speaks from experience because Award lost its independence to Bausch & Lomb, which, despite falling soft lens and cleaning solution sales, still had the financial muscle to make an irresistible bid for the company. The acquisition refreshed Bausch & Lomb, which expanded production and belatedly embraced the concept of daily disposable lenses, while freeing Hamilton and Seden from the constant pressures of competing against the giants of the industry. It is worth remembering that for every Cisco—itself now a dominant company—there are dozens of Awards—entrepreneurial companies whose mission terminates in assimilation by one of the power players of the new global economy.

The Dynamics of Laggard to Leader

Laggard companies come in many shapes and sizes. They all, however, exhibit a lack of dynamism compared with the leading companies in their field. They are not disasters, but they suffer from weak sales growth and loss of market share. They are rarely product or process innovators; they follow trends and imitate market leaders rather than setting the pace themselves. Their profitability varies. Very few of them earn profits above the norm. Some are average, but the majority are poor performers. Their inability to innovate and capture the imagination of customers means that in many cases, though not all, they trade at the lower end of the market and compete on the basis of a good price for standard quality and features. Management's orientation is tactical and responsive rather than strategic. In effect, the past, in one way or another, tends to have a big effect on the present and on projections for the future.

There are three main scenarios for laggard companies when they are examined in relation to Figure 4.1. First, in markets that grow or remain stable for a long period of time, such companies continue to tread water. They generate sufficient cash to renew their capital base and provide modest returns to shareholders, but not much more. The amount of organizational, human, social, and symbolic capital that is at work is perhaps adequate and often fits the needs of the past, but seldom goes beyond this base.

Second, in markets that have turned down or come under fire, such companies enter a downward spiral of negative growth and capital erosion. They lack the human and social capital needed to innovate, change, and develop fresh income streams. Profits turn to losses as revenues decline, and in order to survive, they reduce their physical capacity and dismiss employees.

Third, such companies may recognize the limitations of their current position and seek to break out through the adoption of a laggard-to-leader strategy. This requires the conception of a far more compelling value proposition than what they are currently offering and the simultaneous adoption of a brand-new business model. Only when these conditions are met can a laggard company enter once more into a beneficial cycle of growth and capital accumulation.

The history of Computer Sciences Corporation (CSC), founded in 1959 by two software engineers, Fletcher Jones and Roy Nutt, illustrates the difficulties facing laggard companies and how these can be resolved through strategy and effective management of the capital-accumulation process to turn a laggard into a leader. During its early years, the company depended on the software-development capabilities of its founders, who understood before most others that the rate of development of raw computing power would outstrip the capacity of the computing industry to develop intelligent business solutions. They worked on a project-by-project basis, leveraging their skills by partnering with bigger companies such as Western Union, and over time they gained a reputation for innovation and reliability.

CSC was still a small company compared with the likes of IBM, but its originality and its willingness to take on complex problems resonated with government and other public-sector clients. Indeed, the business accumulated considerable social capital through its relationships with the public sector, but many of its clients were cash-strapped, and CSC often had to buy difficult, customized work at relatively low prices. As a result, it never developed the strong free cash flow characteristic of the most successful breakout companies, and from time to time—as in the early 1970s—the company experienced near-fatal cash crises. This pattern of spasmodic growth and periodic financial crises, so typical of laggard companies, continued until 1980, although the company could claim some major technical successes, for example, in the development of time-sharing software.

The breakthrough for CSC came with the development of a major strategic theme: systems integration. The idea, in a nutshell, was that rather than developing individual software programs for major applications, the company should focus on "combining globally standardized best-in-class components with industry- and client-specific components." The advantage of developing business solutions in this way, of course, is that components can be recycled, leading to significant economies of scope.

In order to realize its vision of being an integrator, CSC pursued an active acquisition program to capture new knowledge and expertise, precisely the approach later used by Cisco Systems. Human capital came in the door with each acquisition. The value proposition had morphed into providing customized solutions at affordable prices using standard components, and it was well received both by CSC's traditional public-sector clients and increasingly by large private corporations. In a rising market, revenue growth became stronger and more reliable, and CSC had the free cash flow needed to enter into an upward spiral of growth and capital accumulation.

Key acquisitions strengthened the company's organizational and human capital bases, and by winning contracts with prestigious clients such as JP Morgan and DuPont, CSC gained immensely through symbolic association in a way that it had never done when it was working mainly for government agencies. In due course, its network of partnerships with leading software providers such as Oracle and SAS added to both its knowledge base and its social capital. As an integrator, CSC found itself in an exceptionally strong position to respond to the burgeoning outsourcing market, signing its first major contract with General Dynamics (a 10-year deal worth $3 billion) in 1991. A major new business was spawned in which CSC invested heavily, running systems and managing data on a global basis.

By 2005, the company had grown to employ 80,000 people across 80 countries, generating sales of $16 billion and a net profit of $810 million. The laggard had become a vision-led, strategically directed industry leader. And to do this, the company cycled through each of the major capital transformations, sometimes simultaneously, to keep the momentum going. Thus, understanding the four types of capital and how they are interrelated can be seen as a critical part of breakout, something that would-be breakout leaders must attend to right from the beginning of their initiative.

The Dynamics of Expanding Horizons

In many ways, international expansion is a logical next step for companies that have proved their value propositions and business models in a national context. By going international, and ultimately global, companies have the opportunity to develop ever more significant economies of scale and scope, creating additional value and accelerating the process of capital accumulation. As is so often the case, however, this is simpler in theory than in practice. International expansion invariably creates a raft of unforeseen challenges that require the acquisition of fresh skills and capabilities. Problems of coordination and control frequently are compounded as lines of communication are extended. Employee relations become more complex as personnel from different cultural backgrounds, with varying expectations and assumptions, are hired in ever-larger numbers. Ignorance of the history, politics, legal systems, and cultural practices of different nations can serve as a barrier to the development of productive relationships with local suppliers, partners, and power brokers. In addition, brands and other forms of symbolic capital, along with the messages that they convey, must be reestablished time after time in a myriad of cultural contexts for breakout to be successful.

Furthermore, pursuit of an expanding-horizons strategy is easier at some times than at others. The original international expansion of the McKinsey management consulting business between 1958 and 1970 is a great illustration of this point. Under the resolute leadership of Marvin Bower, McKinsey had built up a formidable reputation in the United States since the 1930s. The firm was known for hiring the best young people from top business schools and for having particularly strong capabilities in the related fields of strategy, restructuring, and management systems. It gained terrific kudos from its blue-chip client list and had won a reputation for cutting-edge thinking. At every turn, Bowers emphasized professionalism, consistency, and attention to detail.

The identity of McKinsey, deliberately constructed, was spelled out in its particular blend of conservatism and innovation. By 1958, with 150 consultants and sales in the region of $7 million, the company had accumulated significant organizational, human, social, and symbolic capital and was poised to export its value proposition and business model to Europe and beyond. It opened its first overseas office in London in 1959; Geneva, Paris, Amsterdam, Düsseldorf, and Melbourne soon followed. By 1970, the company employed 600 consultants, and its sales had grown to $50 million.

McKinsey's international breakout took place in the most advantageous of circumstances. During the 1950s and 1960s, U.S. companies were becoming increasingly international in outlook and were extending their operations across Europe and the non-Communist world. This development meant that McKinsey had a ready-made market. It also had a second big advantage: almost as soon as a new office opened, its consultants found a warm welcome in the boardrooms (private and public) of local organizations. The preeminence of U.S. companies and the U.S. economy meant that other countries had a hunger for U.S. management knowledge. Demand was buoyant despite the parlous finances of companies and governments and the "high-fee, high-value-added, high-quality, high-prestige" value proposition offered by McKinsey.

Yet even in these most favorable circumstances, the transition from national to international business could not have been accomplished without creative adaptation and positive engagement with the cycle of capital accumulation. The way was paved in 1956, when McKinsey became a corporation instead of a partnership, enabling a large proportion of free cash to be invested in support of growth. Even so, it was particularly difficult for

McKinsey to recruit large numbers of culturally attuned elite knowledge workers outside the United States. Other countries simply did not have high-caliber business schools to act as a ready source of supply. This required McKinsey to build new relationships with different types of elite educational institutions and to invest more heavily in training and human capital development. Likewise, it was necessary to recruit local heads of office, such as Sir Alcon Copisarow, an ex-government official appointed in 1966 as London managing director, with the social networks needed to put McKinsey in a position to receive lucrative contracts.

Hence, even for a firm such as McKinsey, the cycle of capital transformation is at work and needs to be harnessed if the firm is to be successful at breakout. And each of the four types of capital plays a role—organizational capital by raising cash flow to fund expansion, human capital by populating the rank-and-file consulting class, social capital by engaging with power brokers and elite groups, and symbolic capital by providing a presence in boardrooms and government offices alike.

Breakout through expanding horizons remains demanding. Reduced tariff barriers and the progressive lifting of restrictions on capital mobility have created fresh international investment opportunities, as have the phenomena of privatization and outsourcing. The international breakouts of CEMEX, Mittal Steel, Sodexho, Eléctricité de France (EdF), and a host of other companies in recent years reflect an increasingly favorable climate for aspiring global companies. Yet liberalization is not the only force at work. Nationalism, environmentalism, religious fundamentalism, and corporate social responsibility pose challenges for internationally expansive companies.

In the energy sector, for example, the performance of giant companies such as ExxonMobil and BP increasingly depends on their being able to navigate fraught and troubled waters. In these circumstances, there is a rising premium on social and symbolic capital. BP's success in securing a significant share of the Russian oil and gas industry, for example, can be attributed in no small measure to the company's social and diplomatic skills, instilled from top to bottom by its CEO, Lord John Browne. BP is the only oil supermajor to have been granted ownership rights in Russia, with the purchase of a 50 percent stake in TNK-BP in 2003. This historic deal was signed in the presence of Russian President Vladimir Putin and British Prime Minister Tony Blair. Putin has since praised BP as "a good corporate citizen of Russia"—a fitting accolade for a company that under Browne's leadership has worked harder than most to demonstrate its ethical and environmental credentials.[6]

The Dynamics of Shifting Shape

The underlying perception behind any shape-shifting strategy is that the world is changing and changing fast. According to this view, products, processes, business models, and relationships are all, in one way or another, transitory, open to question, and subject to change. This is the classic business stance of power players, but it is also a position shared by early adapters, who perceive the need to get out of one market space and into another. Implicit in this way of thinking is an analysis of how and why markets are evolving and how these changes will affect individual companies.

Culture, ideology, politics, technology, demographics, institutions, regulation, and environmental change, together with many other variables, are factored into predictive scenarios. The straightforward aim is to see the next big thing before it happens. In the words of Patricia Turck-Paquelier, president for prestige international brands at L'Oréal, the philosophy in play at her company is to "anticipate what is about to start."[7]

Correctly anticipating and shaping what is about to start is fundamental to shape shifting. It requires a profound sense, again in Turck-Paquelier's words, of "what people want without them even knowing it." This instinct goes very deep at L'Oréal, dating back to the 1960s, when the company moved out of soap production and into "selling beauty" under the leadership of CEO François

Dalle, who had succeeded the company's founder, Eugene Schueller, in 1957. Dalle recognized that the cosmetics market could be segmented by both income and lifestyle and that to serve such a market, a stable of brands was needed. Each brand could have its own value proposition, character, and associative attributes. In order to realize this vision, Dalle pursued an approach of acquire and assimilate, taking over leading French brands such as Lancôme and Garnier and incorporating them into the L'Oréal stable. A remarkable period of growth ensued, beginning under Dalle and continuing for more than two decades under Lindsay Owen-Jones, who was appointed CEO in 1984 at the age of 38.

Few companies exemplify better than L'Oréal the way in which power-playing companies can shift shape organically through growth and progressive capital accumulation. At the heart of the business is the L'Oréal stable of brands. There can be few more compelling examples of the power conferred on a company by the possession of symbolic capital. Each of the main brands is kept fresh and is redefined periodically by interpreting and implementing the results of extensive market research, and advertising extensively to communicate the character and related attributes of the brand. Some classic advertising catchphrases—especially "Because you're worth it" from 1973—have lasted for decades and have become emblematic of the L'Oréal master brand.

Owning a stable of luxury brands that command premium prices has made the company extremely cash generative, and it has continuously reinvested its free cash flow to stay ahead of the competition. The company has bought and rejuvenated numerous brands over the years, including Redken, Maybelline, Softsheen-Carson, and Matrix and Kiehle's in the United States, as well as the Italian brand icon Giorgio Armani and the Japanese product range Shu Uemura. The most recent acquisition is the environmentally sensitive British brand The Body Shop.

Key to the rejuvenation of many of these brands has been the investment that L'Oréal has made in social capital. The company makes no secret of using its associations with designers and other cultural icons, along with more conventional market research, to discern what is driving the market. With this knowledge, the appeal of each L'Oréal brand is up to date, rather than languishing somewhere in the past.

Investments in organizational capital—in product research and information technology, for example—are a further source of competitive advantage and ultimately growth. Finally, L'Oréal, from the days of François Dalle down to the present, has used its financial muscle to hire the best talent—human capital—available to keep the business moving forward. Patricia Turck-Paquelier, for example, was lured to the company after five years in a senior position at Yves Saint-Laurent to rejuvenate the Giorgio Armani brand. Within the space of a few years, she had used her formidable knowledge of brand tuning, leveraging, and communication to increase sales fivefold. Overall, L'Oréal, as a matter of ingrained strategic practice, has long driven its business forward through application of the principles of capital accumulation and growth.

Breakout Dynamics in Historical Perspective

It is through breakout that companies are lifted to a higher plane. The compound effect of double-digit growth and capital accumulation over a sustained period is organizational transformation. Small companies become large. Laggard companies become leaders. National companies become multinational enterprises. Companies known for one thing suddenly become famous for others. These transformations are fundamental to economic growth, and one of the most important lessons of business history is that companies must break out repeatedly if they are to survive and prosper over the long haul, as GE, Siemens, Michelin, and Toyota have done. The fact that the vast majority of companies fail to do so bears witness to the power of markets to punish companies that fail to move with the times.

Yet breakout should not be confused with continuous change. Rather, breakout represents discontinuity, rapid change over a relatively short period that takes a company from one place to another. The pattern in long-lived companies, seen time and time again, is one of periodic transformational change: relatively long periods of stability punctuated by intense periods of growth and corporate renewal.

There are few better examples than that of Rio Tinto, the British-based multinational mining company that in 2005 employed 32,000 people and had capital of $31 billion, generated sales of $19.8 billion, and had a pretax profit of $7.6 billion. In its long history stretching back to 1873, Rio Tinto has experienced four breakout episodes, each one fundamental and transformational.[8]

The company was founded in 1873 to exploit the Rio Tinto mines in southern Spain, which were known to contain vast deposits of the complex mineral pyrite, a rich source of sulfur, copper, and iron. Its first breakout lasted approximately a decade and saw the company come from nowhere to become the source of 10 percent of the world's copper and 50 percent of the sulfur that Europe's burgeoning chemical industry needed. At the time, breakout on this scale was virtually unprecedented, rivaling that of the great railway companies of the world. The founding entrepreneurs, led by the London merchant Hugh Matheson, had raised several million pounds (a vast sum at the time) to purchase the mines, build a 30-mile railway and a modern shipping pier, and introduce modern mining and smelting methods. They had to do this in the teeth of fierce opposition from rival mine owners, who were quick to denounce Matheson as a charlatan. His scheme, they claimed, was so ambitious that, if it were successful, the markets would be flooded with so much sulfur and copper that prices would fall to uneconomic levels, making the financial projections put before the public baseless.

In a press battle of epic proportions, fought in the newspapers of Europe and the United States, Matheson won the day by demonstrating that price deflation would be mitigated by rising consumption and that Rio Tinto's costs of production would in any case be a fraction of those of existing producers.

There is something timeless in this story. Matheson had a compelling vision of what Rio Tinto might become, a value proposition predicated on much lower prices, and a business model based on cost reduction through economies of scale. He also had the leadership capabilities and social capital needed to propel Rio Tinto into a spectacular upward spiral of growth and capital accumulation. He was connected by family ties and business dealings with several of the most powerful trading and banking families in the City of London—including the Jardines, the Smiths, and the Keswicks—and through them he had privileged access to the leading investment banks in France and Germany.

It was the social capital and symbolic capital derived from association with some of the biggest City names that enabled Matheson to put together the original Rio Tinto consortium and to launch the company through the stock exchanges of London and Paris. With the funds thus provided, he was able to purchase the mines and invest heavily in plant, equipment, and other forms of organizational capital. He hired many of the best mining and metallurgical engineers from around the world, an investment in human capital that resulted in costs falling well below the levels originally projected. Matheson, as chairman (until his death in 1898), had to hold the business together for three difficult years before full-scale production began, but thereafter sales boomed and free cash flow was strong. The company reinvested heavily, and by the early 1880s, Rio Tinto had emerged as the dominant player in the world markets for both sulfur and copper—a spectacular illustration of the dynamics of taking by storm.

The first Rio Tinto breakout was a radical and disruptive act that propelled the company into a dominant market position. Once the company was firmly established as the market leader, its strategic orientation changed. The new goal was to consolidate and reap the advantages of domination. The company focused its attention on driving down costs and improving the technical efficiency of the mining and metallurgical processes. A market-sharing agreement led to an improvement in sulfur prices, and Rio Tinto took the lead in various schemes to drive up the price of copper, most notoriously the Secrétan copper corner of 1888. In all essentials, Rio Tinto's strategy of making the most financially of its mineral assets and dominant market position remained constant until after Sir Charles Fielding joined the board in 1900, serving as chairman from 1904 to 1922.

It was Fielding who led the second Rio Tinto breakout through his pursuit of an expanding-horizons strategy. His goal was to double pyrite sales by opening up the U.S. market on the eastern seaboard. This required the creation of a new subsidiary and the construction of major treatment plants at Roanoke, Virginia, and Wilmington, Delaware. In fact, the growth in pyrite sales exceeded expectations; sales rose by nearly 150 percent during the early years of the twentieth century. Rio Tinto, already massively profitable, went from strength to strength, funding its expansion entirely through internally generated funds.

The third Rio Tinto breakout followed the appointment of an outstanding strategic leader. During the late 1920s and early 1930s, Sir Auckland Geddes, chairman between 1925 and 1947 and former British ambassador to the United States, pursued an ambitious shifting-shape strategy. Geddes was an astute political observer who recognized at an early date that the forces of nationalism and socialism that were growing ever stronger in Spain ultimately would be very costly for the company. His solution was to invest heavily in promising mining, metallurgical, and chemical projects outside the country, using the company's free cash and stock and bond issues to fund new ventures.

Between 1925 and 1931, before the world depression had turned high operating profits into serious losses, the company plowed millions of pounds into new research, exploration, and production companies. Project opportunities almost invariably came through the dense social network of Geddes and his associates, including the Rothschilds, who were major shareholders in the business. The most significant of these stemmed from the discovery of rich and extensive copper deposits in northern Rhodesia (now Zambia).

Through astute maneuvering and the deployment of its best technical brains to appraise prospective mines, the company was able to serve as playmaker for the copper belt. Various interests were merged into the Rhokana Corporation under the leadership of Rio Tinto, and Geddes was appointed chairman.

Rio Tinto's investments in Rhokana and other copper-belt companies proved to be its lifeline. In 1954, when the company finally sold its Spanish assets, dividends from its copper-belt investments represented more than 95 percent of its net profits. The decision to shift shape had proved wise.

However, the successive batterings of the 1930s recession, the Spanish Civil War, World War II, and postwar dislocation had taken their toll. By the early 1950s, Rio Tinto, by the standards of multinational mining companies, was a laggard, not a leader. It fell to Val Duncan, appointed as managing director in 1951, to lead Rio Tinto's fourth and, in many ways, most remarkable breakout, turning the company into a big improver and setting the strategic direction of the company for more than 50 years.

Duncan began by taking stock. There was plainly no future in Spain, and northern Rhodesia might become another political minefield. In the medium term, these assets had to be disposed of and the receipts applied elsewhere. He spelled out a bright vision of the future. Rio Tinto would become an engine room for the discovery and development of large-scale, low-cost mining properties. It would operate a portfolio of mines covering a wide spectrum of minerals. Its properties would be in politically stable countries that respected private ownership, such as the United States, Canada, Australia, and other Commonwealth countries. The company would manage its portfolio wisely, buying and selling companies without sentiment as circumstances dictated. Rio Tinto, as a result, would be stable and profitable.

Within little more than a decade, Duncan had realized his vision and turned Rio Tinto from laggard to leader. This was done smoothly and with steady confidence through the consistent application of four strategic practices. First, Duncan was extremely solicitous in building long-term relationships with financiers, exploration companies, governments, and international agencies. Rio Tinto was seen as having the highest professional and ethical standards and became the trusted partner of many organizations. Second, the company was loyal to its employees, fostering commitment and team spirit. The best people in finance, mining, and metallurgy from around the world were attracted to work for Rio Tinto. Third, Duncan put robust and easily comprehended structures and business processes in place. A small head-office team concentrated on planning, finance, and corporate services, with subsidiaries and associate companies having complete operational responsibility. This gave the business flexibility by legitimizing joint ventures and different patterns of ownership while making it easy to buy and sell companies and properties as the portfolio evolved. Fourth, the company, quietly and discreetly, cultivated its reputation through sophisticated public relations and association with high-profile initiatives launched by governments and international agencies.

Rio Tinto under Duncan was a pioneer of corporate social responsibility well before the term had been coined. Through application of these practices in pursuit of a clear vision, Duncan was able to lift Rio Tinto out of the doldrums of the early 1950s. Asset sales released funds for exploration and the purchase of new mining properties around the world, at first in copper, iron, and uranium. The company's rapid advance inspired confidence and led directly to a friendly merger with the Zinc Corporation in 1962. Other major acquisitions followed. When Duncan died in 1975, he left behind a company that was admired around the world for its management and its culture.

The history of Rio Tinto is replete with lessons. The most obvious is the connection between breakout strategy and breakout leadership. Breakout strategies demand creativity in construction and dedication in execution; they are conceived and executed by individuals who can take others on a long strategic journey. In their own unique ways, Matheson, Fielding, Geddes, and Duncan commanded respect and commitment to the cause. The same is true of the other breakout leaders considered in this book.

It is also evident from Rio Tinto's experience that breakout, both in inspiration and in substance, is path-dependent. All breakout strategies are affected by their starting point, and equally, their content is shaped by the realities of the world around them. It is worth remembering that companies that survive for long periods invariably have played a part in some of the most momentous events in human history. Just as strategies shape the world, so world events shape strategies. It is also salutary to note that breakout would not have been possible at Rio Tinto during any period—whether under the leadership of Matheson, Fielding, Geddes, or Duncan—if its leaders had not had an intuitive understanding of the vital interplay among organizational, human, social, and symbolic capital.

Matheson staved off crisis and won the support of Europe's financial elite for a massive capital program by virtue of his social capital. Fielding leveraged the business's organizational and symbolic capital to open up lucrative new markets. Geddes drew freely on Rio Tinto's human, social, and symbolic capital to win the lion's share of the northern Rhodesian copper belt. And Duncan, a master breakout strategist of the modern era, freely traded organizational assets to secure the resources needed for reinvestment in all four forms of capital. The most remarkable breakout leaders, it would seem, both have their heads in the clouds and have their feet solidly planted on the ground.

Conclusion

What lessons emerge from this analysis of breakout dynamics, when companies experience an exceptional spate of growth and transformation? The first is that breakout companies of all types enter an upward spiral of growth and capital accumulation that raises them to a higher plane. Breakout companies—whether entrepreneurial or already established—can make their move from any starting position. The capital base needed for breakout can be organizational, human, social, or symbolic. In many cases, the initial vision or innovation stems from human capital, but other times it could come from symbolic capital (as in L'Oréal's incredible brand reputation or Peter Orton's coup in grabbing the HIT name), social capital (as in the Cisco founders' prominent position in the social network of universities or Hugh Matheson's central place in London's business elite), or organizational capital (as in the huge resources that conquistadores such as CEMEX and Mittal Steel have brought to bear as they consolidate their respective industries on a global scale). Where you start is not as critical as where you go with the capital you have.

This brings us to the second important lesson from this chapter: no matter where you begin, you cannot succeed unless you generate capital across all four major domains. In each of the companies profiled in this chapter—and many others featured elsewhere in this book—breakout required the generation of multiple types of capital. Could Award have brought the concept of daily disposable lenses to market if its founders had not understood how to leverage its intellectual property by association with a major brand and by applying themselves to creating a first-class manufacturing organization? Where would L'Oréal have been if it hadn't had the capital to acquire leading brands, the connections with leading designers or other cultural icons to promote those brands, and the talent to pull all this off? How would Rio Tinto have survived the trials and tribulations of military conflicts and strident nationalism had it not been able to recycle and redeploy its capital with such aplomb? The same rule applies to all the breakout companies studied here: success is predicated on the ability to summon the capital you need from each of the four core sources.

Who is responsible for directing the breakout company toward capital accumulation and creating the capabilities to realize that accumulation? The answer is clear: the breakout leader of the enterprise. In fact, the importance of leadership is paramount throughout the entire breakout strategy process, and there can be no breakout strategy without effective breakout leadership. In virtually all our examples, we refer to individuals who have played a central role in accumulating the capital needed for breakout. It is the leader—whether that leader is an entrepreneur or an appointed CEO—who drives the entire capital-accumulation process. We saw that with Hamilton and Seden at Award, Bosack and Lerner and then Chambers at Cisco, and Dalle and later Owen Jones at L'Oréal, and the list goes on. The Rio Tinto story, covering more than 130 years, eloquently reinforces what we have learned from others. Without its four brilliant strategic leaders—Matheson, Fielding, Geddes, and Duncan—in all likelihood Rio Tinto would have long since sunk without a trace. As we will discuss again in Chapter 9, the most effective leaders have the necessary capabilities to see an opportunity and build momentum toward realizing it, and they use capital accumulation as a tool in this process.

The successful breakout leaders we have studied invariably have had good strategic instincts, skills, and abilities. This is not to say that such people think alike or act alike. Indeed, thinking independently and pursuing an original course are two of the hallmarks of breakout leadership. Equally, though, there are commonalities that jump out from our research. In all cases we find breakout to be contingent on having a sound understanding of the forces driving the chosen markets. It is only on this basis that realistic yet inspiring visions of the future can be formed and communicated effectively, as we shall see in Chapter 5.

Similarly, breakout leaders understand the necessity of being fully tuned into the markets they serve, even to the point of being able to "anticipate what is about to start." This is expressed in being able to devise value propositions with a "wow factor" that is strong enough to initiate breakout. We turn to this topic in Chapter 6.

A value proposition, of course, is useless if it cannot be delivered, and our research demonstrates that successful breakout leaders focus on constructing robust business models that can regularly deliver on the promises made to customers or clients. This topic is the subject of Chapter 7.

Constructing a robust business model is neither a mechanical nor a one-time affair. It requires constant vigilance and regular, targeted investment in both systems and people. This is what is meant by strategic enactment or execution, and it is an area in which successful breakout leaders invariably excel. This theme forms the substance of Chapter 8.

Finally, breakout leaders have the skills needed to manage high-speed change, overcoming difficulties and limitations to take full advantage of the upward spiral of capital accumulation and growth discussed in this chapter. We return to this topic in Chapter 9, exploring in detail the capabilities of breakout leaders and how these might be deployed to best advantage, both individually and within teams.

In the chapters that follow, we present a powerful set of models, tools, and techniques that simulate the practices of the world's most successful breakout leaders. By applying these tools and learning from these leaders' experience, you have the opportunity to refine and develop your own breakout strategy skills, both to your own advantage and to that of your company.

Endnotes

1 Interview with Ron Hamilton conducted on March 27, 2006.

2 Bausch & Lomb was in the news in 2006 when the company was forced to remove its lens care solution from the market after reports that the solution was associated with potentially severe eye infections. This problem was unrelated to the disposable lenses developed by Award, a different product with the health advantage that it eliminates the need for lens-cleaning solution.

3 The model presented here is a variant of that first presented in Mairi Maclean, Charles Harvey, and Jon Press, *Business Elites and Corporate Governance in France and the UK*. London: Palgrave-Macmillan, 2006, pp. 24–32.

4 The capital-accumulation idea is derived originally from the work of the French sociologist Pierre Bourdieu, who applied it to a social rather than a business or managerial context.

For further reference, see his seminal work, *Distinction: A Social Critique of the Judgement of Taste* (trans. R. Nice). London: Routledge & Kegan Paul, 1984.

5 Interview with Edmund Martin Green conducted on April 27, 2006.

6 As reported by the Associated Press on April 22, 2005. The occasion was a meeting of Lord Browne with President Putin on that day. Few global business leaders command the respect that Browne does.

7 The L'Oréal story as told here comes from the speeches given by Patricia Turck-Paquelier at the Paris international conference of the Association to Advance Collegiate Schools of Business (AACSB) and the European Foundation for Management (EFMD) on April 24, 2006.

8 The Rio Tinto case history presented here stems from the research of Charles Harvey, originally published as *The Rio Tinto Company: An Economic History of a Leading International Mining Company, 1873–1954*. London: Alison Hodge, 1981.

Chapter 5

PUTTING VISION TO WORK

For many of us, the name Harley-Davidson conjures up images of open roads, the wind at our backs, and the low growl of a 1,200-cc motorbike engine "Made in America." It evokes feelings of freedom, independence, and even patriotism in its million or so devotees. The Milwaukee, Wisconsin–based company has a unique image and a distinct tie to American society and history. Thus, it is hard to believe that just over 20 years ago, Harley-Davidson almost went out of business. Although it was a cultural icon, in the early 1980s, Harley-Davidson's market share was slipping and its product quality deteriorating. It wasn't long before it became a laggard in the industry it had helped to found.

What caused such a dramatic decline in the fortunes of one of America's great companies? Many specific errors and oversights can be pinpointed, but behind them all was one dominant flaw: Harley-Davidson's vision of what it was and where it wanted to be was stale and out of touch with its customers. Then, through a series of coordinated initiatives, Harley-Davidson revolutionized its product offering and redefined itself as a lifestyle company. It revitalized its vision and altered its strategic objectives dramatically, implementing quality improvements and enhancing employee relations.

By extending its brand into related businesses such as motorbike accessories and unrelated areas such as financial services, Harley-Davidson moved from industry follower to industry leader. By restyling its vision and delivering it in a way that met the needs and aspirations of its workers and shareholders—and, above all, its customers—the company reestablished itself as one of America's most dynamic companies.

How did this happen? How did Harley-Davidson deliver its revitalized vision in a vigorous and comprehensive way, enabling it to regain market share and recapture the industry high ground? This is just one of the stories we tell in this chapter to illustrate how vision is not something that can be relegated to the sidelines by bottom-line managers, but rather is central to any breakout strategy and fundamental to market success. The Harley-Davidson story also shows that vision must be both dynamic in nature and inclusive in form if it is to achieve its goals.

So far in this book we have laid out the idea of strategic breakout, illustrated its four main forms, and showed you how to find the route to rapid transformation that best fits your abilities and aspirations. We also have described the capital-accumulation cycle, which makes breakout such a dynamic process and provided examples of how that cycle unfolds for each type of breakout. Armed with this knowledge, as would-be breakout leaders, you may already see some of the levers for transforming your organization that are at your disposal. Regardless of your company's size, level of maturity, profile, or location, it can be transformed from an industry nobody into a market celebrity. In this and the following four chapters, we describe in detail the five key practices that all breakout leaders must master and give you the tools you need to make it happen in your own world.

In this chapter, we begin to explore the process by which a company reaches and maintains breakout growth. The first step requires a focus on *vision*—what it is and how it can be harnessed and put to work in a way that releases high-growth opportunities. The challenge of "doing vision" confronts all businesses, whether they are aware of it or not. Some fail to do it very well until a breakout leader, such as Pfizer's former CEO Edmond Pratt, arrives on the scene. Pfizer, which had been a laggard for most of its 150 years in business, grew dramatically under Pratt's stewardship. It went from being a top-20 pharmaceutical company in the 1980s to being the largest and most dynamic global player by the early 2000s. Key to this transformation was the redefinition of Pfizer's vision.

This was captured in a simple but aspirational statement:

Pfizer will strive to achieve and sustain its leading place as the world's premier research-based pharmaceutical company.

This clear statement of intent implies that Pfizer is anything but complacent and intends to maintain its number one status. It also emphasizes the company's focus on research and development as the engine of growth.

To realize this vision, Pfizer has outlined several core values that serve as building blocks for delivering its vision. These values include customer focus, innovation, respect for people, teamwork, integrity, and community. This list captures Pfizer's intention: to appeal to the needs and aspirations of as many stakeholders as possible. The key stakeholders, as with any pharmaceutical company, are employees, patients, health care professionals, customers, investors, business partners, and the communities in which these people work and live, and also governments around the world. Making this disparate group feel included and valued is an essential part of "doing vision" and making it add real value. This chapter describes the key steps required to redefine your vision and make it more—much more—than just another slogan.

Coming to Grips with Vision

On occasion, old ideas are worth revisiting and repackaging. For this very reason, we take this opportunity to look again at the often-used and much-abused notion of *vision*. Despite the ubiquity of the term, the concept of vision remains shrouded in misunderstanding and misapplication. It has become accepted practice to speak of a corporation's vision and to express this to stakeholders as the embodiment of the organization's purpose and goals.

The method for determining vision, however, is unsystematic at best and arbitrary at worst. More often than not, the professed vision is a direct reflection of the leader's personal aspirations and intentions. Foresight and imagination are subjugated to individual ambition. It is vital to avoid the tunnel vision that overtakes so many leaders in their rush to succeed. To be effective strategists, leaders must ensure that their vision is refreshed and supported by the continuous application of imagination and logical thought.[1]

In this chapter, we illuminate and enliven the hazy and often dull world of *strategic vision.* To add real value, entrepreneurial leaders and executive teams must adopt a practical approach to the formulation and execution of vision. Vision is more than the conceptual underpinning of a corporate strategy; it captures the spirit of the enterprise. It is a tangible and indispensable element of a strategy process. To establish a strategy that is robust and adds value, leaders must define and communicate a clear, consistent, and inclusive vision. This chapter gives tangible form to vision, shows you how to create a new vision or revive an old one, and demonstrates how to put a vision to work at the heart of a breakout strategy.

The word *vision* elicits a variety of responses from business leaders, but few of them convey any sense of enthusiasm or clarity. Most managers equate *visionary* with complexity at best and impracticality at worst.[2] They see little value in adopting a vision-led approach to running their business. Experienced executive teams usually can express their company's vision—either as a built-to-order sound bite or in an intuitive, value-driven sense. But few of them can see how to put that vision into practice. A lot of the problem is that vision is shrouded in ambiguity.

In this chapter, we put an end to the confusion and provide four learning points for the executive who wants to make vision real and value-adding. First, forge your own vision, one that captures your company's unique identity, direction, and aspirations. Do this before you do anything else. Do not fabricate a vision in response to competitors' posturing, management ambition, or market fads. Second, ensure that your vision captures the imagination and loyalty of all key stakeholders, from workers to shareholders. Third, be open to change. You should always maintain and nurture you values and core strengths, but you should change the purpose or direction of your vision if you need to. Fourth, keep your vision uncomplicated and easy to remember. "Less is more" should be your motto. Also, make sure that you strike a balance between what it is realistic for you to achieve and what will inspire your people and partners to strive for ever better results. Reaching too far too fast can lead to dejection when you fail to deliver. Remember, though, that lack of ambition or challenge also can cause discontent and underperformance.

We talked about the British retailer Marks and Spencer (M&S) in Chapter 3, classifying it as a failed *boundary breaker*. In fact, its problems began well before its lackluster international expansion efforts. By the mid-1990s, M&S was out of step with the changes that were taking place in the retail market and with customers' expectations. Its vision of good-quality products at an affordable price was not obsolete, but customer expectations had evolved, particularly in the areas of product style and design. While M&S was busy developing new stores and new products that were intended to take the company from *laggard to leader*, its competitors (including Tesco) were strengthening their core identities and offerings. Diversification was a key initiative, but in diversifying, the company lost its focus on its core business—the exclusive M&S brand.

Despite his financial success, then Chairman and CEO Richard Greenbury failed to realize that the chain was falling out of step with its customers. The M&S vision had become unclear—particularly to its customers. If you mentioned M&S to a British shopper in the late 1990s, the most common responses were "poor quality," "lack of vision," and "dire." Many investors and consumers turned their backs on the store. In essence, M&S lost sight of a key stakeholder—the customer. The M&S customer base was essentially mature, but customers in their fifties began to feel that M&S was no longer catering to them. In addition, the dynamics of retail spending were changing, with older people becoming less likely to dress the way their parents had done.

M&S's failed *expanding-horizons* breakout was blamed in part on increased competition as more foreign retailers entered its home and overseas markets. Retailers such as The Gap from the United States, Sweden's Hennes and Mauritz (H&M), and Spain's Zara provided a more contemporary look that was targeted at younger audiences, while M&S continued to do the same old thing. As a result, M&S was being attacked on one side by foreign retailers and on the other by supermarkets such as Wal-Mart-Asda,[3] Tesco, and Sainsbury.

By 2004, Wal-Mart's U.K. acquisition, supermarket chain Asda, had knocked M&S out of the top spot as Britain's number one clothing retailer. This was a big blow for M&S and its CEO, Stuart Rose, because Rose had just fought off a 9 billion pound takeover bid from retail mogul Philip Green on the strength of his promise to improve the clothing side of the business.[4] "A bit boring" is how Rose described some of the products that M&S sold—a stinging indictment from the company's own boss. Although when Rose took the helm, he emphasized a back-to-basics approach, strengthening and rejuvenating the company's main areas of competency (such as women's underwear), something happened along the way that blurred this message to stakeholders. The result was the continuation of strategic ambiguity and of a vision that contained mixed messages and failed to catch the imagination of either employees or customers.

M&S failed on all four of the vision tests laid out in this chapter. First, it remodeled its vision out of necessity rather than by choice. This occurred under successive CEOs, each of whom took the company in a slightly different direction, but none of whom did so proactively or in a nondefensive way. Second, by the mid-1990s, the M&S vision was no longer inclusive. It had lost the involvement of an essential stakeholder—the customer. As customers drifted away, M&S found that its vision was increasingly out of touch with the market. Third, rather than deepening the company's know-how and expertise at a time when the subsequent market leader, Tesco, was doing just that, M&S expanded into product and geographic markets where it had no natural advantages or known abilities. The company was open to change—it just did not change in the direction of what it was good at and known for. Fourth, the M&S vision became blurred and unrealizable. Quality inconsistencies in the product line meant that customers were not sure of what M&S stood for anymore, and constant change at the top resulted in uncertainty and concern about the future among employees in the lower echelons of the company and even among supply-chain partners. These anxieties were exacerbated by the company's global expansion in the 1990s, which many M&S workers and partners considered to be too far and too fast. None of this makes for a feasible and inspirational corporate vision that drives breakout success.

So just how should vision be put into practice in a way that adds real value and delivers the much-sought-after strategic breakout?

Translating Vision into Practice

Every corporate leader has a mental picture of where he or she wants to take the business. For some, such as John Sperling, founder of the Apollo Group and its farsighted market offering, the University of Phoenix, or Jim Koch, the entrepreneur behind the Boston Beer Company and its flagship product, Sam Adams Boston Lager, this vision of the future is clear and beyond doubt. For many, however, it is hazy and uncertain. A lot of senior executives fail to make their vision statements sufficiently inclusive, far-reaching, and tangible.

In fact, this should not surprise us. There are very few tools and techniques that can help business leaders make their vision more explicit. Cognitive mapping approaches[5] are logical and methodical, but they are too complex and time-consuming for many leaders to use effectively. There are also dynamic approaches to vision, based on showing executives how to bridge the gap between the current reality and a future vision.[6] Although these approaches are useful, they emphasize the development of visioning competencies among executives and fail to capture other dimensions of or factors contributing to a successful visioning process. Some people use the balanced-scorecard approach to translate vision into action.[7] This is a novel approach, but it overemphasizes the hard, process-led (what we call *techno*) dimensions of vision and underestimates the softer, people-focused (*socio*) dimensions, such as culture. We demonstrate later how the idea of strategic vision can be made clear, inclusive, and dynamic, a valuable starting point that can take a company forward by striking an appropriate balance between the techno and socio dimensions and internal and external influences and interests.

Instead of the widely held emphasis on vision as a combination of purpose and values,[8] we prefer to think of vision as being based on stakeholders' interests and aspirations. The idea is to ensure, first, that a company's purpose reflects the needs and objectives of all those who have a stake in the business (both inside and outside the enterprise) and, second, that it is dynamic in expression, enabling the senior management team to modify the vision in accordance with changing stakeholder demands or desires. The vision will remain constant and consistent in most instances. Sometimes it may have to change fundamentally, particularly when the company's very existence is at stake. When Lou Gerstner took over an ailing IBM, he had little choice but to transform everything, including the vision. In most cases, however, what will change is how the vision takes into account and integrates certain stakeholder interests.

For example, suppose that a company—let's call it Nuts 'n' Bolts, Inc.—has a relationship with its supply-chain partners that is based on high quality, high price, and slow delivery. As a components manufacturer, Nuts 'n' Bolts consistently produces products that are leading edge in design and high quality in finish. The company charges a premium for these products and is notoriously late in delivering its goods to the wholesalers that constitute its immediate supply-chain business partners.

Before too long, a competitor enters the market. The new supplier produces similar products, but with a difference: although its products are not comparable in quality of design and build specification, they are cheaper, and the company's deliveries are on time. How does Nuts 'n' Bolts respond? At the vision level, it needs to alter its relationship with wholesalers. It must do so in a way that maintains its image as a high-quality provider that charges a premium price. If it can do this, the vision remains constant. To maintain its business, however, Nuts 'n' Bolts needs to do more. It needs to infuse the vision with a dynamic that illustrates its adaptability and its willingness to change. It can do this by improving its manufacturing time frames and logistics to provide its supply-chain partners with on-time delivery of their orders. If it is successful in doing this, the company is likely to retain most—if not all—of its customers, despite having higher prices.

The wholesalers already subscribe to Nuts 'n' Bolts' vision, and although they are not always pleased with the delivery time, they like the products and accept the price as fair. A competitor may siphon off those customers that want lower prices, but it will not satisfy those that want reliable and durable leading-edge components. By reengineering its business model to deliver its products on time, Nuts 'n' Bolts is modifying its vision to satisfy the stakeholder interests of its supply-chain partners, namely, the wholesalers that sell its products to the end customers.

Vision as Stakeholder Needs and Aspirations

It is important to know what a vision is and how its core constituents fit together. But how many people actually know how to create a vision statement? Not only that, but can you be sure that your vision statement is inclusive, incorporating the short-term requirements and long-term objectives of all relevant parties? The usual response is confusion at best and misguided or misdirected action at worst.

We provide a method for fixing this problem and cutting through the confusion surrounding strategic vision and its formulation. The logic employed is straightforward: vision is derived from a creative equilibrium between a company's internal and external influences or stakeholders. A successful vision is generated through responding to the internal organization and culture, together with the external dimensions of markets and relationships. Figure 5.1 defines corporate vision in terms of these four main dimensions, each of which, in turn, is defined by a set of attributes.

Each segment of the vision wheel has three spokes. These are chosen carefully to address crucial microcomponents of the overall vision. For instance, the culture of an enterprise is a vital component of its vision. But how do we determine culture and, more important, how do we make it dynamic rather than static? Our

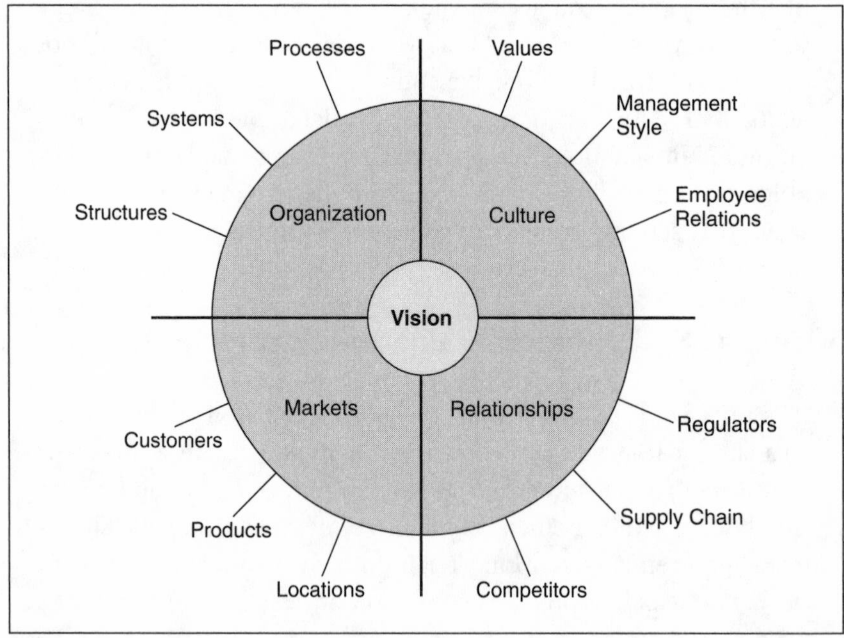

Figure 5.1 The Vision Wheel

approach is to break culture down into its three core ingredients: values (the standards and ideals embedded in the business that shape its interaction with the outside world), management style (are the managers flexible and responsive, accessible and open to advice?), and employee relations (do workers feel valued and empowered, and is there a team ethos between management and workers?).

By looking at each of these ingredients in turn, we can identify the essential elements that must be reflected in the overall vision. For example, the flat hierarchy and team philosophy of budget airlines such as Southwest Airlines, easyJet, and jetBlue are key vision determinants, as are values such as sustainable development and the nonuse of animals in product testing to companies such as The Body Shop. The vision-wheel approach ensures that none of a company's key influences—internal or external—is missing from its vision. When taken together, the 12 spokes of the wheel ensure that the corporate vehicle is going forward with direction and purpose.

The second advantage of our approach is that it enables a *static* and a *dynamic* interpretation of each spoke and of the overall vision. When Robert Louis Dreyfus was appointed CEO of the failing sporting goods manufacturer adidas in 1993, one of the first things he did was change the company's management style to make it less hierarchical. A second change was in the relationships dimension, where he shook up the supply chain and sought new partners in lower-cost countries. These dynamic adjustments became part of the revived vision and put adidas on the fast track to becoming one of the two leading sports brands in the world. As we will see later, the static vision for Harley-Davidson was to be a motorcycle manufacturer; the dynamic vision was to be a lifestyle company offering a range of related merchandise and services. The catalyst for change appears to have been greater competition from cheaper motorcycle producers and hence the need to reinforce the brand image and concentrate on the more lucrative stages in the value chain.

Far from being an imprecise idea that is difficult to carry out, developing a vision can be used as a practical tool of strategic management by specifying a set of *state transitions* from now to the future. This gives visioning a dynamic and forward-looking quality. The premise is straightforward: each quadrant of the vision wheel is worked through separately, generating a static and a dynamic scenario. The *static* scenario indicates how stakeholders view the existing situation and identifies specific components of the vision, assuming that the vision will remain constant. The *dynamic* scenario is the opposite: it represents stakeholders' best-case or ideal scenario for each element, with the presumption being that the overall vision is vibrant and is constantly adapting to stakeholder needs and aspirations.

The two states can be the same—not everything has to change. Once you have assessed all four quadrants, you are left with four overarching sets of objectives. When these are integrated and the essential change actions are distilled, the result is an inclusive and robust vision statement that is imaginative but realizable, that inspires and unifies all stakeholders, and that guides the organization in setting a direction and coordinating its activities.

Reviving the Harley-Davidson Vision

Let's return to the breakout company mentioned at the beginning of this chapter. We can deploy the vision-wheel idea to frame and explain how a vision was put to work at Harley-Davidson.[9] After several decades of faltering growth and unclear vision, the iconic American motorcycle company emerged into the twenty-first century with a refreshed look and a revitalized corporate mission. It put forward a compelling vision that captured, in simple terms, what Harley was about and where it was going:

> *We fulfill dreams through the experience of motorcycling by providing to motorcyclists and to the general public an expanding line of motorcycles, branded products and services in selected market segments.*[10]

Despite serious changes in its production methods and product offerings, Harley-Davidson did not deviate from its core identity: freedom, distinctiveness, passion, independence, and toughness. This identity, coupled with the company's external image as an American icon, resonated with customers and turned out to be one of the driving forces in the company's revitalization.

The revival began as far back as 1983, when Harley-Davidson formed HOG (Harley Owners' Group) to keep its customers loyal and involved. This quickly became, and still is, the world's largest motorcycle club, with chapters all over the world and close to one million members. Factory-sponsored rides, gatherings, parades, and charity events create a highly visible presence, serving both marketing and customer service functions.

HOG also fostered and encouraged the community and camaraderie for which Harley-Davidson is world renowned, positioning the brand as a lifestyle, not just a motorcycle. HOG sponsors and runs national events and state rallies for Harley-Davidson owners every year. In 2003, more than one million people worldwide participated in 100th-anniversary events. The Harley-Davidson brand frequently is cited in marketing books, top 100 lists, cult brand lists, and enthusiast lists for its ability to generate loyalty beyond reason and profits beyond projections. This has enabled Harley-Davidson to capture market share and mind share, extracting a premium in each.

To further develop the Harley-Davidson lifestyle, the company focused on complementary products as well as motorcycles. These consisted of both motorcycle parts and accessories ("Genuine Parts") and general merchandise. Motorcycle parts and accessories include items such as chrome oil pan covers and performance engine components. General merchandise includes riding attire, such as leather jackets and helmets ("MotorClothes"); nonriding attire, such as T-shirts and baseball hats; and household goods, such as branded pet accessories and barbecue tools. Since the mid-1990s, the parts and accessories division has grown from $127 million in sales to $816 million, and the general merchandise division has grown from $71 million to $248 million—and sales are still climbing.

Diversification was another component of Harley-Davidson's breakout from industry laggard to leader over the past 20 years. Its purchase of Eaglemark (now Harley-Davidson Financial Services) allowed the company to extend credit to both retail and wholesale customers, and also to underwrite motorcycle insurance. The financial services business also sells asset-backed securities on the market.

Harley-Davidson Financial Services continues to show strong growth and contributes an increasingly large part of the company's net income. Operating income went from $61 million in 2001 to almost $192 million in 2005, and sales continue to increase at rates higher than the core motorcycle unit's 6.2 percent per year. To further the lifestyle image, Harley-Davidson now offers a branded VISA card, extending the brand in strategic and financial areas.

The company also offers motorcycle rider training, a branded version of the nationally recognized Motorcycle Safety Foundation course. Now customers can learn to ride a motorcycle at a Harley-Davidson dealership. At some dealerships, customers also can have an extended test ride by renting a Harley-Davidson, in addition to having the option to "fly and ride" at various vacation destinations. Harley-Davidson is also in the business of providing extended service plans and sponsoring motorcycle racing. Additionally, the company partners with Ford trucks and the Washington, DC, police force for presidential inaugurations.

Now let's translate all this into something you can use and learn from—a state-transition approach to vision creation. Figures 5.2 through 5.5 illustrate how Harley-Davidson has transformed its vision and its business, with a view to meeting the needs and aspirations of all key stakeholders.

The Harley-Davidson organization had been a multilayered, fragmented command-and-control system with an overly bureaucratic approach to routines and procedures. Decisions were made at the top and passed down the line for implementation, with little or no input from the lower ranks or from middle management. This did not fit well with the company's new dynamic and responsive vision, so Harley-Davidson needed to revamp its organization.

	Static	Dynamic
Structure	Multilayered and fragmented	Delayer management and establish synergies between divisions
Systems	Top-down; lack of feedback loops or bottom-up input	Empower middle managers and encourage them to feed information upward as well as downward
Processes	Bureaucratic	Cut the red tape; reduce the number of approvals needed for minor decisions

Figure 5.2 State Transition for Harley-Davidson: Organization

	Static	Dynamic
Values	Tell the truth, be fair, keep your promises, respect the individual, encourage intellectual curiosity	Continue these values
Management Style	Top down, focused on short-term returns, slow to adapt to change	Proactive and positive, concerned with continuous improvement, flat style
Employee Relations	Passive participation in company decisions and actions	Create self-autonomous work-groups (established Harley-Davidson Learning Center); greater involvement of employees; engage with trade unions

Figure 5.3 State Transition for Harley-Davidson: Culture

This resulted in a flatter and better-integrated structure, systems that were less hierarchical and more inclusive, and increased flexibility in practices and procedures.

On the softer side of the internal vision, the Harley-Davidson culture also was in need of improvement. Not everything needed to change—the values of truth, fairness, integrity, and respect for the individual had served the company well over time and would continue to do so. However, management style needed improvement, as Figure 5.2 indicated. In particular, the vertical approach and short-term orientation were phased out in favor of a more

	Static	Dynamic
Regulators	Protective (tariff on Japanese large motorcycles)	Aiming to be free from the protection of the regulators
Supply chain	No strong connections	Introduce just-In-time system to reduce inventory, with the full cooperation of suppliers
Competitors	Relatively poor relationship management and development	More extensive, creative, and better managed relationships

Figure 5.4 State Transition for Harley-Davidson: Relationships

horizontal, continuous-improvement focus. In the area of employee relations, employees were encouraged to take a more active role in product and service innovation, and trade unions became partners rather than antagonists.

Harley-Davidson had significant room for improvement when it came to relationships. Since the early 1980s, its relationship with government regulators had been focused on protectionism, with the company using its status as de facto national champion status to encourage the government to erect tariff walls that increased import costs for foreign competitors. Twenty years later, the world had changed and the public panic over Japanese imports had largely receded, making such protectionism harder to justify. On top of that, the World Trade Organization had phased out most such tariffs. It was in Harley's best interest to embrace free and fair competition and to break free from the stifling arms of the regulators. In another area, like many companies, Harley had poor supply-chain management in place. To reduce costs and improve responsiveness, it needed to introduce a just-in-time (JIT) system and work more cooperatively with supply-chain partners. Relationships with competitors also were in need of updating. The old animosity or, at best, indifference was replaced by a more practical approach based on cooperation when that was both possible and mutually profitable.

Finally, in the markets quadrant of Harley-Davidson's vision, the company had significant room for improvement. Its

	Static	Dynamic
Customers	Limited customer base (only for late 30s to 50s male customers)®	More extensive, creative and better managed relationships (Especially HOG)
Products	Limited products line®	Line expansion to women and younger generation
Locations	US-centric with an export-led heritage®	Global expansion and emphasis

Figure 5.5 State Transition for Harley-Davidson: Markets

traditional customer base had been narrow, focusing on American men, mostly in their late thirties to late fifties. Through the HOG, Harley was able to extend this base and reach out to women and a younger generation of appreciators. This worked hand in hand with Harley's product line extension—developing Harley-branded toiletries, clothes, and other merchandise—which reached a younger market than the motorbikes alone. Also, Harley finally shook off its U.S.-centric approach to the world and invested heavily in reaching a more global audience.

A word on process: changing an organization's culture or altering people's long-held behavior is not an easy task, especially when the people do not believe that the organization is in crisis. This was Harley-Davidson's situation in the late 1980s. After a long period of decline, the company had just regained confidence in its business and was once again on a steady growth path. But there was plenty of scope to realize the vision and to do even better—much better. When Richard Teerlink was appointed president and chief operating officer (COO) of the motorcycle division in 1987, the hard work of saving the company had been done, but Harley still was not a breakout business by any stretch of the imagination.

Teerlink immediately saw the need for a new kind of leadership—one that would be the polar opposite of the command-and-control model that had carried the company through its turnaround.[11] During his time as president and COO, and subsequently as Harley-Davidson CEO, Teerlink launched several programs designed to elicit interest, ideas, and, above all, vision inputs from employees. These initiatives helped to transform Harley's culture and made it the breakout success story it is today.

Teerlink believed passionately that people were a company's most important asset, and he sought to ensure that every Harley employee played a part in leading the company through his or her ideas and actions. Together with organizational consultant and coach Lee Ozley, he built a change process based on this radical premise of cooperative leadership, driven by what came to be called the "joint visioning process." The essence of this process—based on the work of psychologist Abraham Maslow—was that employees could be persuaded to take ownership of the vision if they helped to create it. This meant that the old approach of giving the workers answers had to be replaced by a new approach of asking for their advice and queries. Compliance had to be replaced by commitment if the new method was to work.

The joint visioning process did not come naturally to Harley-Davidson, which had long been used to a rigid hierarchical structure and a culture of bosses versus workers. But Teerlink was determined to succeed, and he reached out to the company's unions to try to bridge the traditional divide and to get them to work with management in devising the company's future. This included formal partnerships with the International Association of Machinists (IAM) and the Paper Allied-Industrial Chemical and Energy Workers (PACE). He and his management team also emphasized effective communication, which included reviving old "town hall" formats that gave those at the plant level direct contact with corporate leaders. A further element of the joint visioning process was the introduction of lifelong learning programs for Harley employees and dealers to encourage intellectual curiosity at all levels and in every corner of the corporation.

The joint visioning process ensured the input of employees who had previously been excluded, such as those at lower levels of authority, including plant workers, who were very close to the end product and often had a better sense of what was truly needed to revitalize, reshape, and transform the company. Although this was very commendable, the process did not succeed at first. It laid the groundwork for a strong culture of employee participation, but it took some time for this new culture to take hold. However, managers gradually found that the nonhierarchical, team-based structures vastly improved employee motivation and accelerated innovation and learning. To embed this new ethos and attitude, Harley-Davidson's leadership reduced the traditional hierarchy and layers of management and implemented an open-door policy, ensuring easy access to senior management.

The success of these efforts soon became apparent through employees' strong commitment to their jobs, which led to more efficient and effective manufacturing and business processes. Gradually the joint visioning process took hold and created a stakeholder-led vision that set Harley-Davison firmly on the path to strategic breakout.

The overall result of Harley-Davidson's revived and more inclusive vision was substantial. By the early 2000s, the company's annual growth rate was averaging 15 percent. In 2003, Harley-Davidson's 100th anniversary, consolidated revenue for the business was $4.62 billion, a 13 percent increase over 2002, with net income of $760.9 million, a 31.1 percent increase over the prior year. The company shipped 291,147 Harley-Davidson motorcycles in 2003, a 10.4 percent increase over 2002 and nearly double the 150,818 motorcycles produced just five years earlier. Retail sales of Harley-Davidson motorcycles for 2003 grew 8.8 percent in the United States, 11.8 percent in Europe, and 8.3 percent in Japan, outpacing the growth of the heavyweight motorcycle industry in those markets. Harley-Davidson Financial Services, Inc. (HDFS), recorded impressive gains in 2003, with operating income increasing by 61.1 percent to $167.9 million.[12]

Harley-Davidson firmly reestablished itself as one of the world's leading producers of heavyweight motorcycles, with a 25 percent global market share and a 50 percent share in the United States. In financial services, the company rapidly captured over 40 percent of the securitized loan market for new bikes sold at retail. By 2005, its two main divisions—Motorcycles and Related

Products and Financial Services—were outperforming almost all other Standard & Poor's (S&P) 500 Index automobile and components companies.[13] Despite a slowdown in 2004–2005, growth remained strong across the company. The company was particularly successful in the areas of international motorbike sales and motorbike sales to women, indicating that the more-inclusive Harley vision was working.

Now that we have discussed vision in a breakout context and advanced a technique for putting it into practice, we turn our attention to each of the major breakout types to see what special issues arise. In so doing, we provide extensive illustrations of vision in action to further sharpen our thinking. In many ways, as you will see, designing a compelling vision has been a key impetus for bringing breakout strategies to market.

Taking Vision by Storm

The vision wheel and its prevailing logic—that breakout is based on meeting stakeholder needs and aspirations through a vision that appeals to and inspires all—is at the heart of all breakout types. A company that takes by storm uses its vision to *revolutionize* and *reach out.* The idea is fresh and promises to transform the market, but *taking-by-storm* companies often are new and must sell their vision aggressively to anyone who will listen—especially potential customers.

The New York–based low-fare airline jetBlue Airways illustrates this perfectly. Since its launch in 2000, jetBlue has shaken up not only the budget airline sector but the wider air transport industry, causing it to refocus on customer service—but only on a base of cost-efficiency and low fares. In so doing, the company spurned the U.S. airline industry trend away from providing service and established its vision as original and driven by its own unique values and objectives. The company's senior management team successfully delivered this vision through a nonhierarchical, people-centered, customer-focused strategy.

Just like Richard Teerlink at Harley-Davidson in the late 1980s, jetBlue's founder, David Neeleman, was acutely aware from the outset that vision must be inclusive and that giving all employees a stake in shaping the vision results in much more effective delivery of the vision. The airline business has seen more than its fair share of companies entering and exiting the business rapidly. The industry is infamous for not making money and for failing to deliver on strategic visions. Margins are tight, costs are high, competition is fierce, and demand cyclicality is constant and often dramatic. There are notable exceptions to the rule, however, and these companies have become household names.

These success stories have one thing in common: each has an inclusive and proactive vision that forges an aspirational and deliverable corporate strategy. This vision is clear and consistent to all stakeholders and is straightforward in its manifestation, both as a customer value proposition and as an organizational business model. In the United States, both Southwest Airlines and jetBlue Airways are synonymous with value for money and good service. Both companies base their success on a clear and consistent vision and value offering, balancing low prices with efficient operation and friendly service. Still, jetBlue differentiates itself from Southwest in several ways, most notably in service, where it generally provides greater passenger comfort and amenities in return for a marginally higher average fare. In Europe, a similar game has been played out, with Ryanair and easyJet mimicking the Southwest-jetBlue rivalry and market positioning. Ryanair remains the cost and price leader, whereas easyJet's commitment to and delivery of customer service tends to be superior, although its fares are rarely lower than Ryanair's.

The vision at jetBlue is clear and straightforward: to provide high-quality customer service at low fares. This emerged from the simple but often overlooked or underexploited idea of creating an airline that would treat customers with respect and provide everyone with high-quality service at affordable fares. The company also wanted to create a positive environment, one in which crew members would feel respected and would be excited about coming to work every day. As CEO Neeleman has pointed out, jetBlue's vision is predicated on a belief in the three P's: great *people* drive solid *performance*, which generates *prosperity* for all.

Central to the company is a conviction that the airline business is fundamentally one of customer service. When hiring new "crewmembers" (Neeleman and his management team shun the more hierarchical word *employees*), jetBlue does not necessarily look for people with experience in the air transport business. Instead, the company places a premium on people who have worked in customer service at high-quality companies such as Ritz Carlton or Nordstrom's.

Unlike many other airline companies, jetBlue has focused from the beginning on meeting the needs and demands of all its stakeholders. Good employees strengthen a brand; bad employees ruin it. Customers perceive the brand through what they see and feel—the airplanes, the service, the attitude, the efficiency. The jetBlue ethos mirrors the long-established Southwest Airlines creed: if your people are happy, the customers will be happy, and if the customers are happy, the shareholders will be happy. The company also has been successful in courting New York City and state legislators, who for years have demanded improved fares and service for their constituents. Relations with global suppliers such as Airbus have been excellent because jetBlue paved the way for Airbus's entry into Boeing's home market. Profitable from its first year of operations, the airline has had growth figures higher than those of any other U.S. airline.[14]

The airline is also a service leader, having been named "best U.S. airline" by the 2003, 2004, and 2005 Airline Quality Awards, a respected annual survey conducted by the University of Nebraska at Omaha Aviation Institute and the W. Frank Barton School of Business at Wichita State University. Also in 2005, for the fourth year in a row, jetBlue was named best low-cost carrier and best U.S. domestic airline by the readers of *Condé Nast Traveler*, with almost 28,000 travelers voting. Going one step further, the Skytrax 2005 Airline of the Year Survey named jetBlue the "world's best low-cost airline." The company clearly delivers on its vision to be a leading low-fare, low-cost passenger airline offering high-quality customer service and a differentiated product. A stakeholder approach to vision creation has been instrumental in this success.

Laggard-to-Leader Vision

At the heart of a laggard-to-leader breakout is the need to *revive* and *reconfigure* a company's vision. Most laggards remain so because they fail to grasp the need for a top-to-bottom shakeup. This includes revisiting the company's vision. Does it still work in a modern business context? Does it take the interests of all key stakeholders into account? Is it attractive both internally and externally? Is it easy to understand and consistent across markets? Do you need to modify or overhaul it? These questions must be uppermost in the mind of any management team pursuing a laggard-to-leader breakout.

The renaissance of Texas Instruments (TI) was just such a breakout. It was a two-stage process that was begun in the early 1990s by then Chairman and CEO Jerry Junkins and was completed after his untimely death in 1996 by his successor, Tom Engibous.[15] Under Junkins's leadership, TI executed a series of transitions that repositioned each of its major businesses so that it could better compete in the 1990s and beyond. Junkins changed the image of TI, leading its transition to a company that was focused on its customers. He was highly respected and was known for his ability to motivate people to seek excellence in performance, setting high standards and rewarding accomplishment by individuals and teams at all levels. A strong supporter of individual development and team empowerment, he championed the company's team structure and set the example from the top. In late 1993, he set up the Office of the Chief Executive, which he shared with TI Vice Chairmen William P. (Pat) Weber and William B. (Bill) Mitchell. At the same time, TI's Strategy Leadership Team (SLT), consisting of the company's senior officers, was created. Both these structures embodied a management philosophy and vision process based on teamwork and partnership.

Reaching out to stakeholders in the wider society, Junkins was deeply committed to the issue of education at many levels. He helped initiate and support the landmark involvement of TI and the TI Foundation in model Head Start programs in south and west Dallas, which were recognized as vehicles for systemic change in early-childhood education.

When Tom Engibous took over as CEO in 1996, he inherited a company that was in good shape, but still not quite at breakout level. His predecessor had rationalized the corporation, getting rid of TI's once-mighty consumer electronics business and its also-ran home computer division. Before his sudden death, however, Junkins had not finished grappling with the essence of what TI needed to be if it was to regain market leadership. This required even tougher decisions and a further overhaul of TI's vision of being an innovative, customer-focused global electronics business.

Engibous went further than Junkins, divesting TI's memory chip (D-RAM) and defense electronics businesses. He rationalized the corporation's complicated web of joint ventures and began a major cost-cutting initiative. Engibous and his successor, Rich Templeton, also set out to further transform the TI culture, which had been a significant stumbling block during previous turnaround efforts. In particular, they focused on reducing bureaucracy and increasing decentralization, giving engineering units the ability to pursue innovation. Operating groups were given the freedom to make their own choices about technologies and products. This complemented Junkins's efforts at fostering teamwork and management-worker partnership in delivering the vision.

The result was a smaller, decentralized, and more efficient semiconductor company that sold chips mainly to consumer electronics and telecom companies. The company also was more focused technologically, having identified digital signal processing and analog technologies as its main strengths in terms of engineering skill, market position, and growth.[16] Engibous's vision for TI—an efficient, flexible, and creative company focused on the design and manufacture of innovative and specialized microchips—proved decisive in the reversal of TI's fortunes. It took a few years for investors to catch on, probably because the revival had been proclaimed too often during the previous decade. This time things were different: TI won over the key stakeholder—the customer—and established a real edge in digital data and analog chips, and this propelled the company to the forefront of the market. It had learned to build new businesses to supplement this competitive core. For example, its chips now were used in profitable, high-growth markets such as big-screen televisions and hi-fi amplifiers.

Today, TI is again one of the world's five largest semiconductor companies. It designs, manufactures, and sells semiconductors for the communications, computing, automotive, military, industrial, and consumer markets. By building on a long-standing and proven vision centered on innovation and costumer-focused design, TI adapted its structure and focused its strategy to deliver what the modern market wanted and what its people, partners, and investors needed. After years of trying, the Texas conglomerate had emerged from the wilderness to reclaim a leadership position.

Shifting Shape but Not Vision

A *shifting-shape* breakout vision often—but not always—will remain constant at the core but dynamic and flexible in how it is expressed to the customer and delivered to the market. As we noted earlier, companies such as IBM have shifted shape radically to ensure their survival, and this has included altering their vision to capture their new direction and ethos. In most instances of shifting shape, though, the breakout company must *reinforce* and *relate* its vision to ensure that it remains true to what it is good at but is able to extend this into a different corporate form, product offering, or customer proposition.

A perfect example is EMI Music's shift into digital music downloads. An iconic British music company whose artists have included The Beatles and David Bowie, EMI Group's music division entered the twenty-first century as an industry laggard. It lost over 40 percent of its market value in 2000–2001, and its profit was declining by as much as 20 percent year over year. In 2001, Eric Nicoli, chairman of EMI Group, appointed former Polygram CEO Alain Levy as CEO of EMI Music. The appointment proved inspired because Levy turned out to be a music industry visionary. While never straying from EMI's core vision of providing innovative, high-quality music for a discerning global audience, Levy realized immediately that the company urgently needed to change its form and approach. Responding to emerging customer needs and aspirations was crucial.

As we discussed in Chapter 3, companies that pursue a strategy of shifting shape in an emergent-market context are *early adapters*. Levy recognized the limitations and dangers of remaining wedded to EMI's existing markets and business models and resolved to shift position to take advantage of emergent-market developments. In doing so, he set the company on a path to market leadership. Levy immediately began researching how to make digital music pay. At that time, digital music accounted for a very small portion of the music business, and the industry received little return on what digital music did exist because of the preponderance of illegal downloading.

Circumstances, related product innovations, and changing market trends came to Levy's aid. Legal action led to the closure of illegal file-sharing pioneer Napster in 2001. This sent a well-publicized warning shot across the bows of digital music pirates around the world. The action was followed by a 2005 U.S. Supreme Court ruling that companies whose software enables the trading of free music can be held liable for theft.[17] These legal decisions were reinforced by market research indicating that most consumers would prefer to buy their music legally if the process were more user-friendly. These findings led Levy and his team to gamble the family jewels by announcing at the end of 2002 their intention to license all of EMI's legally available music to anyone who would pay the company's set wholesale prices and meet its terms regarding use, sharing, and so on. Although some of its catalogue—most notably The Beatles—remains offline, EMI Music encouraged all its artists to make their music available online.

The company's digital strategy received a major boost from the development and success of a related product—Apple's iPod. As we discuss elsewhere in this book, the iPod and Apple's online music store, iTunes, proved to be a bigger success than anyone could have anticipated and brought millions of customers into the downloadable music market. Having invested heavily in the new technology and market channel ahead of its rivals and before it became attractive to more than a small, technologically savvy group of music lovers, EMI stole a march on its competitors. By not compromising on the company's long-standing vision but being willing to change the interpretation and delivery of this vision, Levy and his team shrugged off their straggler reputation and captured the vanguard position in the modern music business.

Digital music revenues are now expected to grow from 6 percent of sales in 2006 to 25 percent in 2010, and EMI has the pole position in maximizing this income stream. Success is already evident. In 2005, EMI reported growth for the first time since 2000[18] and saw its global market share rise, largely through a massive surge of 142 percent in digital sales.

Despite being the world's largest independent music company and the owner of the world's largest catalogue of songs, EMI is not resting on its laurels. Instead, it is looking to exploit new opportunities in the fast-moving world of cellular phone downloads. The potential here is even greater because of the ubiquity of cell phones and the market demand for ringtones and, increasingly, complete song downloads (so-called ringtunes). EMI has begun to capture this emerging market, forging an alliance with leading wireless telecom provider T-Mobile to make more than 200,000 songs and music videos available to T-Mobile's 60 million European customers.

Driven by a powerful vision of quality and creativity and a strategy geared toward delivering music to consumers in any form, at any time, and in any place, EMI's early-adapter strategy is keeping it at the forefront of market trends and industry evolution. Levy and his team have achieved breakout by proactively embracing a new and unproven sales medium before its main rivals did so, and by building on its reputation for innovation and nonconformity to capture the more sophisticated and demanding customers typical of the new online music market.

Expanding Horizons, Extending the Vision

Stakeholder needs and aspirations vary from country to country, but the fundamentals remain constant: workers want to be valued, customers want to get value, and shareholders want a good return on their investment. A breakout company should not deviate from a winning formula just because it is operating in a different country; however, it must be aware of variations in rules, norms, market conditions, and customer preferences. It is vital to *replicate* and *revise*—deliver on what you do best, but be willing and able to modify aspects of the way you configure this, package it, or deliver it to the consumer.

When Dell Computer first entered the Chinese market, its vision of low-price, high-quality branded personal computers built to order and sold directly to customers hit a number of problems. In particular, rolling out the Dell Direct model proved difficult in a market where few people had credit cards and Internet access was limited. There also was a cultural reluctance to pay for goods not only before you got to test them out but as much as two weeks before you received your purchase. Dell had to be creative if it was to deliver on what we described in Chapter 3 as the boundary-breaker form of the *expanding-horizons* strategy—successfully carrying the winning Dell Direct formula from one geographically defined market space to another.

The company rose to the challenge, intent on capturing the advantage in the largest emerging information technology (IT) market in the world. An early solution was to make an arrangement with local post offices; Dell would ship the computer to the post office, and the customer would come to see the product there and then pay for it. This was not an ideal scenario for Dell, but it allowed the company to build a presence in China. Later on, in Beijing, for example, the company's delivery drivers began to carry wireless debit-card machines so that customers could pay when their computers arrived, a system that solved the credit-card problem. Dell stuck to the essence of its vision of selling direct to the customer, but it had to tailor its implementation to overcome local constraints. Dell's perseverance has paid off, with its share of the Chinese market climbing from zero in 1998 to 5 percent within four years.

Many American boundary breakers have had equal success in international markets, some (such as McDonald's) by tailoring their product offerings to meet local needs, and others (such as Dell) by modifying their business models to ensure market reach and delivery. All have had one thing in common: clearly understood and consistently executed breakout visions that resonate with customers around the world.

Starbucks, the global coffee retailing giant, offers a vision that combines an emphasis on selling only the finest coffee in a relaxing and welcoming atmosphere with a strong commitment to a friendly working atmosphere, thus making a contribution to society and the environment. The Starbucks vision, rooted firmly in responsiveness to stakeholders, has enabled the company to grow rapidly around the world. Customers want Starbucks outlets to look and feel the same or similar wherever they are located. Product offerings vary slightly from location to location, but the vision remains consistent in both principle and practice.

Best Western's vision is straightforward: to be the world's preferred midlevel hotel chain. A common inspection system ensures that all members meet the chain's basic quality and service requirements, and a user-friendly Web site and globally integrated loyalty program help to maintain customer allegiance. Best Western's international expansion has been stealthy but steady, and it has captured the three-star market segment in numerous countries around the world. It is striving for global domination in a very specific market niche and is integrating its front- and back-office activities to maximize cost-efficiencies and customer awareness. It has resisted the temptation to diversify into related markets, such as lower- or higher-quality hotels, and has retained its focus on a vision that serves it well.

Finally, on occasion there can be movement between the two main forms of expanding-horizons breakout—but even so, the corporate vision should remain constant. HSBC started life in 1865 as the Hong Kong and Shanghai Banking Corporation; its purpose was to finance the growing trade between China and Europe. It has since grown to become one of the world's largest banks, second only to the U.S. giant Citigroup.

Expanding mainly through acquisitions, the company has steadily extended its global reach and reputation. Following a major expansion and consolidation in mature markets during the 1990s and early 2000s (its *conquistador* phase), the group began to focus on carrying its winning formula from established markets such as the United Kingdom to emergent markets such as Brazil, China, and India (going into boundary-breaker mode). In particular, it is looking at the high-earning new elite in these countries. The group invested more than $4 billion in China alone between 2001 and 2005, buying stakes in Chinese financial institutions. With its catchphrase, "The world's local bank," supported by a clever and appealing advertising strategy, HSBC's vision remains straightforward and consistent: it aims to be the world's leading financial services company.

Everything that HSBC says and does indicates that this is a company that takes a stakeholder approach to vision creation and strategy implementation. This approach has paid off handsomely: HSBC's asset base increased from $472 billion in 1997 to $1.5 trillion by 2005, and its share price reached a level almost double that of Citigroup. Going forward, the company is likely to place increased emphasis on its boundary-breaker approach in emergent markets, firmly fixed on its winning vision to be the world's bank of choice for quality, customer-responsive products.

Conclusion

Every lone entrepreneur or top-management team needs a vision, but more important, it needs guidelines for developing and delivering that vision. The vision wheel, which is critical to developing a breakout strategy, provides these guidelines. It requires a fresh look inside the company at organization and culture and outside the company at relationships and markets. This can precipitate a rethinking, restructuring, and repositioning of the enterprise to put it firmly on a high-growth trajectory.

There are four key requirements for using the model as a practical tool within a business:

1. *Create your vision proactively, not reactively.* Don't be forced into changes by competitors or stakeholders, creating a vision in haste and adapting it to protect rather than promote your product and position.
2. *Ensure that the vision is inclusive.* If you do not do this, you run the risk of the vision's not being attractive externally or deliverable internally.
3. *Keep the essence constant.* Be true to yourself and build on your strengths, but make sure that you build in flexibility and adaptability so that you can deal with market change and customer evolution.
4. *Don't overcomplicate or overclutter the vision.* Keep it simple, clear, and consistent, and above all, ensure that it is both realizable and motivational.

Strategy without a clear, purposeful, and dynamic vision is doomed to mediocrity at best and failure at worst. Vision is not a hazy and confused idea concocted by a senior management team to appease shareholders or bolster its own ego. Instead, it is a clear and coherent notion that drives an entire breakout process and remains consistent despite a constantly changing business environment. The ways and means of delivering a vision may change, but in most cases the core vision principles and values should not.

When it is designed correctly, a strategic vision can deliver value to all stakeholders. By employing our multistakeholder vision-wheel method, companies can develop a vision that appeals to different constituencies in different ways. The result is happy customers, contented employees, satisfied regulators, positive supply-chain partners, and delighted shareholders. Thus, a stakeholder vision results in high-growth shareholder value. Harley-Davidson, jetBlue, Texas Instruments, and others illustrate that regardless of the nature of the industry or the age of the company, a clear, dynamic, and inclusive vision, consistently delivered, can take any company to industry prominence and market success.

In Chapter 6, we continue our account of how to deliver on strategic breakout. Once a vision has been clarified, communicated, and embedded, the next step for any business leader is to turn to the enterprise's value proposition.

Endnotes

1 This was K. Ohmae's argument in "The Secret of Strategic Vision," *Management Review*, April 1982, p. 10.

2 See I. Wilson, "Realizing the Power of Strategic Vision," *Long Range Planning* 25(5):18, 1992.

3 "High Street Woes," *Economist*, July 26, 2001; www.economist.com/displayStory.cfm?Story_ID=710209.

4 Terry Macalister, "Asda Overtakes M&S as UK's Top Clothing Retailer," *Guardian*, August 23, 2004.

5 P. Cossette, "A Systematic Method to Articulate Strategic Vision: An Illustration with a Small Business Owner-Manager," *Journal of Enterprising Culture* 9(2):173, 2001.

6 In particular, this is exemplified by the work of L. Grattori, "Implementing a Strategic Vision: Key Factors for Success," *Long Range Planning* 29(3):290–303, 1996.

7 For example, see C. J. Pineno and C. R. Cristini, "The Balanced Scorecard: A Vision Report Card," *Management Accounting Quarterly* 4(4):28–40, 2003.

8 Advocated by J. C. Collins and J. I. Porras, "Organizational Vision and Visionary Organizations," *California Management Review* 34(1):30–52, 1991, and "Building Your Company's Vision," *Harvard Business Review.* September–October 1996, pp. 65–77.

9 Thanks are due to Dora Fang, Takashi Kimura, Jamesa Rogers, and Kiyoshi Saito, Tuck 2005, for their input into this case study.

10 Stated in Harley-Davidson's annual reports and on the company's Web site.

11 For further details of this process, see Rich Teerlink and Lee Ozley, More Than a Motorcycle: The Leadership Journey at Harley-Davidson. Cambridge, MA: *Harvard Business School Press*, 2000.

12 "Harley-Davidson, Inc.," *Datamonitor*, November 2004, pp. 23–24.

13 Harley-Davidson, Inc.'s corporate governance quotient as of July 1, 2005, was better than 86.3 percent of the S&P 500 automobile and components companies (Yahoo! Finance, July 26, 2005).

14 The company hit some turbulence in 2005, suffering losses for the first time in its five-year history. Fourth-quarter net losses of $42.4 million caused jetBlue to post an annual loss of $20.3 million at year-end. The reasons for this dramatic change in performance were in part beyond the carrier's control. The devastating hurricanes that ravaged the Gulf of Mexico and the neighboring U.S. states during the fall of 2005 forced many flight cancellations, sapping revenues, and also brought about severe disruptions in oil supplies, causing oil prices to skyrocket. The company was at fault insofar as it had not made adequate provision for rising fuel costs, having failed to enter into price hedges as rivals such as Southwest had done. The airline also expanded too far, too fast during 2005, increasing overall costs for the year (up 43.3 percent over 2004) and putting strains on network efficiency (e.g., during several months of the year, jetBlue

ranked last out of 19 airlines surveyed by the U.S. Department of Transportation in terms of on-time arrivals). Despite these setbacks, jetBlue's traffic numbers continued to climb during 2005, and revenue was up 34.5 percent over 2004. At the risk of speculation, we would anticipate that this was only a temporary setback, largely attributable to a combination of growing pains and the forces of nature.

15 Simon London, "A Highly Calculated Recovery Act," *Financial Times*, October 26, 2004, p. 13.

16 Ibid.

17 Thomas K. Grose, "Sing When You're Winning," *Time*, February 27, 2006, p. 41.

18 Ibid., p. 40.

CHAPTER 6

BEING A MAGNET COMPANY

Few companies succeed without a powerful, compelling vision. This is a prerequisite for business success. But is it enough? The answer to this question is an emphatic no. Developing a vision, as we discussed in Chapter 5, involves managing the perceptions and preferences of multiple stakeholders to develop an internal and external raison d'être that attracts adherents. This is essential, but it is not enough.

It is time to turn our attention directly to the customer, the key to making any business thrive. To take the vision forward and make it the inspiration for a strategy process, a company must listen to its customers—both real and potential—very carefully. It is crucial that you adopt a customer-focused approach to everything you do. In pursuing rapid breakout, deep customer focus is needed.[1] Deep focus is not about buying customer relationship management (CRM) software to track customers' purchases and habits, nor is it about designing leading-edge products or processes. It is about becoming indispensable to customers by constantly thinking about better, quicker, easier ways of doing things that they need.

Samsung's breakout in the early 2000s stemmed from this type of a deep customer focus. The design team at Samsung Electronics has been intently focused on meeting customer needs. A visit to the company's U.S. offices, beside a highway in northern New Jersey, reveals a team that is dedicated to improving customer value at every opportunity.[2] It is common to see engineers trying out equipment to find out how it could be made more user friendly. One engineer watches as colleagues stuff the contents of several bags of groceries into a refrigerator. Afterward, having photographed the crowded appliance to see where the "shoppers" had put the various items, the engineers trade opinions on several different configurations of drawers and compartments. "We want to know the tastes of American customers because we need to develop products that fit their lifestyle," comments engineer Lee Byung Moo. The effort has paid off. Samsung has risen rapidly from a "me too" producer of electronics and appliances to become one of the world's leading brands, winning a raft of design awards along the way.

Deep customer focus is especially about becoming a *magnet company*, one that attracts customers to its unique offerings. A strong magnet exerts a force that draws metallic objects to it. The imagery is apt: magnet companies make themselves indispensable to customers by developing a world-class value proposition. Customers are drawn to such companies and are kept there for as long as the magnetic field surrounding the value proposition holds. In this chapter we describe what such a value proposition is and provide guidance on how to think about each component of it independently and all the components as an interconnected whole to drive strategy and maintain the company's magnetic pull.

Let's first be clear as to what a value proposition is and what it isn't. Surprisingly, research indicates that managers still do not agree on what a value proposition is or how a company can make its value proposition convincing and appealing to customers.[3] When we use the term, we refer to the offer of a product or a set of related products that a company makes to a customer, including all the experiences that go with making the purchase—before, during, and after the purchase itself. To be useful—and that is the litmus test for all the ideas in this book—a value proposition must go far beyond the usual calls to "get close to your customer." Such truisms tell us little. Of course we must get close to the customer, but how? And in what ways?

A value proposition offers an answer to these essential questions. In many ways, the most fundamental challenge for any business is to put together a value proposition that is both attractive to existing and potential customers and unique to the business. *Unique* does not mean that the value proposition is one of a kind and totally inimitable. It means that this market offering is configured more effectively and delivered more efficiently than anyone else's. It is an offering that gives customers what they need—and then some. It involves consistently providing what you promise and augmenting this with extra "free" value, be it a more obliging sales team than anyone else has or a more flexible returns policy than any competitor's. And it involves ensuring that you are offering customers something that is different enough from what competitors offer in some important way to give customers an incentive to buy from you and not from someone else.

It is astonishing how many companies go to market without a carefully constructed and clearly defined value proposition. Part of the problem may be that managers often are unsure about how a value proposition is configured. What factors define a value proposition? How can these factors be merged in a balanced and appealing way?

A value proposition includes two key types of assets—tangible and intangible. Specifically, for customers, the added value of any product or service is equal to the value of the tangible and intangible benefits of purchasing that product or service, minus the price paid. The tangible benefits of a product or service are straightforward: it has appropriate technical attributes, it meets the customer's needs, it fulfills a function that is important to the customer—in a word, it works.

Depending on the model you choose, an Apple iPod can store up to 15,000 songs and 25,000 photos and supports as much as 150 hours of video. Its battery lasts as long as 20 hours on a single charge, and—depending on the car you drive—you can integrate it with your car's stereo system. On top of this, and the iPod's trump card in many ways, there is a seamless connection between Apple's iTunes Music Store software and the iPod players—a real advantage in an industry that is held back by the divisions among hardware, software, and online music providers. These are all practical and appealing features that are tangible benefits.

The intangible benefits are just as critical; indeed, they are vital to defining and distinguishing an enterprise. These may include brand or lifestyle choices. Several rivals now can match or come close to the iPod in design, features, and functions—and undercut it on price—but they fail to equal it on reputation and image. As IBM and Hoover did in the past and as Microsoft and Intel have done more recently, Apple has successfully established the iPod as the industry yardstick and cleverly implanted it in the minds of consumers as a "must have" product. By doing so, the company has captured over 80 percent of the market.

When adidas realized that its brand had to mean something—that it was leading edge in both technology and fashion—it broke out of its downward spiral and recaptured its glory days. Richard Branson's Virgin Group and its various subbrands leveraged their advantage by amplifying the intangible benefits of their products. Being a Virgin customer always has been as much about an image and the identification with an attitude toward life as it has been about the actual product or service in and of itself.

Intangible benefits may also include friendly and accommodating customer service. The success of airlines such as Southwest and jetBlue is based in large part on their people-centric view of the world and their personalized treatment of their customers. Why else would such companies thrive in an industry that has a relatively standardized product and is notorious for its lack of profitability? Some companies—notably Dell Computers and Starbucks—effectively harness a range of intangible benefits, from lifestyle choice to customer experience. In crowded markets, it is these intangibles that ensure and sustain breakout.

Together, the tangible and intangible benefits of a product or service must exceed the price that the customer pays for that product or service. When they do, added value is created for customers, and the value proposition defines precisely what it is about the product or service that accomplishes this goal. Hence a value proposition enables customers to preferentially differentiate your company from your competitors. Breakout cannot occur unless you have developed a compelling value proposition.

The Six Pillars of a Value Proposition

Our research, as well as our work with dozens of companies in a consulting capacity, has enabled us to identify the six key pillars of a value proposition that most closely reflect the "hot buttons" that customers look at when they are considering engaging with a company and its products and services. These pillars are distinct but highly interrelated. As illustrated in Figure 6.1, they are price, features, quality, support, availability, and reputation. The organization distinguishes itself from the competition through its unique configuration of these systemic variables. Moreover, an organization can identify its relative strategic weakness by seeing which of these variables require additional attention and resources.

It is important to keep in mind that customers perceive where you stand in relation to each of the six pillars *whether or not you perceive it yourself*. In other words, every company conveys a message to customers in each of these areas, intended or not, and when this gets out of control, the consequences are dire. Breakout strategy absolutely requires companies to take hold of their value propositions and actively manage them as a core strategic function. Active management of a value proposition involves three related requirements:

1. *Explain what you are and what you offer.* An effective value proposition makes clear to customers what it is that you are offering them. It ensures that the tangible and intangible benefits exceed the price paid. Once your vision is clear and consistent, developing and delivering a compelling value proposition becomes easier. Customers who know what you are and where you are going as a business are more likely to consider your product or service offering. It is then up to you—through the value proposition—to make the sale, close the deal, and lock in customer allegiance.

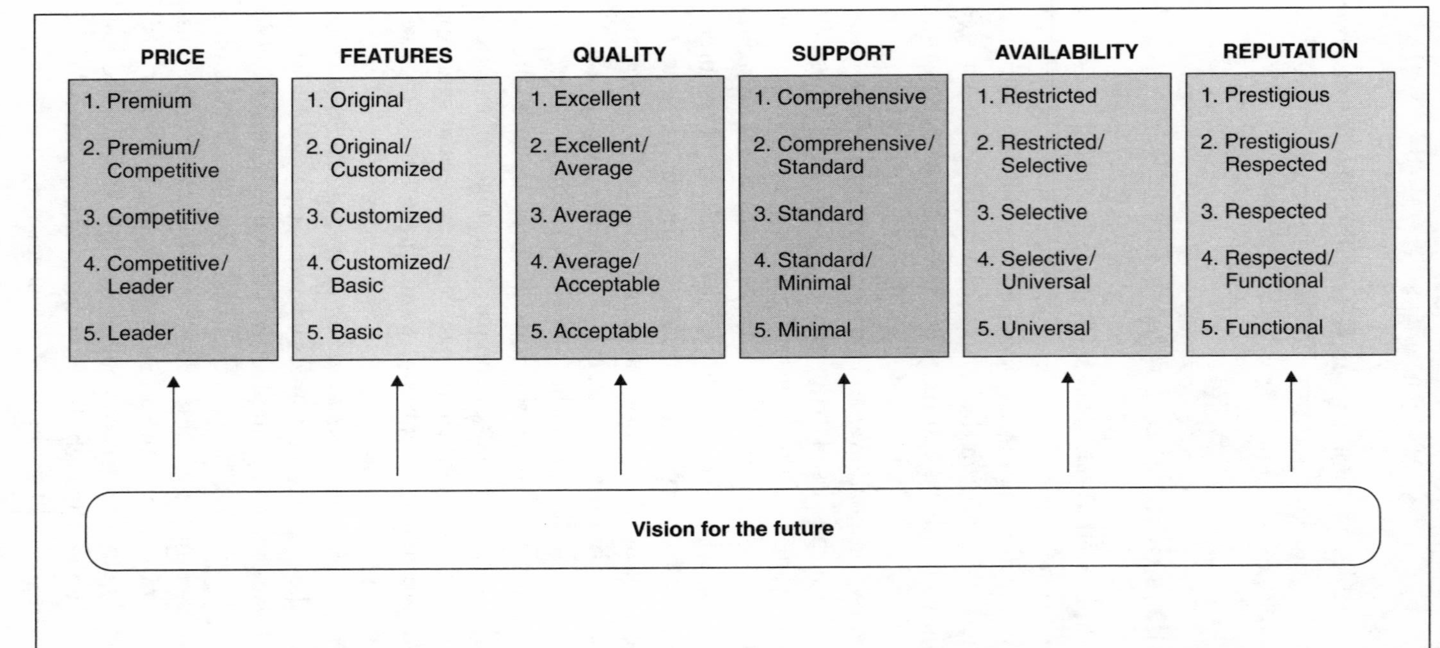

Figure 6.1 The Six Pillars of a Value Proposition

2. *Ensure clarity and consistency to the customer.* It is critical that the company consider each of the six pillars from a customer perspective and align them to ensure that the customer's needs and expectations are met. If a consumer looks at a company and sees the highest-priced—premium—provider, then he or she will expect certain value offerings to offset the above-average price. These will be top-of-the-line features, quality, and support, compounded by a lifestyle statement embodied in the reputation of the product, brand, and company. Similarly, if a consumer pays the lowest price possible for a product or service, he or she will expect the minimum features, quality, and support and will not expect to obtain any kudos or image enhancement from association with the product. The key, from a business perspective, is to ensure that customers know precisely what they are buying into and receive exactly what they expect each and every time they interact with the company. Ambiguity and inconsistency are the sworn enemies of an effective value proposition.

3. *Leverage up to gain competitive advantage.* The value proposition is also an analytical tool that breakout companies can use to help identify attributes of the customer experience that are ripe for further exploitation. Especially when you are assessing your own value proposition relative to those of competitors, new opportunities to extend your position with customers can emerge. *Leveraging up* refers to enhancing one or more of the six pillars in ways that can further strengthen your value proposition at the expense of competitors.

For instance, the market breakout of premium guitar maker Paul Reed Smith Guitars is based in large part on its leveraging up of features, quality, and support relative to market leaders Gibson and Fender.[4] As we have seen in many other industries, these much larger competitors had grown complacent, losing their innovative edge and allowing quality to slip as they became mass-production businesses. They also became disengaged from serious guitar players and their individual needs. Paul Reed Smith saw an opportunity to take the best of what his rivals were offering and improve on it. His passion for quality and continuous improvement was real, and the care and attention that went into building each guitar—as well as his willingness to customize—won over demanding and discerning customers such as guitar legend Carlos Santana. These customers were willing to pay top dollar for a premium product that met their specific demands. When you add in the company's willingness to sell only through retail stores that provide expert sales support and service, you have a winning formula. Despite its much smaller size, Paul Reed Smith Guitars has risen to become number one in the premium segment of the market, capturing 60 percent of top-end sales and doubling its turnover in the process.

Let us illustrate these points by looking closely at one of the biggest cultural phenomena to take hold in recent years—the rise of the iPod. Steve Jobs and his colleagues at Apple Computer understood these principles when they launched the Apple iPod. Demand for these iconic miniature digital music and information devices quickly outstripped supply, causing product shortages and waiting lists at some outlets. Despite establishing an early lead in the MP3 market, Apple was quickly besieged by a number of lower-priced rival devices. Apple retained its premium pricing strategy, however, and also maintained its market leadership position. How did this happen in a world where price appears to be the dominant element in market competition?

The reason is clear: Apple customers were willing to pay top dollar for iPods because of the other reinforcing components of the iPod value proposition. The iPod's features were essential and highly original. The rotating-jog dial appealed to customers because of its ease of use. The long-life battery ensured that someone who was traveling a significant distance could have constant music or audio books to break the tedium of the journey. Most of all, the miniaturized memory chip at the heart of the iPod could store more data than any of its predecessors. Even the mini version—designed for ultimate portability—could hold as many as 1,000 songs.[5]

The iPod's quality was excellent. Along with having pleasing aesthetics, the iPod was extremely robust and able to withstand the rough and tumble of fast-moving, energetic lifestyles. The

Apple brand further enhanced the perception—and reality—that the iPod was made with the utmost attention to detail and composed of the highest-specification parts.

Support was comprehensive, consisting of a user-friendly and interactive Web site, a telephone support hotline, and well-trained and approachable advisors in the dedicated Apple stores. The stores, found in selected urban locations around the world, are stylish and accessible. They not only sell Apple computers, iPods, and other devices and peripherals, but also offer training and advice to Apple customers.

So far we have seen absolute consistency in Apple's value proposition: premium price, original features, excellent quality, and comprehensive support. For the remaining two pillars, the same holds true. Availability is a little down the scale; it is best described as "selective/universal." You might ask why it is not universal. The answer is simple: to maintain the allure and cachet of Apple devices, they should not be available in every mall or supermarket outlet. This is a clever ploy to get people to travel some distance in order to physically try out the Apple product that they are interested in. Human nature dictates that the harder we have to work to gain access to or obtain something, the more we want it—assuming that it is worth having, of course. So it is with the Apple product line. Although the number of Apple stores has proliferated, the expansion has been gradual and cautious. Apple is a long way from striving to achieve blanket coverage of even core markets.

On the final pillar, reputation, it should be clear that Apple specifically positioned its iPod MP3 players at the top end of the scale—"prestigious." Buying an iPod was not just the purchase of a state-of-the-art digital music device; it also was a fashion statement, a lifestyle choice. People bought the iPod as much for the brand and what this said about them as they did for its features, quality, and support. The bold colors on the iPod mini product line helped to convey this evocatively to anyone who cared to look. It was hard to miss the lime green, shocking pink, or sky blue color of the mini iPod as it flashed by you strapped to a jogger's arm.

The clarity and consistency of the iPod value proposition ensured that its market leadership approach would succeed—despite the high prices. What's more, this was part of Steve Jobs's deliberate strategy to leverage up the wider Apple value proposition after the wilderness years of the 1990s. Despite a loyal following and a high-quality offering, Apple previously had been unable to break out of a niche position. So what did Apple's top management team do differently to leverage up the company's value proposition and create broad competitive advantage?

Returning to the six pillars, there was no significant change in price, features, or quality. Apple remained a premium-priced competitor that distinguished itself through innovative high-specification products. Instead, there were changes in the remaining three pillars. As Figure 6.2 illustrates, Apple leveraged up its offering to customers in the areas of support, availability, and reputation. Its support always had been among the best, but by expanding into dedicated Apple stores with in-house training and advice, Apple took the value to customers up a notch, from "comprehensive/standard" to "comprehensive."

At the same time, by increasing the number of Apple stores, the company shifted its availability from "selective" to "selective/universal"; its products became easier to try out and to buy than they had been previously, when they were sold only via direct order or at select Apple dealers, but they still were not available at all computer stores.

Hand in hand with these two shifts, Apple expended enormous resources on both technological transitions and advertising and marketing to move it definitively to the top of the reputation scale. Apple always had been trendy among its core constituency, but everyone else saw it as a "walled off" company, accessible only to those who were willing and able to operate on its exclusive platforms. As the company moved toward compatibility between its systems and standard PC operating platforms, however, its appeal broadened. At the same time, Apple spent heavily on selling the idea of Apple as a fashionable, user-friendly choice that did not require retraining and that allowed the integration of

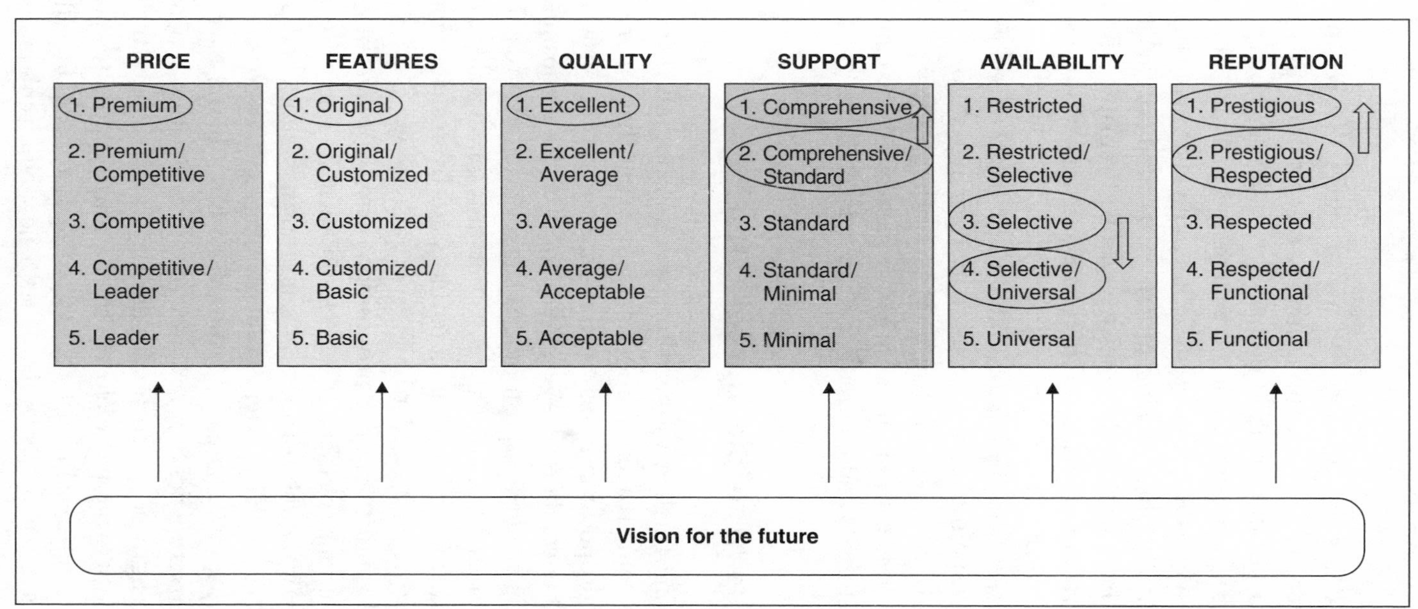

Figure 6.2 Leveraging Up the Apple Value Proposition

Apple products and other electronic products that you owned. The effort worked, and Apple quickly came to occupy the top reputation spot in its market domains.

This case demonstrates how a company can adopt a dynamic approach to its value proposition, deliberately increasing the scale or scope of its value offering to gain market advantage. It also shows us that this shift does not have to be dramatic. Apple did not move from minimal to comprehensive support, for instance; it merely increased its support from a relatively comprehensive but incomplete service offering to a fully comprehensive support service. In fact, in most cases, such short- to midrange shifts are likely to prove more successful than total repositioning (e.g., moving from price leader to premium price), which can cause confusion among customers and contradictions in market offerings.

Reconciling Multiple Market Offerings

Before going further, we need to answer a question that might now be in some readers' minds: is it possible to have more than one value proposition in play at the same time? The answer is a definite—but conditional—yes. We recognize that companies can have multiple value propositions, as suggested in Figure 6.3, but we believe that if the company is to pursue a successful breakout strategy, all these propositions should stem from shared vision, values, culture, and standards.

In our formulation, value propositions exist in *families* in which the propositions are more or less closely related. There are associations between the corporate, brand (business unit), and product levels, although the extent of these linkages varies considerably from company to company. Products within a brand have very similar characteristics but vary in degree of association depending on the strength of the corporate identity. The stronger the corporate identity, the more closely the various brands are related, and the greater the similarity between value propositions will be. For instance, when Disney launches a new children's animated

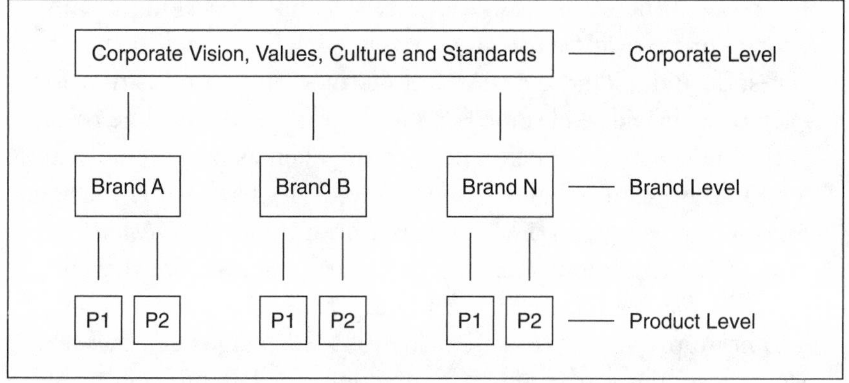

Figure 6.3 Reconciling Different Value Propositions

movie, the Disney identity often trumps the product characteristics (*Mickey, Donald, Goofy: The Three Musketeers*) or the brand (Mickey Mouse and Friends) in the minds of customers. Parents buying the DVD for their kids are reassured by the Disney stamp of quality and reliability and often are not as concerned about the theme or content of the actual movie. Thus, the value proposition for Disney's animated children's movies is constant and varies little from product to product.

In contrast, HIT Entertainment, introduced in Chapter 3 and discussed in some detail in Chapter 7, has the opposite experience. Although it competes in markets similar to those served by Disney, HIT's corporate identity is not as well known among end users of its products. Parents—and children—do not tend to go into a store to purchase the latest HIT Entertainment DVD, soft toy, or other branded product. Instead, they purchase *Bob the Builder*, *Barney*, or *Angelina Ballerina* on the strength of each product's individual value proposition. Sometimes brand association helps with sales of new products (*Bob Saves the Day* sold well in part because it was a clear follow-up to *Bob the Builder: To the Rescue!*), but there is scant evidence that either sold well because of the HIT identity. Only a very well-informed customer makes the connection between HIT and *Bob*. This makes life more difficult for HIT because it is not leveraging significant equity from one brand to another and therefore has to invest in and promote a new and distinct value proposition for each of its brands and sometimes each of its products. The result is that Disney can launch a new brand, such as *Mulan*, and win a sizable portion of sales based solely on its having the Disney logo, whereas when HIT launches a brand such as *Rubadubbers*, it is unable to capitalize on the fact that it comes from the same stable as *Bob the Builder*, *Barney*, and *Thomas the Tank Engine*.

The implications are self-evident at this stage, but they are worth spelling out. First, if your company has multiple value propositions, to avoid confusion or contradiction, they all should start from an explicit common vision, values, culture, and standards. Second, a robust and constructive corporate identity can make a family of value propositions more cohesive and enable goodwill spillover between brands and products when consumers are making their purchasing decisions.

As with so many things in strategy, and in life, there are exceptions—or so it seems. A larger and more diversified organization, particularly one operating across a number of different geographic markets, can reconcile different configurations of value propositions. Typically, however, there is little variation among them once you look beneath the surface. The key to pulling this off is ensuring, first, that the different propositions are all synchronized with the overall corporate goals and identity, and second, that there are no contradictions between different offerings for different markets. Three contexts leap to mind.

The first is the multibrand global conglomerate that adopts different guises in different countries or markets. Procter & Gamble (P&G) can be Folgers coffee to one consumer, Crest toothpaste to another, and Duracell batteries to a third. These products are in different markets and face different competitors and potentially different consumers. But the value proposition is broadly the same: a good-quality, respected product that is priced at the upper end but not the top of the market and is available widely around the world.

Variations can exist, but often they are superficial. Unilever sells men's deodorant under the Lynx name in Australia and the United

Kingdom and under the Axe name in France and the United States, but the product is essentially the same. Sometimes the value proposition may seem to differ: P&G hair products, sold under the Pantene or Wella brand, may be cheaper to buy in Turkey than in France. Does this mean that these brands are price leaders in Turkey but merely price competitive in France? No—it means that country income differentials and market realities necessitate different prices, but in all markets these brands are somewhere in the middle—well-established, widely known, and widely available brands that command respect and a good price.

The second context is the company that occupies different segments of the same market and appears to be different things to different people. This tends to occur most often when a company's product brands resonate more with the customer than the corporate brand. Take the ice cream business as an example. Unilever sells Ben & Jerry's and Breyers ice cream in the United States and Wall's and Ben & Jerry's ice cream in Europe. As a consumer, you can purchase a bar of chocolate ice cream, a frozen yogurt, or a carton of Chunky Monkey and never leave the Unilever stable.

Unilever looks as if it is employing a set of value propositions rather than just one. Let's look a little more closely, though. What we find is variations but no radical departures. To ice cream lovers, Ben & Jerry's is a premium-priced product with unique features, excellent quality, comprehensive support, selective availability, and a prestigious reputation. Wall's ice cream, on the other hand—including such favorites as Magnum and Solero—is a rung or two lower on the ladder but still not at the lower end of the market. Unilever is occupying more than one position in the same market and has to adjust its value proposition accordingly because customers will pay a premium for Ben & Jerry's ice cream but will not pay more than the market average for a Wall's or Breyers' product. There is no brand association with the company, and therefore no confusion arises.

In fact, if you go to Ben & Jerry's or Breyers' Web sites, you will be hard pressed to find a mention of Unilever anywhere. But if you go a little deeper, you will find that all the business units share common objectives and values predicated on all-around customer satisfaction, investment for growth, business integrity, and the safeguarding of reputation. The point is that through a combination of brand separation and behind-the-scenes harmonization of vision and values, a company such as Unilever can make several offers simultaneously and successfully to customers in the same market.

The third context in which more than one value proposition may appear to be in existence at the same time occurs when there is a group or holding-company structure, where a variety of different businesses, sometimes with apparently little in common, coexist. Bridgestone, Virgin, and Moët Hennessy–Louis Vuitton (LVMH) are all cases in point. These are very different entities, but each is united by a shared vision, a common culture, and a common set of values. Bridgestone is the world's largest tire and automotive service network, but it also manufactures building and industrial products, synthetic polymers, and fibers and textiles. The result of a 1990 merger between Bridgestone USA and Firestone Tire and Rubber Company, the company is Japanese-owned, but much of its market is in the United States. Although it operates in different markets, the company is united by its excellence in rubber technology, values that emphasize superior quality and product innovation, and a culture that continually reinforces being the best at what the company does.

The Virgin Group is involved in planes, trains, finance, soft drinks, music, mobile phones, holidays, cars, wines, publishing, and bridal wear. You might well ask how all these can have any common features. Virgin argues that what ties all these businesses together are the values of the brand and the attitude of the people. The Virgin vision is about service innovation and value for money; the values are centered on quality, creativity, and customer focus; and the culture is one of fun, flexibility, and empowerment. Whether it's Virgin Atlantic, Virgin Money, or Virgin Mobile, the value proposition—what the customer sees and likes—has some variations but is broadly consistent. You buy Virgin, and you get a consistent and reliable product that is configured creatively, priced fairly, and delivered in an accommodating way to meet your needs. And on top of this, you get a brand that indicates that you are someone who knows his or her own mind and appreciates fun and friendliness.

LVMH Group has a portfolio encompassing 50 brands, ranging from wine and spirits (including Moët & Chandon champagne) to fashion goods and perfumes (Louis Vuitton, Thomas Pink, Kenzo, and Dior, to name just a few). What unites them? All are prestige brands, all blend elegance and creativity, and all strive for product excellence within a decentralized group structure that emphasizes individual responsibility and rewards constant improvement and personal initiative. The result is a group that sees breakout across its divisions and collectively achieves double-digit growth in revenue, operating profit, and net profit.

In all these contexts, breakout companies either appear to have multiple market offerings but actually do not or have numerous propositions but ensure that each hinges on common vision, values, culture, and standards—and in some cases market positioning. In so doing, they avoid brand conflict or contradiction and realize customer contentment.

Being a Magnet Company via Breakout Strategy

We have seen that value propositions are essential for successful breakout strategies. Building a compelling value proposition is the surest path to becoming a magnet company, and mastery of the six pillars is critical to this endeavor. The same six pillars are at the heart of value propositions in all breakouts, yet there are crucial differences in the circumstances surrounding the creation and enhancement of value propositions in different breakout types. And these factors play a role in how managers should think about the process of developing value propositions and the form the value propositions should take. In the following sections, we consider some of the more crucial of these differences by looking at value propositions in each of the four focal breakout types, beginning with taking by storm.

Taking-by-Storm Value Propositions

The hallmark of the *taking-by-storm* breakout strategy is speed and surprise. In emergent markets, *true originals* usually are first movers or close to first movers in a marketplace. In classic entrepreneurial fashion, they see an opportunity and act quickly to capitalize on it. For example, Google saw the potential for Internet search long before mainstream players did. The company moved quickly to develop a one-stop search engine that was free to users and relied on advertisements to make money. Google's streamlined, user-friendly interface, sophisticated software, and range of different but related features, such as Google Finance and Froogle for online shopping searches, propelled the company to the forefront of its market.

Similarly, Genentech, the first biotechnology company ever, is an example of an original enterprise that came from nowhere to achieve prominence in the therapeutic industry within a few short years. Genentech was shaped by founders Herbert Boyer and Robert Swanson's ability to seize and exploit the creative disruption brought about by new genetic technologies. Genentech's growth resulted from an aggressive attack on the market that enabled the company to capture a significant share, redefining the entire industry and forcing old, established pharmaceutical giants to respond and reconfigure. In both these instances, as for most true originals, there is a premium for carving out a position before others can react.

Revolutionaries may feel compelled to move even faster. These companies follow a taking-by-storm strategy in established markets, and thus they have even more to fear from incumbents who find themselves outflanked by nimbler players. Speed and surprise are almost required if these companies are to be successful. Vodafone, the world's largest telecommunications company, was founded in 1982, and by the beginning of 1985, it had made the first-ever cell phone call (on a Motorola handset). Catching the large but slow European telecommunications providers unaware, Vodafone continued to be at the forefront of every new mobile telephony innovation, from the first roaming cell phone call to the notion of prepay phones to leading the market in offering SMS (text messaging) services.

In the same way, when Reed Hastings and Mark Randolph launched Netflix in the late 1990s—offering an Internet-based unlimited rental subscription service for DVD movies—the business took off like wildfire.[6] A key aspect of Netflix's success was a value proposition that included original features and comprehensive support—a novel idea in an industry characterized by rental stores that usually stocked little beyond the most recent blockbuster movies and had very loose relationships with their customers. For instance, the Netflix recommendation software suggested new movies to customers based on their prior rental choices. A user-friendly queue management and rating system ensured that customers could have their own personal box office online; for a fixed monthly fee, they could have a steady flow of movies delivered to their homes. Even better, the company operated a no-hassle free-delivery-and-return service and allowed customers to keep movies for as long as they liked.

This focus on innovative features, individualized and flexible customer support, and universal availability (within the U.S. market) has proved to be a winning combination. These were revolutionary ideas in an industry characterized by an increased uniformity of service and product. Netflix experienced double-digit growth from the beginning and rapidly developed a loyal clientele and an iconic reputation. It has grown rapidly to become the world's largest online DVD movie rental service, offering more than 60,000 titles to four million members across the United States.

For taking-by-storm breakouts, speed and surprise are a key challenge. The value propositions that these companies offer must be sufficiently differentiated from and superior to what already exists in the market to make customers pay attention. This is no place for marginal improvements. These companies are defining and redefining the rules of the game in their industries, and their value propositions must reflect this aggressive stance. A classic illustration of this came from British startup Direct Line, launched in 1985. The company originally offered a single product—car insurance—that could be purchased only by telephone. Today, the company has in excess of 9,000 employees serving more than five million customers and offers a broad range of products and services (including personal loans, mortgages, and credit cards). Business is still conducted mostly over the telephone, but more and more is being done via the Internet. The company also has spread into Germany, Italy, and Spain.

Direct Line's initial appearance sent a ripple of unease through the traditional insurance industry. It was the first British insurance company to use the telephone as its main form of communication and as a direct conduit to its customers, which proved to be revolutionary. Out went the indirect insurance sales model and all that it entailed: brokers with offices, large commission fees, and long and tedious application forms. In came low prices, speed, simplicity, and a common-sense human touch.

Direct Line's value proposition was easy and attractive: cutting out insurance broker intermediaries and expensive front-office premises allowed the company to be a price leader; the product was basic, and added features—for example, extra drivers on a designated car—usually required additional charges; the quality of Direct Line's policies was average—nothing special, but comparable with other, more expensive products; and support was not comprehensive—there were no brokers to walk you through the options and implications or personalize a package for you—but it was standard, offering pleasant and helpful telesales agents who were trained to take as much time as necessary to explain all the options to you over the telephone. The result was a value proposition that delighted the customer: the lowest price around at that time; basic but easy-to-understand policies; above-average quality and support, given the price you were paying; limited but sufficient access; and a reputation that didn't bestow any snob value but assured you of honest and efficient treatment if you needed to avail yourself of your insurance policy.

Although today several new companies are competing vigorously with Direct Line on price, the overall package remains superior in the minds of many customers. The company itself argues that the secret of its success rests on a combination of great products and services, competitive pricing, outstanding customer service, and a real belief in its employees. Its continued growth (often through acquisition) and high customer retention rate suggest that the Direct Line breakout is continuing unabated.

In addition to speed and surprise, taking-by-storm breakouts also require flexibility and learning. Great taking-by-storm companies such as Google and eBay develop a winning value proposition to get into the game, but they are seldom content to stay put and wait for often stronger and more established competitors to come after them. Their game must continue to evolve, or their advantage will erode. One of the best ways to do so that builds on your core value proposition is to seek ways to strengthen and diversify your offerings to customers in precisely those areas where you have already laid a claim.

Search engine supremo Google does just this. Although it is already at the top in its business, it resists the temptation to sit back and enjoy being number one. Instead, it continues to look for new ways to offer customers more value. Already a leader in features, the company continues to add additional ones—maps, an academic search portal, videos, and even online matchmaking software and dating listserves. This makes it very difficult for Microsoft to use its much deeper pockets to leapfrog Google.

While using flexibility and adjustment to enhance a value proposition can be an incredibly powerful way to stay ahead of competitors, it is critical to ensure that your position on the six pillars creates a true value proposition that preferentially differentiates you from your competitors. We need only consider the example of Webvan to see what can happen when a company that is attempting a breakout strategy (in this instance, as a revolutionary) fails to establish a compelling value proposition but continues to constantly adjust and refine this failing proposition.

Webvan was the California e-business startup that offered online ordering of groceries, with reliable delivery the following day. Although it was founded by Louis Borders (of Borders Bookstore fame), had a raft of top-notch investors (including Goldman Sachs and Yahoo!), and was run by the ex-head of Andersen Consulting (now Accenture), George Shaheen, Webvan never created a value proposition that appealed to enough customers or provided an advantage over competitors. This was true because the combination of huge expenditures for automated warehouses and the ease of replication by established grocers meant that Webvan had no differentiation, but high costs. Yet, despite the company's inability to make the model work, it continued to complicate and expand it, adding new products, setting up numerous alliances with partners, and offering faster delivery time to an even wider area. Thus flexibility and adjustment do not work when the core value proposition is fundamentally flawed.

Essential differences persist between true originals, where breakout requires a brand-new value proposition, and revolutionaries, where the company expands or refines an existing value proposition. In both instances, though, taking-by-storm breakouts are made easier when there are major discontinuities or disruptions in the environment. This is when the big opportunities for taking by storm emerge. Looking forward, it may well be that major demographic changes among baby boomers will create new opportunities for revolutionaries in home health care, nursing homes, and other industries focusing on seniors. After all, it was not that long ago that the rise of the green movement and environmentally conscious shoppers allowed Anita Roddick to adopt her revolutionary breakout strategy for The Body Shop.

Laggard-to-Leader Value Propositions

Rather than involving new, nimble companies that are moving aggressively to establish value propositions that the dominant companies in a market have not even considered, the *laggard-to-leader* breakout is all about the resurrection of a once-languishing company to a position of strength, if not dominance. Laggard-to-leader companies build new strategies, guided by a rebirth of vision that translates into new value propositions. As we saw in Chapter 2, there are two types of laggard-to-leader companies. First, there are *wave riders*, companies that spot an opportunity in an emergent market and exploit this opening to rise out of their straggler status. Sony pursued a wave-rider breakout during the 1970s when it spotted the rise of a global market for affordable consumer electronics and the trend toward ever smaller but feature-intensive products. Investment in miniaturization technology and product design enabled Sony to leave its business in low-technology electronic household appliances behind and capture leadership in global consumer electronics.

Second, there are *big improvers*, businesses that transform a mature industry or market by introducing an enticing new value proposition or business model that attracts customers from rival companies, draws new customers into a market, or causes existing consumers to increase the frequency of their purchases. If you wanted to fly with Singapore Airlines in the early 1970s, you could go only from Singapore to London and back again. The company was an industry minnow, trailing far behind giants such as Pan Am and TWA. Three decades later, Pan Am and TWA have been consigned to aviation history, and Singapore Airlines is a driving force of the world's most powerful airline alliance (Star Alliance), owns 49 percent of Richard Branson's Virgin Atlantic, and is proclaimed the world's best service airline by customers, partners, and rivals alike. In the interval, Singapore Airlines redefined customer service, delighting customers and establishing itself as the point of reference for service-led companies the world over.

These breakouts are as much turnarounds and transformations as anything else. Therefore, it is critical for companies to develop radically different value propositions if they truly wish to make the leap from laggard to leader. Fine-tuning will not do here.

Even big improvers such as Gucci and Texas Instruments went to customers with a substantially upgraded value proposition that required changes in multiple pillars and usually a leveraging up of some components of the value proposition. In the case of Italian fashion house Gucci, investment in people, design, and image, combined with a revamped business model, saw the company leap ahead of global rivals and capture the frontier of the notoriously fickle fashion industry.

What did Gucci do to bring about such a transformation of its value proposition? In the golden days of Hollywood, stars such as Audrey Hepburn and Grace Kelly established Gucci as the label best associated with sophisticated, cosmopolitan chic. However, Gucci lost its luster during the 1970s and 1980s, as the world changed and Gucci failed to keep pace. Its designs were no longer fresh or original, and its products and brand failed to capture the imagination of buyers and critics. Gucci became a follower rather than a leader in the cutthroat world of haute couture; its value proposition became stale and ordinary and appealed to fewer and fewer customers, bringing the company to the brink of bankruptcy by the end of the 1980s.

Impending doom can lead to a heightened sense of urgency, focus people's minds on what needs to be done, and give breakout leaders the opportunity to push through change and even radical transformation. This was what happened at Gucci. Gucci's strategic acceleration was spearheaded by CEO Domenico De Sole and chief designer and Gucci newcomer Tom Ford. Under De Sole and Ford, Gucci was transformed from an also-ran to a trendsetter. De Sole focused on reviving and repairing the business model, particularly the brand. Much of his approach focused on reducing customers' access to Gucci products, on the assumption that this would increase the mystique and therefore the market desire for Gucci goods. He bought back franchises that took Gucci into stores and markets that undervalued the brand. He also closed almost half of Gucci's own stores around the world.

Meanwhile, Ford focused on modernizing the value proposition, emphasizing a leveraging up of features, availability, and reputation. He did what he did best—designing eye-catching new products and building interest in and enthusiasm for the brand. One of Ford's innovations was that every season he created an "it" piece, a must-have, a season-defining trend. He also created a ready-to-wear line, something that Gucci had previously lacked and that was a key factor in the brand's extension beyond a narrow, select market. When Ford designed a new look, it was photographed for every magazine, paraded down the red carpet, and then photographed some more. Ford didn't just make over Gucci; he gave it a radical face lift. Generating desire is an awkward business, but Ford made it into an art form. Ford's first collection was rolled out in 1996, and the money started rolling in soon after.

Despite Maurizio Gucci's initial misgivings about the young Ford's audacious ideas, Gucci rapidly became a $3 billion megabrand and a trend-setting culture club for jet-setters. Although Ford and De Sole extended Gucci's value proposition and market reach beyond a narrow, high-end market niche, they remained faithful to the company's original vision of international sophistication and clever, high-quality craftsmanship. Together they transformed a staid and stuffy brand and provided the momentum for building the group into what it is today. The industry now terms this type of breakout revival as "doing a Gucci," and fashion houses such as Burberry and Dior paid close attention to the Gucci model when orchestrating their own breakouts.

Laggard-to-leader breakouts do not always require radical changes in value propositions. However, the question of just how a weak company can get into a position to dominate where once it was subordinate still arises. Central to this challenge is developing much better sources of data about what is going on around the company and in the industry in general. Scanning of the environment must be increased to the point that all managers are given this responsibility. Changes are always going on, but not everyone will see them in a timely fashion, or even see them at all. It is essential to search actively for inflection points that signal a break with the past. Both wave riders and big improvers must devote resources and create incentives toward this goal.

Consider Bacardi, the world's leading privately owned liquor company, best known for its light-bodied, smooth rums that define the category of premium rums. Bacardi rums are distilled three times, aged, blended, and filtered more than five times, providing the benchmark by which all other rums are measured. Since the company was founded in Cuba in the 1860s, however, it has had to adapt in order to survive on more than one occasion. Most dramatically, during the 1960s, growth almost halted when the company's Cuban assets were confiscated by Fidel Castro and the Bacardi family fled the island. Relocating to Bermuda, the family formed a new Bacardi company and struggled to get it back on track.

Traditionally, Bacardi's value proposition rested on producing premium-priced light rum, known for its original distillation and blending features and excellent quality, that was often available only at selected bars and stores, and that had a prestigious reputation. This began to evolve when the company began a concerted assault on Asian, European, and U.S. markets during the 1970s, pushing Bacardi rum as a drink that "mixes with everything but driving." Bacardi rose from a laggard to become the best-selling distilled spirit in the United States.

Bacardi's more interesting evolution occurred during the 1990s, often described internally as the decade of acquisition and adjustment. The acquisition of Martini & Rossi, Dewars, Bombay Gin, and Disaronno Amaretto made Bacardi the largest supplier of alcoholic beverages in the world at that time. This was followed by the 2004 purchase of Grey Goose vodka, giving the company control in the superpremium vodka category.[7] The company's wave-rider breakout came with the recognition that a new and potentially more lucrative market was arising in the ready-to-drink—sometimes dubbed "alcopops"—business. Bacardi was one of the first to spot changing consumer tastes, particularly in the younger market segments, and in 1991 it launched the Bacardi Breezer, a drink that was available in a range of fruit flavors but always had light rum as the key ingredient. Bacardi swiftly captured the lion's share of the new emergent market and transformed the alcoholic beverage industry, as the demand for alcopops increased at a rapid pace.

Today, Bacardi has a portfolio that includes more than 250 brands and labels, employs over 6,000 people, and has a presence in 170 countries. Despite this product extension, the Bacardi value proposition has endured. Although its pricing has become more competitive and Bacardi products now can be purchased quite easily all over the world, the company's excellent quality, high-end reputation, and market influence endure. What better indication is there that this is so than the fact that many people no longer ask for a rum and Coke (the traditional Cuba Libre mixed drink), but instead request a Bacardi and Coke. In the highly competitive global liquor industry, Bacardi has continued to add additional original features, introducing flavored rums such as Bacardi Limon and Bacardi Spice, as well as ready-made margarita mixers.

As the ready-to-drink market slowed, Bacardi took on global giant Diageo on its home turf, launching a cream liqueur, Kalyr, to compete with Bailey's, the leading liqueur brand in the world. Bacardi has never been a company to shy away from change or to miss an opportunity to occupy a fast-expanding market area.

Expanding-Horizons Value Propositions

In contrast to the challenges faced by companies seeking breakouts of the taking-by-storm or laggard-to-leader types, which often are driven by these companies' weak positions in the marketplace, companies that start from a more dominant position have more bullets in the barrel. Breakouts that expand horizons and shift shape are less about land grabs and short-term survival and more about foresight and the desire for growth. Companies in dominant positions do not have to do many things that are different to keep on generating earnings, at least in the short term, but they most definitely must be aroused to action if they are to grow. And here is the key point: without growth, it is only a matter of time until the very existence of the company is threatened.

The business landscape is littered with enterprises that overstated the strength of their competitive positions. One need only consider General Motors, Kodak, and Marconi, to name a few. What is now a dominant position may quickly turn into something very different. Breaking out to growth actually is more difficult for such businesses precisely because they don't have to do it. But we must not operate under any illusions as to the consequences of strategies that are devoid of breakout potential.

Companies that seek breakout by *expanding horizons* already have a relatively strong position in a market, but within a limited space. How do such businesses expand into new markets? First, they must embrace a vision that extends the company's reach. But after that, what's next? The answer is that they must craft a value proposition that has meaning beyond the company's original borders—that defines its relationship with customers who may no longer share identical attributes.

The eBay case is instructive. The company has grown from a small California Internet auction start-up to one of the most profitable high-tech companies in the world in less than 10 years. What has been the key to its success? In essence, it has been more concerned with the entire experience than just with the facilitation of an online transaction. Just as people are drawn to Starbucks for its coffee-shop experience, so people are attracted to eBay for its online community experience. The eBay value proposition is, of course, about universal availability—it is a conduit through which you can sell anything at any time to anyone anywhere in the world. This is what made it different from traditional auction sites.

However, the eBay value proposition is also about price (you pay a small commission for listing and selling items), original features (a self-regulatory system and an easy online payment mechanism), comprehensive support (unique customer forums and surveys, to which eBay is highly responsive), and excellent quality (a technologically reliable Web site where transactions are consistently smooth). On top of that, it is about a high-end reputation that confers a certain technologically savvy image and even "armchair entrepreneur" status on members of the eBay community. This winning proposition has proven appealing not just to Americans but also to sellers and collectors all over the world as eBay leverages itself into more and more international markets through a combination of acquisition and investment.

This discussion of eBay only hints at how complex the issue of value propositions can be when a company is breaking out with a *boundary-breaker* form of expanding-horizons strategy. For eBay, the value proposition was definitely the same across regions and countries, but for other companies, it may be necessary to tailor the value proposition somewhat to accommodate the demands and expectations of customers in different locations. As we noted earlier when we discussed taking-by-storm breakouts, the essence of the value proposition should remain constant. However, there is room to adjust and accommodate at the margin to make sure that customers in different places continue to experience superior differentiation.

For instance, in the United States, Starbucks offered a "third place" where people could meet or relax outside the home and outside work. This social function, a feature of the Starbucks experience that was highly original in its home market, is much more commonplace in traditional coffee cultures. Cafés have been around for decades in France and Italy, for example, so providing a third place was not an original feature in these countries. Instead, in these countries, Starbucks emphasized other aspects of the value proposition that were true differentiators for the company relative to competitors—an open, purposely nonexclusive environment that meant universal access for customers, a reputation as a purveyor of especially high-quality coffee (although the actual quality of the coffee probably was not a differentiator), and comprehensive/standard support supplied by friendly, helpful baristas, as well as the option of purchasing your own coffee beans for home use. In Europe and Asia, these attributes of the customer experience were not as common as they were in the United States, and hence they helped to differentiate Starbucks from its competitors in a positive way.

The second type of expanding-horizons breakout is what we labeled *conquistador* in Chapter 3. Unlike the boundary breaker, which latches onto emerging trends and market opportunities, the conquistador restructures and integrates established and nationally or regionally distinct markets on a global basis. Usually, this can be successful only if the value proposition for the customer in each market improves. Established purchasing patterns, brand loyalties, and even national company allegiances can be replaced, but only if there is a leveraging up of the offering and value for the end consumer.

An interesting case of conquistador breakout and leveraging up of a value proposition is Mittal Steel. Operating on four continents, with headquarters in London, incorporated in the Netherlands, listed on the New York and Amsterdam stock exchanges, and founded by an Indian business family, Mittal Steel is the world's largest and most global steel company. Lakshmi Mittal, who founded the company with his father in 1976, is one of the few entrepreneurs to have built a thriving, high-growth business in a declining, unprofitable industry.

The secret of Mittal's success is the very essence of conquistador breakout: he restructures and integrates once nationally distinct steel markets on a global basis. He has a remarkable ability to repackage and relaunch failed or failing businesses under the Mittal Steel banner. For instance, he bought Mexico's loss-making Sicarsta mills in 1992 for $220 million—a fantastic deal considering that the Mexican government had spent more than $2 billion to build the complex fewer than 10 years earlier. His approach is to identify struggling, often loss-making steel companies, many of them state-owned. He then purchases these at a low price, replaces the management team with his own world-class people, and makes major investments in new facilities, equipment, and processes. At the same time, he bargains hard with supply-chain partners to cut the costs of raw materials and with workers to increase productivity.

The clincher is Mittal's approach to the market. Rather than having the national or regional orientation of traditional steel manufacturers, Mittal Steel views the world as a single market and ships steel to wherever prices are at a premium. By transforming and integrating business models, Mittal harmonizes and leverages up the value proposition in the areas of availability, quality, support, and reputation. As a result, the company is able to command a higher price for a lower-cost but superior product. The outcome is consistent double-digit growth and the strongest overall market performance in the industry.

Shifting-Shape Value Propositions

On occasion, leveraging up is not enough to achieve breakout. Sometimes a company has to either overhaul its value proposition completely or even disguise that value proposition if it is to succeed. This happens when the business is *shifting shape*, making a transition from one type of market or identity to another. It doesn't matter whether the market is established or emergent. What matters is that the new value proposition is very different from the value proposition in the market you are shifting from—for instance, Samsung Electronics moving from the low end of the consumer electronics business to the high end of the mobile telecom market. Alternatively, the value proposition has a unique configuration that has little or no association with what the company looks like elsewhere—a good example is consumer goods giant Unilever's takeover of the socially activist Vermont-based premium ice cream maker Ben & Jerry's.

The shifting-shape breakout is one of the most difficult types to pull off, mostly because so many companies never try! Dominant enterprises often pass up new opportunities for fear of the effect of pursuing these opportunities on their core business. Classic examples ranging from disruptive technology (e.g., Motorola with digital cell phones) to slow decline (e.g., General Motors) are evidence enough that shifting shape is among the most demanding of all leadership challenges. Our research suggests that in many of these cases, senior executives are aware of the changes that are going on around them, yet fail to act. They retain old value propositions for old customers and fail to shift to the new opportunities that require new value propositions. So what is needed for this breakout strategy to lead to growth?

The first answer actually emerges from some of the things we have already addressed in this chapter. Dominant companies sit at the top of the pyramid and are natural targets for more aggressive companies that are seeking growth of their own. It is essential that companies that wish to remain open to shape-shifting opportunities aggressively monitor potential competitors that are trying to move into their positions. There are two primary threats: other dominant players that expand into new markets or restructure existing markets (the expanding-horizons strategy) and once-subordinate but large competitors that move quickly to take advantage of new opportunities or introduce a compelling new value proposition (the laggard-to-leader strategy).

In both situations, the space occupied by large, dominant organizations is the natural growth target. Hence a shape-shifting breakout really requires extreme attention to competitors and how they are approaching customers. The good news is that shape shifters need not be the first to recognize these new opportunities; their deeper pockets and greater resources ensure that they can respond. But respond they must. For example, Wal-Mart was heavily criticized for not immediately jumping onto the e-commerce bandwagon when the Internet start-ups were on the march. However, the company had the luxury of waiting to see whether the Internet had legs and the heft to move forward powerfully when it became apparent that it did. But let us not be too sanguine about a strategy of waiting. Yes, it is possible, and sometimes quite sensible. Nevertheless, waiting too long to adapt is virtually certain to be a losing formula.

The second requirement for implementing a shape-shifting breakout is to recognize that what business-to-business customers are interested in above all else is that vendors contribute in a substantive way to the achievement of customer goals in their own business. Stated differently, customers inevitably migrate toward companies that can help them solve their own business problems. IBM is the classic example. IBM's shift from hardware giant to multifaceted integrator of hardware, software, and services for customers, made under the leadership of CEO Lou Gerstner in the 1990s, dramatically changed the company's position in the marketplace. With the move from a customer perception that IBM sold its own hardware because it could to a new perception that IBM would do what was needed to help customers build IT systems that supported their ultimate business objectives, the transformation was complete. As a consequence, by leveraging up customer support and product features, IBM was able to retain a value proposition built on premium price and prestigious reputation.

As we have already seen, shape shifters come in two forms: *early adapters* that migrate into emergent markets, intent on reaping the rewards of their initiative and maximizing the profit potential, and *power players* that move into, shape, and dominate established but high-growth market arenas. On occasion, these two types coalesce, with power players shifting the shape of their value proposition and using their new identities and position to seize a leading role in both established and emergent markets. The main point here—and the third requirement for implementing a shape-shifting breakout—is that being big and influential is not enough to succeed with breakout; you also must be flexible and fast.

Early adapters often are underperforming—or failing—companies that need to do something dramatic if they are to get back on the fast track to growth. We saw this in the case of the Irish airline Aer Lingus, which was one of the first state-owned carriers to shift its business model—and consequently its value proposition—in the direction of the low-cost operators. Sometimes early adapters are companies that see the writing on the wall for their way of business. HIT Entertainment knew that U.S. regulatory changes that facilitated direct dealing between broadcasters and content providers would make life much more difficult for intermediate distributors like it. Ahead of its rivals and before being pushed, the company made the conscious decision to shift into originating and exploiting its own content, offering its customers—the broadcasters—a more sophisticated and complete market offering.

In the case of power players, the challenge of change often is greater because these companies usually are well-established, large businesses that tend to be performing at or near market expectations. Their value propositions tend to be clear and consistent, and their customers are relatively satisfied. Why bother rocking the boat? This is precisely the attitude of companies in this position.

The answer is simple: if you don't keep moving forward, at some point you're going to fall over. And the bigger you are, the harder you fall. Corporations such as IBM, Motorola, and Texas Instruments have learned this lesson only too well. A power player is a company that understands this logic and constantly strives to innovate and excel. Its value proposition evolves as customer needs or expectations change and as markets emerge or accelerate. These companies are poised to reap the rewards of any growth in established—and sometimes emergent—markets.

A terrific example of this type of enterprise is the Korean giant Samsung Electronics. Part of the Samsung Group of companies, Samsung Electronics is a global leader in semiconductor, telecommunications, and digital convergence technology. Founded in 1969, Samsung Electronics originally began operations as a manufacturer of black-and-white televisions and gradually shifted into emergent markets such as washing machines, refrigerators, telecommunications, semiconductors, and personal computers.

As a large business with a sizable, diversified revenue stream, Samsung Electronics did not seem to be a likely candidate for breakout. But in 1993, company Chairman Kun-Hee Lee outlined his vision for the twenty-first century. His new management philosophy stressed quality over quantity, with a declaration of strategic values that encouraged intellectual capital, organizational creativity, innovation, and employee empowerment. The new strategy advocated the concept of continuous change at both a personal and an organizational level and necessitated a fundamental reengineering of the company's operations.

Led by CEO Yun Jong Yong, Samsung Electronics shook off its traditional cheap but low-quality image and broke out to become a successful global leader in several fast-growing high-tech markets.[8] The company did so by shifting shape within both existing markets such as microchips and emergent markets such as cell phones and liquid-crystal display (LCD) products. In both types of markets, the company was flexible and creative in how it approached customer needs and aspirations and quick to respond to their demands. But at the core of Samsung Electronics' successful and sweeping shape shift was a fundamental realignment of its value proposition (Figure 6.4).

With regard to price, Samsung knew that it had to move up the value chain to avoid direct competition with emerging low-cost products from China. It also wanted to make more of an impression in the developed consumer markets in Europe and North America. But realism, combined with strong premium-end competition from Japan, Europe, and the United States, ensured that the company did not strive to be the most expensive—the middle to upper end of the market was perfectly acceptable.

In features, Samsung knew that it had to radically improve its product design and market offering. The company invested heavily in innovation and research and development (R&D) and gave its design teams considerable flexibility and control in new-product development. This proved to be an essential part of its successful breakout in both established and emergent markets. It was augmented by a concerted effort, across product families and business divisions, to promote total quality management. For instance, Samsung adopted the "line-stop system," which allowed any employee to stop the entire production line if he or she discovered a product defect; the line could not be restarted until the source of the defect was identified and eliminated.

The managers' performance also was rated and rewarded based on to quality criteria. The result was a substantial drop in the product defect rate, giving a huge lift to the company's

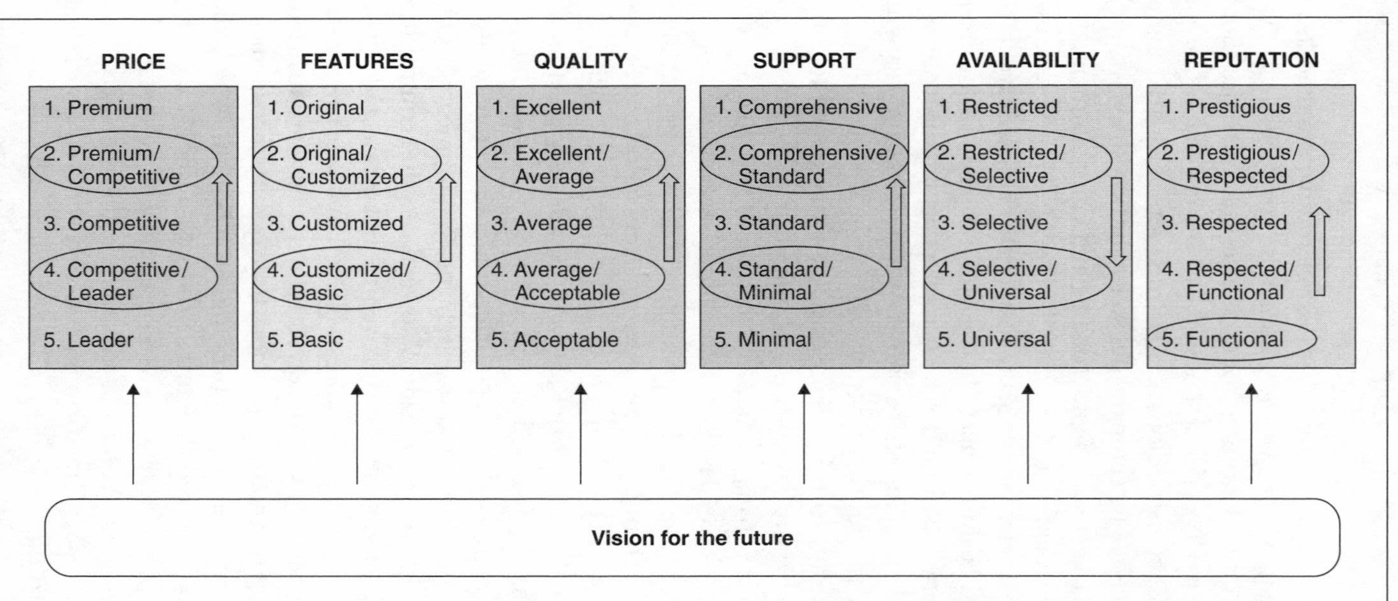

Figure 6.4 Leveraging Up Samsung Electronics' Value Proposition

credibility in the area of product quality. Linked to this, the company invested heavily in customer service and retention, particularly in after-sales service and support. On the availability front, Samsung Electronics increased the number and global reach of its distribution networks and entered into alliances and joint ventures with IBM, Microsoft, Sony, Time Warner Cable, and Yahoo! to make its products accessible and attractive to a wider audience.

Finally, all these efforts inevitably fed into and improved Samsung Electronics' reputation—probably further and faster than even the company itself had anticipated. Samsung promoted its brand aggressively and pursued a much more targeted and systematic marketing campaign than it had ever previously undertaken. Samsung became the world's fastest-growing brand in 2001, and its brand value increased 30 percent, moving from forty-second to thirty-fourth in the world. Over the next five years, Samsung Electronics coursed ahead to take the number 20 spot in the rankings of best global brands.[9] The company posted the biggest gain in value of any of the top 100 global brands, with a 186 percent overall surge. In 2004 Samsung surpassed Sony, a far more entrenched rival that once dominated the electronics category in terms of brand value.

Samsung's increase in brand equity and customer awareness was mirrored by its financial performance, with overall revenue often rising by over 30 percent a year and revenue in emergent markets such as the LCD and cell phone businesses rising at double that rate. In the cell phone market, the company jumped from nowhere in 2000 to a position rivaling Nokia and Motorola by 2005. Gross profit margins reached 84 percent, despite constantly falling unit prices in some businesses. By responding quickly and efficiently to customer needs and by overhauling its business model and reconstituting its value proposition, Samsung Electronics had orchestrated one of the most daring and successful shape-shifting breakouts ever seen.

Conclusion

The message of this chapter, driven home through our six-pillars value proposition model, is that it is essential for breakout leaders to grasp, deeply and completely, the bases of competition within their fields and how their organizations might steal a march on their rivals. What matters is not which company in the field is "best" in terms of pure product or process quality, but which can put together and sustain the most compelling and consistent offering to customers. This is the key to winning and retaining market share—nationally and internationally—and delivering double-digit growth.

Two other important and related learning points emerge. First, when you are generating more than one value proposition—for different markets, perhaps—you are more likely to succeed, and to avoid sending mixed signals to customers, if these value propositions emerge from shared vision, values, culture, and standards. Second, if you are presiding over a cluster, or family, of value propositions, shaping and leveraging a strong corporate identity can boost sales by instilling cross-brand and cross-product confidence in customers.

It may be a cliché to say that the customer is king, but in dynamic, hotly contested markets, this remains an inescapable fact. Any business that does not put the customer at the heart of its strategy is doomed to failure. The demise of Webvan and thousands of other dot-coms is evidence enough of this reality. But breakout does not happen just because you focus on the customer. As we have seen throughout this chapter, companies such as Apple, Bacardi, Google, Samsung Electronics, Starbucks, and Unilever achieved market breakout by not only listening closely to their customers, but also responding in ways that made their products indispensable to consumers. By understanding the needs and aspirations of their markets and using this knowledge to leverage up their value proposition, these companies have ensured that the customer always prefers their product or service to those offered by competitive rivals.

In Chapter 7, we explore the construction and refinement of the breakout business model. This is essentially the value proposition's Siamese twin, since knowing what the customer wants and ensuring that the customer has a positive experience when getting it, each and every time, are two inseparable elements that are at the core of any successful breakout strategy.

Endnotes

1 The idea of "deep customer focus" is derived from the work of Sandra Vandermerwe. In this instance, we are referring to "Achieving Deep Customer Focus," *MIT Sloan Management Review*, Spring 2004, pp. 26–34.

2 David Rocks and Moon Ihlwan, "Samsung Design," *BusinessWeek*, November 29, 2004, pp. 38–43.

3 James C. Anderson, James A. Narus, and Wouter van Rossum, "Customer Value Propositions in Business Markets," *Harvard Business Review*, March 2006, p. 91. Authors who agree with us on fundamentals but ultimately take a different approach include George S. Day, "Which Way Should You Grow?" *Harvard Business Review*, July–August 2004, pp. 24–26, and Carla O'Dell and C. Jackson Grayson, "Knowledge Transfer: Discover Your Value Proposition," *Strategy & Leadership*, March–April 1999, pp. 10–15.

4 Thanks are due to Viren Gupta, Matt Kummell, Justin Phillips, and Matthew Waterbury, Tuck 2006, for their contribution to this case.

5 Such features helped Apple to come out on top in a Boston Consulting Group survey of more than 1,000 senior executives in 63 countries to list the world's 25 most innovative companies; *BusinessWeek* special report, April 24, 2006, pp. 63–76.

6 Thanks are due to Prashanth Kamath and Sungsook Hong, Tuck 2006, for their contribution to this case.

7 Elaine Walker, "Bacardi to Add Grey Goose Vodka to the Mix," *Miami Herald*, June 21, 2004.
8 Thanks are due to Echo Chong, Tanaka 2005, for input into this case.
9 *BusinessWeek* special report, "The Best Global Brands," *BusinessWeek*, August 1, 2005.

CHAPTER 7

DELIVERING THE PROMISE

Can it really be only a few short years since the dot-com boom? Not only did Google, eBay, and Amazon vault into the ranks of household names, and thousands of companies, large and small, adopt the Internet as a business process and a distribution and advertising vehicle, but the boom also gave us a new business lexicon. Rather than competing in a market, companies competed in a "space"; rather than focusing on customers, companies counted "eyeballs"; and rather than speaking about strategy, companies boasted of their "business models." Gradually, this new lexicon lost currency, with one important exception—the *business model*. This ephemeral concept is now used to refer not only to strategy, but also to all sorts of other business activities too numerous to catalogue. And this is a shame because business models are at the core of breakout strategies.

Promising customers the world can be a risky undertaking because eventually you have to deliver on your pledge. Countless strategies run into trouble at this point, as it is easy for a gulf to open up between good intentions and business realities. The breakout enterprise has the solution: build a vibrant business model that delivers on or even exceeds customer expectations. At the heart of a successful strategy is a symbiotic relationship between what the customer wants and what the company can deliver. The system for delivering the value proposition to customers is the real "business model" that all breakout organizations must master if they are to be successful.

There is a dynamic essence to a business model; it is the constant, yet ever-changing mechanism for ensuring that a company delivers on its promise to existing and potential customers. A business model is the unique configuration of resources and processes that enables the organization to deliver its value proposition,[1] synchronizing market perception and corporate reality. In other words, *a business model is the vehicle for delivering a value proposition*. Shaped by the corporate vision, the essential components of any business model are illustrated in Figure 7.1.

The balance that a company strikes among cost, innovation, reliability, relationships, channels, and brand determines the configuration of the business model. A business model is constant but changing: it is constant because, regardless of the company or the context, it always will be determined by the interaction and tradeoffs among these six core constituents; it is changing because an executive team regularly can choose to alter the emphasis or configuration of these six drivers.

For example, when E.&J. Gallo, the California wine producer, undertook a shape shift from a low-end, mass-production winemaker to a higher-quality, high-technology wine company, it changed the emphasis in its business model from cost (price leadership) to innovation (new methods for producing and bottling wine) and brand (investing more in advertising to discerning wine drinkers who previously would not even try its wines). At the same time, Gallo had to rethink its customer relationships and place greater emphasis on providing customers with more information on its production techniques and scientific investments.

Similarly, in responding to the threat from low-fare airlines, national flag carriers such as Aer Lingus had to redefine their business model to emphasize cost and deemphasize relationships (customer service and support) and brand (advertising to ensure that the customer realized that lower prices also would mean reduced services, such as the removal of free drinks and snacks from in-flight services).

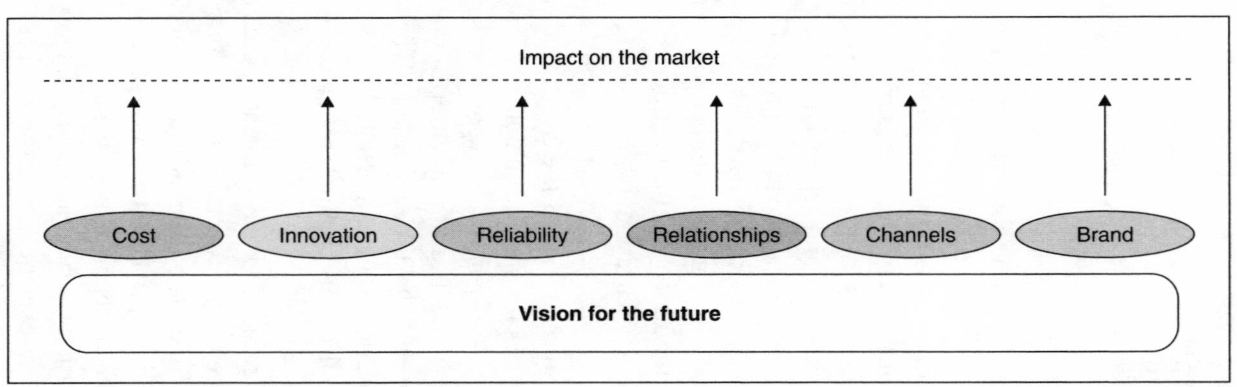

Figure 7.1 Components of a Business Model

Business Models Deliver the Promise of Value Propositions

The strategic implications of this approach and insight are formidable, far-reaching, and of immense practical significance. The previously staid and static notion of the business model is brought to life and given a lively and flexible status at the core of any company's strategy.[2] In Chapter 6, we focused on reconfiguring the company's value proposition to deliver what the customer wants and adjusting the business model to ensure delivery. Similarly, reorganizing the business model first can reanimate a value proposition and attract new and repeat business.

The Canadian live entertainment company Cirque du Soleil adopted this approach. The company develops and launches new circus shows regularly, investing in innovation to ensure that its market offering remains fresh and original. For instance, the *Saltimbanco* show is a celebration of life, *Alegría* explores power and the handing down of power over time, and *Varekai* pays tribute to the nomadic spirit and art of the circus tradition. The company also creates shows for specific audiences. Thus, *Zumanity* is a provocative, adults-only show that you can see only in Las Vegas, whereas *La Nouba* is a family entertainment spectacular and a resident show at Walt Disney World in Florida. In this way, by leveraging innovation, Cirque du Soleil can widen its market relationships and multiply its channels to maximize its appeal and market reach.

In addition, as Figure 7.2 vividly illustrates, each aspect of value that a customer perceives is a function of a specific corporate activity. Thus, price is a function of cost, product or service features are a function of innovation, quality is a function of reliability, customer support is a function of relationships, availability is a function of channels, and reputation is a function of brand. How efficiently and effectively a company manages and exploits these functions will determine its relative value in the eyes of the consumer.

This relationship between the business model, which is internal to the company, and the value proposition, which is external

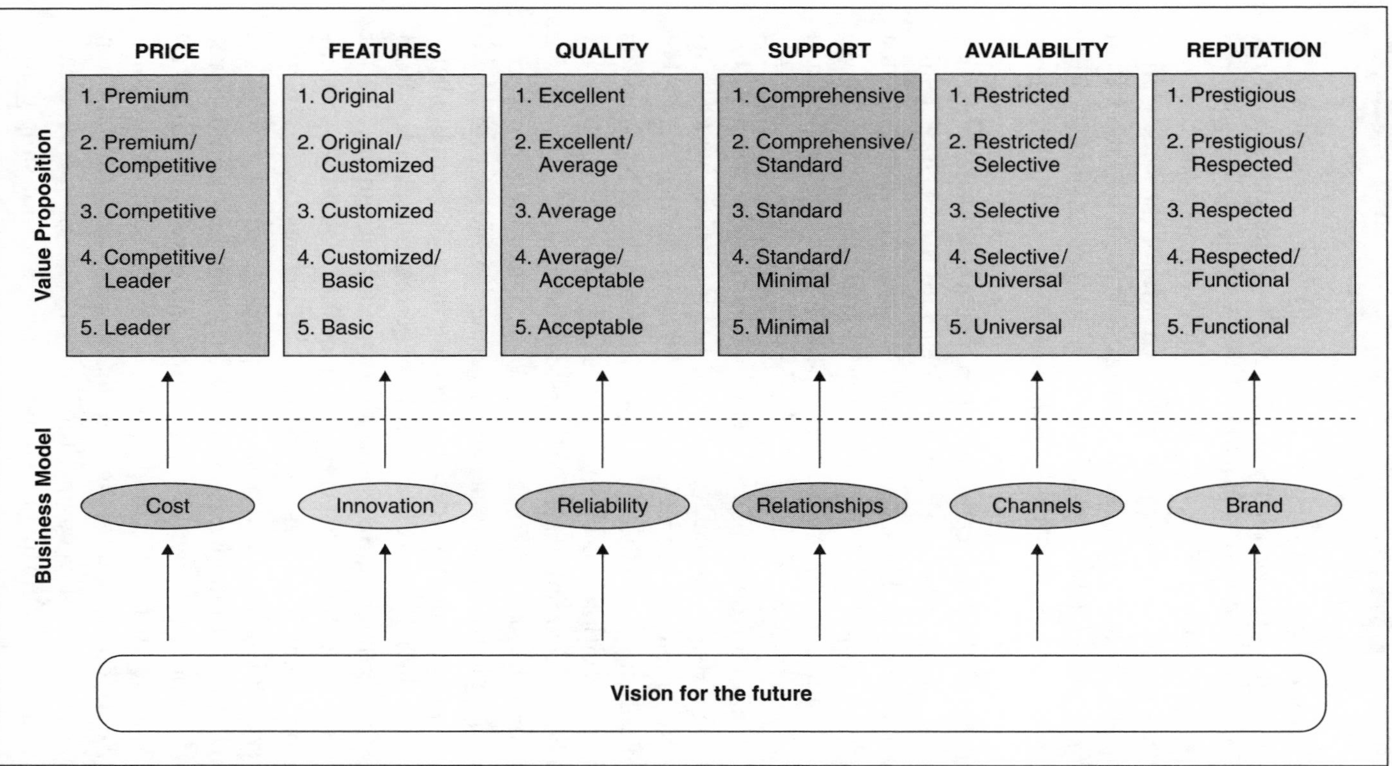

Figure 7.2 Aligning the Business Model and the Value Proposition

in its orientation, is at the very heart of any breakout strategy. By understanding the six pillars of each and carrying out a carefully orchestrated trade-off between the different pillars, a leadership team can ensure a successful breakout. By seeing the business model and the value proposition as two sides of the same coin, a company can avoid the common mistakes of promising more than it can deliver and overinvesting in the wrong areas and activities.

Let's take an example of this dynamic interaction and show how, when managed properly, it can ensure breakout. In the health care industry, medical device manufacturer Smith & Nephew (S&N) was founded in 1856 but remained a laggard for much of its history. During the 1990s, however, S&N transformed itself from a broad-based health care conglomerate into a three-pillared business organization focused on orthopedics (joint replacement and repair), endoscopy (instruments for minimally invasive surgery), and advanced wound management (products and techniques for treating difficult-to-heal wounds). CEO Sir Christopher O'Donnell led a strategic reorganization of the company that resulted in double-digit growth. Taking a closer look at how S&N aligned its value proposition and business model provides a crucial insight into how the company achieved strategic breakout.[3]

Prior to breakout, S&N's pricing was at a premium/competitive level. The company was not a market leader and was unable to command premium prices. By reconfiguring its supply chain, reducing the number of suppliers, and getting a better deal from those that remained, S&N was able to reduce its input costs. At the same time, by introducing higher-quality materials—particularly on products such as hip and knee replacement joints—S&N better positioned itself to push up its prices.

Investment in innovation gave S&N's value proposition a tremendous boost. By increasing research and development (R&D) and manufacturing spending to 6 percent of total sales, the company developed leading-edge products and processes that often were well ahead of its competitors' offerings. Customers increasingly saw the company as having original and not simply customized products and techniques.

In the area of reliability, S&N realized that it was only a middle-ranked company, in part because of the characteristics of some of its products. Traditionally, when assessing the trade-off between product wear and durability, the company had chosen materials that struck a balance between the two—that were somewhat hard wearing and somewhat durable—rather than seeking excellence on both measures. With its breakout strategy, S&N increased its investment in product innovation and ensured consistently first-rate reliability in the production of these high-quality new products that combined both good wear and good durability characteristics.

For the fourth pillar of the business model, relationships, the company had traditionally provided standard customer support. It worked at developing strong relationships with doctors and hospitals, but since its product offering was mediocre, it was difficult for it to motivate doctors to switch their loyalties to S&N. As a means of both retaining and gaining customers, the company adopted an elaborate training and development program for health care professionals, aimed at educating them about the benefits of the new and more advanced therapies and products that S&N had released or was developing.

S&N's strong distribution networks traditionally had been a source of strength for the company. The business had built enduring global ties from an early point in its history. Even so, there remained room for improvement, and S&N developed its capabilities further, to a point where it was operating in more than 30 countries and working with 60 other companies. The company expanded into most regions of Asia and North America and maintained its presence in Europe.

Finally, with regard to brand enhancement, to sustain its price increases and capitalize on its improvements in features, quality, and support, S&N needed to refashion its brand image. The company put more emphasis on innovative marketing and communications and on having a more knowledgeable technical sales force. It accepted the idea that increased activity on the front line was needed. Direct-to-consumer advertising, with television commercials and local advertisements, was launched as a way to improve S&N's image and reputation among those who mattered—existing and potential customers.

The results were spectacular. S&N captured the first or second position in all its markets and became the fastest-growing company in several of its key business areas, such as orthopedics. By understanding the value proposition–business model interaction and trade-offs and reconfiguring one to align with the other, S&N ensured its successful market breakout.

Releasing Business Imperatives

As we have seen, the configuration of your business model provides a framework for delivering the promise of your value proposition. We can go even further, however, in using breakout strategy tools to promote double-digit growth. Putting our value proposition and our business model together releases a set of business imperatives that can be followed through and that determines the projects and programs employed to implement a breakout strategy (Figure 7.3). It is one thing to lay out a value proposition, and even a business model to back it up, but providing a game plan to implement both is essential. Business imperatives are the pathways to breakout success. With the frameworks for strategy presented thus far, any company has the potential to play the breakout game. Let's consider how you might use business imperatives to help guide a breakout strategy for growth.

The needs analysis outlined in Figure 7.3 is an example of several that we have developed for organizations of different sizes and levels of maturity. Here's how to interpret and use it within your own company. Begin with a reconfiguration of the elements of the value proposition to ensure that there is clarity and consistency, positioning the business to gain competitive advantage. Remember that your value proposition must explain what you are and what you are after. In the scenario mapped in Figure 7.3, the product is overpriced and needs to be repositioned slightly, maintaining its premium status but benchmarking itself against competitors to

Value Proposition				Business Model	
Element	***Movement***			***Element***	***Business Imperatives***
Price	1	→	2	Cost	*Need* to become more efficient in the use of resources. *Need* to improve systems for costing, budgeting, planning, and control.
Features	3	→	2	Innovation	*Need* to encourage innovation culturally, systematically, and relationally. *Need* to challenge convention while remaining safe.
Quality	2	→	1	Reliability	*Need* to improve quality enhancement and control mechanisms.
Support	3	→	2	Relationships	*Need* to work more closely with customers to meet their requirements for information, responsiveness, and value for money.
Availability	2	→	3	Channels	*Need* to proactively identify opportunities and sell products and services. *Need* distribution arrangements that fit with product brand image.
Reputation	3	→	2	Brand	*Need* to build image through external engagement, learning initiatives, and citizenship.

Figure 7.3 Business Model Needs Analysis

ensure that it is not too expensive (moving from premium to premium/competitive). To deliver on this adjustment, the cost component of the business model needs to be looked at, and in most cases this means seeking increased efficiencies in resource utilization. Improved business processes and systems can provide a lot of these cost efficiencies. For example, when Iowa-based communications and aviation electronics company Rockwell Collins began its move from laggard to leader during the late 1990s, President Clay Jones sought to make the business leaner and more efficient by focusing more resources on processes that he believed would produce great returns, particularly in marketing, strategic planning, and customer service.

In addition, the features offered in our Figure 7.3 scenario are nothing special and certainly do not justify the premium demanded. These need to be ratcheted up to ensure consistency with pricing and prevent customer dissatisfaction (moving from customized to original/customized). Thus, when Samsung Electronics transformed its business and raised prices, much of its success was the result of putting product and process innovation at the core of everything the company did, across all parts of the company and in every product division. This resulted in radically improved product design, functionality, and ease of use.

Although quality is already a strength, in order to go beyond consistency and gain advantage, the third step is to place even greater emphasis on quality. This means not only meeting but also exceeding customer expectations every time customers interact with your company (moving from excellent/average to excellent). The global success and double-digit growth of Marriott International is due in large part to its consistent emphasis on excellent quality. The company's total quality management processes and its approach to supply-chain management are second to none. It reliably delivers a flawless product time and time again—there is no room for inconsistency or error in how such companies manage product and service quality. This is particularly important for hotel companies that employ franchise agreements for much of their international expansion. When you place your brand in the hands of others, you should seek nothing less than consistent excellence in service delivery.

In the area of support, there is a dip in the value offering; customers are not receiving the first-rate support that would be expected to accompany a premium-priced product. This element needs to be brought in line with pricing, but the support does not have to be the most extensive available because the price has been slightly lowered, and fully comprehensive support would add a significant amount of cost and squeeze profit margins (the company should move from standard to comprehensive/standard). In the personal computer industry, premium-priced Apple retains a significant lead over its rivals in the area of customer support and consistently tops the polls in customer satisfaction ratings. This lead in relationships is an important factor contributing to the company's success.

Other PC sellers, such as Dell, became successful through lower prices and high customer knowledge and service. As Dell grew in the early to middle 2000s, however, it found that its customer approval ratings were falling, partly as a result of problems that customers encountered when the company moved its call centers offshore and partly because people found themselves spending longer amounts of time on hold. Complaints to the Better Business Bureau rose dramatically, and Dell's customer satisfaction rating fell to about the industry average.[4] To deal with this declining value proposition, Dell correctly sought to respond to customer demands for improved support by raising its support to an above-average level, but not trying to match that of Apple, which can afford to provide comprehensive support owing to the price premium it extracts.

With regard to availability, it makes sense to offset the decrease in price indicated in Figure 7.3 by making the product more widely available and easier to access (moving from restricted/selective to selective). This shift needs to be tempered because making the product too widely available can, in many businesses, diminish the brand and undermine its position as a competitively priced premium product. Would you want to pay several hundred dollars for a pair of Gucci shoes that you can also purchase at JC Penney, TJ Maxx, or a factory outlet mall?

Finally, to embed the idea that the product is high end in the minds of consumers, its reputation must be raised, but again, not too far (moving from respected to prestigious/respected). It is important to show restraint and not oversell—customers soon know when the product is not quite as good as they have been led to believe. German skin and beauty care company Beiersdorf—best known for its Nivea skin care products—has achieved this kind of value proposition leverage. With more than 120 years of history, Beiersdorf broke out globally during the late 1990s when it invested aggressively in product range extension (particularly targeting the fast-growing male skin care market) and brand promotion. But Beiersdorf has never overestimated or oversold, making sure that customers realized that it was not vying for the prestige, top end of the market and that its reasonably priced products were viewed as above-average value for money. Further, Beiersdorf built a distinct and higher-than-average brand by being an early mover on corporate social responsibility initiatives, particularly environmental protection and not testing cosmetics on animals.

Turning next to the business model configuration, each element of our value proposition has a root within the resource configuration of the enterprise. By translating each of the value shifts just discussed into a relocation or reemphasis of both static and dynamic resources, we can release a set of business imperatives. These are the strategic priorities that take an enterprise forward and shape how value will be delivered. In Figure 7.3, a slight reduction in price affects the cost element of the business model. More precisely, if profits are to remain strong and cash resources are not to be depleted, a more competitive price can be delivered only if it is accompanied by cost reduction or greater cost efficiencies. Large-scale cost reduction like that pursued routinely by Wal-Mart or Tesco is not needed because the company is not seeking price leadership. Instead, improved performance and better-targeted resources such as those delivered successfully by Clay

Jones at Rockwell Collins are usually the way to go. The consequent business imperative is increased cost efficiencies in resource management and deployment.

To augment features, the company must increase innovation. As a business imperative, this is not just about investing more financial and human resources in innovation (although this can be crucial). It is more important to unleash a concept that encourages everyone in your company to think more creatively about how she or he can deliver value to the customer, challenging convention and trying new approaches, but always being careful not to undermine quality or reputation. Richard Branson has always prided himself on fostering this sort of culture at Virgin, maintaining an open-door policy for good ideas, encouraging employees to try out new service innovations, and rewarding those who consequently raise customer awareness and allegiance to Virgin products.

Slight improvements in quality tend to involve more emphasis on reliability in the development and delivery of the product. The business imperative here is to bring about further refinements of the quality management system and more effective control mechanisms at all stages in the execution of the value proposition. If your value proposition promises unsurpassed quality and reliability, there is no room for errors and no excuses when things go wrong. The Ritz-Carlton hotel group is world renowned for its innovative and first-rate quality of service and product. It employs novel techniques such as the Service Quality Indicator (SQI) grading system, which scores hotel departments, enabling them to monitor key production and guest service processes on a minute-by-minute basis. Departments compete to have the best scores, which they achieve by having the fewest defects and a consistent culture of excellence.

Increasing the amount or the nature of support to customers translates into working harder at the company's relationships, not only with its clients, but also with its supply-chain partners. The business imperative here is to deepen the rapport with customers—particularly repeat purchasers—and ensure a consistent and reciprocal sharing of market and process information, cost-reduction techniques, and value-creation ideas with supply-chain associates. Companies such as Cisco Systems always have been first rate at building and strengthening relationships. On the supply-chain side, innovations pioneered by Cisco include the eHub, a private trading network that provides a central point for planning and executing across the company's extended manufacturing supply chain.[5] It includes more than 2,000 of Cisco's supply-chain partners, and its overarching objectives are to deliver end-to-end supply-chain synchronization and visibility, event alerting, and cost and inventory reductions among them.

To increase the availability of a product, the channels to market need to be exploited and expanded. This expansion can be both physical and virtual. New channels can emerge when a manufacturer sets up its own retail outlets, as Apple did with the selective opening of Apple stores in major cities around the world. It also can be virtual, as when a company shifts from a Web site that provides only information to one that also allows commercial transactions.

Finally, as the Beiersdorf example illustrates, any improvement in reputation requires either investment in brand development or a reconfiguration of the existing brand. Brand is a subset of reputation because reputation is about how all your stakeholders (including regulators, employees, competitors, and supply-chain partners) view you as a company, not just how your customers and potential customers perceive your image and your products. To increase the market reputation of your enterprise and products, however, there is a business imperative to invest more in image building. Spending more on advertising is one way to move toward this goal, but it need not be the only way to build brand reputation. Consider alternative approaches, such as spending time and resources on acts of good citizenship like sponsorship of university basic research initiatives or—like Beiersdorf—displaying corporate social responsibility by employing more environmentally friendly production techniques and packaging processes.

At the end of this exercise, we are left with a game plan that we call *business imperatives.* They may vary in importance and depth of change required, but collectively they are all about achieving strategic breakout. Developing clear, consistent, and dynamic business models is how you deliver the promise of value propositions; together, they suggest a set of business imperatives that can bring that promise home. Breakout strategies don't emerge haphazardly, and they don't need to (and shouldn't) be excessively complex. However, they do require mastery of these fundamental practices.

Delivering the Promise via Breakout Strategy

Now that we have a good idea of the core components that make up a business model, how a business model is the primary vehicle for delivering on the promise of a value proposition, and how the resulting business imperatives provide a blueprint for breakout strategy, let us consider some of the differences in how all this plays out across the four primary breakout types. As we did in the preceding two chapters, we pay special attention to some of the key challenges facing each breakout type and the implications of these challenges for bringing breakout growth strategies to market.

Taking-by-Storm Business Models

In Chapter 6 we highlighted the importance of speed and surprise for *taking-by-storm* breakouts. Inevitably, this leads to some learning on the job as you create your business model to follow through on your customer promises. With your company's vision as your guide, you can turn potential threats into opportunities, and miniopportunities into important learning opportunities. At no point is it safe to simply hope that you are delivering what you promised, but in reality, taking-by-storm breakouts never operate in lockstep fashion.

The early days of Southwest Airlines simultaneously illustrate both the value of a mind-set that constantly seeks to turn disadvantage into advantage and how taking-by-storm business models are seldom fully specified right from the start. The start-up

Southwest Airlines went to market with four airplanes, but quite unexpectedly was forced to take one of them out of service. Facing aggressive competition from industry powerhouse American Airlines, Southwest decided that it could not afford to substantially reduce the frequency of its flights; however, it did not have the resources to acquire another aircraft (a not unusual circumstance for small companies looking for breakout in this way).

The solution that the company eventually hit upon came to be known as its hallmark—exceptionally quick turnaround of flights at the airport. Instead of the industry standard of 50 minutes between flights, Southwest cut this down to 25 minutes. With its short-haul routes, such a dramatic reduction in downtime allowed Southwest to maintain its flight frequency. Today, this short turnaround time is an essential feature of the low-cost business model and is highly valued by customers, who waste less time as a consequence.

The Southwest example should give some solace to would-be taking-by-storm breakout companies, but let us not leave the impression that the expectations for business models are somehow lessened for these breakouts. At some point, and this is a case where sooner is absolutely better than later, your business model must be world class. Customers may put up with idiosyncrasies for a time in exchange for a blockbuster value proposition, but you should never test your customers' patience. When there are alternatives (which there soon may well be for taking-by-storm players as larger competitors seek to get in on the action), if products don't work as advertised, it is very tough for customers to stay loyal to that new, exciting, entrepreneurial start-up that just can't get its act together. Google's early advantage and subsequent staying power in the Internet browser business are due mostly to the company's realization that success is predicated on a robust business model that does not overcomplicate or underdeliver the value proposition. Despite aggressive assaults by enterprises larger and smaller, Google has endured and has grown to become the model that everyone else looks to emulate.

As Google illustrates, it is usually much better to get it right from the start. There are certainly great examples of taking-by-storm companies doing exactly that. Costco is a fascinating example of a taking-by-storm *revolutionary* that has its business model in top-notch working order. Washington state–based Costco refers to its stores as "warehouses" and its customers as "members" and tries to cut out intermediaries by purchasing most of its merchandise directly from manufacturers and passing on the resulting savings to its members. Costco is renowned for paying its employees better than the average and for having higher staff productivity and lower turnover than its rivals. The Costco business model is a winner because it combines cost efficiencies; innovation in product sourcing and sales; consistently reliable quality; strong and enduring relationships with customers, staff, and suppliers; restricted channels to increase interest in its thinly distributed warehouses; and a brand based on quality and integrity.

One of the difficulties for taking-by-storm companies is that their business model may well have original elements that don't seem to match the value proposition. What do we say to a company that chooses not to charge consumers anything for its services? Yet Google, for one, has built a business model that works. In so doing, Google clearly took a big risk. But it also realized at an early date that to sustain the model, money had to come from somewhere, and it had to develop relationships with users and with other companies. The result was the sale of advertising, which appears adjacent to Google search results and on sites maintained by a large network of publishers across the Web who participate in Google's AdSense program (where Google's proprietary software automatically matches advertisements, known as "AdWords," to the content of the page on which they appear). Google may have started with some original elements, but it soon realized the necessity of building capabilities in all six pillars of the business model.

One final point on business models in taking-by-storm breakouts: a degree of innovation across the spectrum of elements that make up a business model is often needed. We highlight the importance of innovation in features, and of course this is critical, but innovative thinking and practices may be needed throughout the business model. Thus, eBay has a remarkably low-cost structure because the Internet is so well suited to its business model. Google continues to innovate on features for consumers. Costco, already strong on quality, keeps pushing logistics, back-office operations, and warehousing to boost efficiency. The Apollo Group continues to shift services and materials online to make life easier for its students. Cirque de Soleil is popping up in more, and original, locations to increase its availability to customers. Finally, easyGroup takes its orange image and its cheap and cheerful reputation into a wide variety of established industries, intent on shaking them up and benefiting the consumer. Hence innovation can be a key weapon for taking-by-storm players as they try not only to establish a beachhead in a market, but also to stay ahead of followers with deeper pockets.

This point is particularly important for revolutionaries. These companies need business models that break the rules along multiple dimensions. Unlike *true originals*, who not only have the advantage of coming to market with something new, but also benefit from the greenfield opportunities they are after, revolutionaries are competing in established markets and hence face a tougher bar for breakout. They must develop business models that redefine the ground rules in a market in many different ways. It is rare for a revolutionary to come to market with just one differentiator, and indeed, the mind-set of revolutionary breakout is to challenge industry convention as a whole rather than just to tinker at the margins.

One of the best examples of this is The Body Shop, the British cosmetics retailer that created a virtually new and highly successful business model in its industry. When Anita and Gordon Roddick launched The Body Shop in the mid-1970s, promoting animal welfare, the environment, and human rights, its feature- and quality-laden value proposition instantly resonated with a sizable section of the market and pioneered a new era of ethical shopping on Britain's Main Streets. To deliver on this, the company took on several of the sacred cows that dominated thinking in the cosmetics business. Rather than creating complicated products using various chemical processes, the company used only natural ingredients. Rather than investing in sophisticated and expensive packaging, it relied on refillable containers with simple identification of the product and its ingredients. Rather than spending millions on advertising, the company did none (it relied on word of mouth and the uncanny ability of the founder/CEO to generate free publicity). Rather than selling through department stores, it opted for a franchised retail model. And rather than pushing the standard industry formula that equates sex appeal with quality and price, the company emphasized honesty and made only modest claims for efficacy. By turning the typical business model on its head, The Body Shop was able to deliver on its promise to customers in spectacular fashion for years.

Laggard-to-Leader Business Models

Companies that have fallen behind in their industries—laggards—face a difficult task. They tend to be reactors. Usually, competitors have taken the lead because the laggards' value propositions are no longer exciting to customers. A compelling new vision is needed, as is a value proposition that takes advantage of changes in the marketplace, be they in a rapidly expanding market space (*wave riders*) or a long-established market (*big improvers*). But none of this will help turn these companies around unless they can back it up with a totally reconstituted business model. The old model provided few advantages, and it is dangerous to assume that some minor tinkering will do the job. To go from *laggard to leader*, formerly stale business models must be rejuvenated. But how?

The big picture answer is that strategic change processes must take hold, and usually new leaders are needed to make that happen. We address these issues in detail in Chapters 8 and 9. At this point, however, we can make an important point: every business model involves implicit assumptions, and companies seeking laggard-to-leader breakout growth will need to start here. What are the underlying assumptions behind your business model? How accurate are these assumptions? If they once made sense, do they still do so? These are tough questions, and laggard-to-leader companies inevitably find that many of the assumptions they have relied on, sometimes for years, are no longer valid. To make the turnaround change needed, it is essential that these companies rethink all of the major assumptions that underlie each element of the business model.

Consider Rubbermaid, a failed laggard-to-leader breakout. Rubbermaid, the manufacturer of innumerable rubber-based products such as children's toys, garbage cans, housewares, and the like, once was a dominant company with a business model that was all about innovation, channels, and brands. Over time, however, and with the rise of big-box retailers such as Wal-Mart, Kmart, and Target, the assumptions behind Rubbermaid's business model began to break down. Wal-Mart and its rivals were less impressed with the added features that Rubbermaid's innovation provided. Controlling shelf space in the major channels was no longer Rubbermaid's birthright, and the brand began to lose its luster as new, more aggressive entrants to the market took away share.

What Rubbermaid failed to do was to question its assumptions and make the commensurate adjustments to its business model required to move toward the big-improver breakout that was the only avenue for renewed growth. In addition, the company's assumption that the other elements of the business model were not as critical proved to be wrong. Cost in particular became hugely important, as the big-channel players demanded lower prices than Rubbermaid could afford to offer. The net result was a greatly diminished company that was unable to become a big improver when it most needed to.

Another company that was forced to question its basic assumptions—on several occasions—was Rockwell Collins. When the company was still Collins Radio, management failed to do so and, just like management at Rubbermaid, neglected to devote sufficient attention to the cost component of its model. The result was a takeover by Rockwell International. When the resulting business, Rockwell Collins, faced similar problems some two decades later, it didn't make the same mistake. Let's take a closer look at this story because it is a vivid illustration of how laggard-to-leader breakouts can succeed only if the company questions and, when necessary, transforms the very fundamentals on which its business model is built.

Founded in 1933 in Cedar Rapids, Iowa, the Collins Radio Company was the creation of 23-year-old Arthur Collins. Collins had risen to national prominence at the tender age of 15 when his homemade two-way radio maintained reliable communication with a scientific expedition in Greenland. No sooner was the company founded than Collins was again in the national spotlight, providing voice communication for Admiral Byrd's historic expedition to Antarctica. Collins continued to set the pace in the area of technological innovation, launching an automatic tuning system that revolutionized aircraft communication and may well have saved the lives of thousands of U.S. pilots during World War II by preventing the enemy from jamming or intercepting radio transmissions.

Collins was a remarkable innovator, and his company was responsible for many of the twentieth century's most historic advances in communication technology. Who doesn't remember Neil Armstrong's inspiring words—"That's one small step for man, one giant leap for mankind"—as he became the first human to set foot on the moon? It wouldn't have been possible without Collins Radio equipment. Collins also transmitted the first image—a photo of President Eisenhower—via satellite, indicating the genesis of the modern satellite TV business.[6]

By the early 1970s, however, the company's limited resources had taken it as far as they could, and in 1973, defense contractor Rockwell International purchased the Collins Radio Company. Within a few months, Arthur Collins was out, and his company was restructured to meet the needs of its new masters. Collins

Radio was a classic taking-by-storm breakout, but ultimately its business model failed it, and the company was taken over. Arthur Collins and his team had tremendous creative ability and produced world-class products, but they did not know as much about running and, especially, growing a business. As the industry evolved and bigger, more aggressive competitors emerged, Collins found itself in an increasingly precarious industry position. In addition to being less skillful at marketing and brand development, Collins displayed particular weaknesses in cost management and financial engineering. As Rockwell Collins CEO Clay Jones comments:

> *For 40 years, Collins Radio was a technology leader, an innovator. It was ruled by engineers who did incredible things as the radio and avionics industry was developing. Unfortunately, along the way they forgot to hone their financial skills.*[7]

The new Rockwell Collins, a division of Rockwell International until its 2001 spin-off, prospered during the 1970s and 1980s as U.S. defense expenditures spiraled during the height of the Cold War. Innovations continued, with the development of the world's first safety-critical Federal Aviation Authority (FAA)–verified microprocessor and pioneering work with the Global Positioning System (GPS) technology, which now has a wide array of users, from pilots to soldiers to fishermen.

The early 1990s proved a challenging time for Rockwell Collins, however. The company was still heavily dependent on government defense contracts for a large portion of its revenues. With the end of the Cold War, defense budgets were reduced under the presidency of George H. W. Bush and then cut dramatically under President Bill Clinton. This was compounded by a U.S. economic recession that hit Rockwell Collins' other main customer base, commercial aviation, particularly hard. The business's growth slumped, and its industry position fell from leader to laggard.

Rockwell Collins retained a lot of its old culture from the days of Arthur Collins; it was an R&D-intensive, technology-focused business. It began to focus greater attention and resources on marketing and market development. However, years of government largesse had resulted in the company's losing its commercial—and even technological—edge, and it had stopped listening to its customers. It bumped along for a few years, but it lacked the leadership needed to reform the enterprise and put it back on the fast track to high growth and market success.

This all changed when the breakout leader arrived in the form of Clay Jones, corporate senior vice president of government operations and international at Rockwell International's Washington, D.C., office. When Jones became president of Rockwell Collins in the mid-1990s, he recognized almost immediately that the assumptions behind the business model had to change. In particular, Jones realized that despite some of the changes set in motion by his predecessor, the resource and business emphases remained heavily biased in favor of R&D and product innovation. Furthermore, little attention was devoted to business planning and strategy development. Jones set about beefing up the resources dedicated to marketing, strategic planning, and customer service. This included setting up a separate unit reporting directly to him that focused exclusively on service.

In terms of our six-pillared business model approach (see Figure 7.1), Jones retained and reinforced the organization's strengths in innovation and reliability but invested heavily in relationships, channels, and brand. He also adopted a more creative and efficient approach to cost management. At an overarching level, Jones placed greater emphasis on making everything fit together, synergistically and strategically. He sought to make the company more efficient and effective by restructuring the business model to reduce the barriers between business activities and encourage greater cross-departmental and cross-functional interaction and cooperation. By placing planning, marketing, and customer service at the core of the business model, cutting across all activities—rather than keeping them in their own functional silos—Clay Jones unlocked an array of creative ideas and process improvements.

At the strategic level, Jones emphasized relationship building and service extension, resulting in a redefined value proposition that moved in the direction of more integrated customer sales and support and network-oriented solutions. As Lou Gerstner had done at IBM a few years earlier, Jones realized that the business was evolving in such a way that future profits would be generated more through sales of parts and services than through sales of products. Thus, in addition to selling clients a traditional hardware product, Jones wanted to push a long-term support contract wrapped around the hardware. His vision was a one-stop-shopping approach, providing customers with more holistic solutions to their business needs.

The other strategic emphasis that Clay Jones introduced to Rockwell Collins' business model was to grow the business around core market strengths and product technologies, rather than just getting bigger for the sake of getting bigger. Unlike his industry peers, he was a vocal advocate of the notion that you don't have to be big to survive and prosper—you just have to be good. The company had been an early leader in GPS technology, and Jones invested in diversifying the market reach of this product beyond the military and aviation sectors and into agriculture and other modes of transport. The company's growth occurred in part through acquisition, but the takeovers that Jones and his team engineered were designed strategically to reinforce or extend existing competencies. For instance, Rockwell Collins bought Hughes-Avicom in 1997 to enter the in-flight entertainment business—a natural extension for a market leader in avionics.

The result of all this was breakout. By transforming its business model, Clay Jones took Rockwell Collins from laggard to leader, recapturing a top spot in its various business arenas. The company's small size relative to giants such as Honeywell meant that it was difficult for it to establish itself as the undisputed market leader, but it certainly was punching above its weight.

Symbolic successes have come its way, such as winning the major supply contracts for Boeing's next-generation 787 Dreamliner passenger jet aircraft. In 2005, *Forbes* magazine named Rockwell Collins as one of the best-managed companies in America, having consistently outperformed the stock market and notching up a five-year total return of over 17 percent. Double-digit growth figures were evident elsewhere as well; the company saw strong revenue and profit growth, consistently outperforming most of its rivals. Looking ahead, Rockwell Collins continues to innovate and has begun a partial shape shift, moving into flight-simulator production and into software development for both commercial and military product applications. But, as always, under the watchful eye of Clay Jones, these new markets are natural extensions that leverage on a common and consistent business model.

As the Rockwell Collins example vividly illustrates, there are times when a radical upgrade of the business model is needed. Companies such as Harley-Davidson, Tesco, and Nissan also were floundering, but each saw enormous opportunities to bypass incumbents with a revised and rejuvenated business model. Unlike other forms of breakout, where business models are relatively fresh and dynamic (taking by storm) or work extremely well and are being adapted for other markets (expanding horizons and some forms of shifting shape), laggard-to-leader breakouts almost always require a major overhaul of business models. Minor adjustments will not do.

In sum, laggard-to-leader breakouts face a tall task; not only do they need to design a new winning value proposition, but they also need to execute across the board in their business model. This is not a trivial change process, as we discuss in Chapter 8. Nevertheless, we have uncovered a number of laggard-to-leader breakouts that provide great examples of what it takes to make this leap. This form of breakout, perhaps more than the others, is amorphous, making it valuable to take a close look at some best-practice cases in action.

Expanding-Horizons Business Models

How do you deliver the promise when your breakout strategy takes you across regional and national boundaries and sometimes even involves massive restructuring on a global scale? The tools we laid out in this chapter apply to these complex challenges as much as they do to the somewhat narrower scope of some of the other breakout strategies, but there is no denying that the task is all the more difficult for companies that are *expanding horizons*.

The first point to make, then, is that an expanding horizons strategy calls for world-class execution of business imperatives across market boundaries. We noted in Chapter 6 that the essence of the value proposition remains the same, even when a company is competing in multiple locations, and therefore the business model will need to be relatively stable across markets. We also acknowledged that companies can have multiple value propositions, but pointed out that if the company is to pursue a successful breakout strategy, all of these propositions should stem from a shared vision and culture.

Customers in different countries, for example, have different expectations concerning what constitutes, say, a "premium" price. Global consumer goods companies such as Procter & Gamble (P&G) and Nestlé realize that in less developed nations, it is simply not possible to go to market with the same high-end prices that their products might command in wealthier markets, even when you are offering commensurate features, quality, support, availability, and reputation. To be successful in such markets, it will be necessary to manage costs in a much more aggressive fashion. Of course, other aspects of your business model may need to shift as well. But just as with value propositions, in most instances these companies strive to maintain a relative consistency in business model configuration across countries. The point we are making is that added complexity and often dramatically different market conditions mean that doing this is more of a challenge for the expanding-horizons enterprise than for other forms of breakout.

A key question to consider for the expanding-horizons breakout is this: why should you expect to gain an advantage in other markets where you currently have no, or little, presence? *Boundary breakers* in particular are faced with this challenge. When both eBay and Starbucks were considering an expansion to Europe, for example, why did they believe they could make it work? Part of the answer was hinted at in Chapter 6, when we demonstrated that eBay's and Starbucks' respective value propositions offered points of differentiation that customers valued. The second part of the answer comes from considering how business models themselves can be sources of competitive advantage. Consider Best Western International, the world's largest hotel brand. With over 4,200 independently owned and operated hotels in 80 countries around the world,[8] this Arizona-based enterprise clearly has a business model that works well beyond the U.S. home market.

Best Western was founded in 1946 by M. K. Guertin, a California-based hotelier who noticed that servicemen returning from the war were taking their families on road trips but often could not find consistently acceptable lodging along their routes. Spotting a market opening, Guertin began to travel the most popular auto routes in America, stopping each day at what he considered the most reputable hotels. After touring the premises and ensuring that the proprietor was willing to commit to uniform quality standards, he invited the proprietor to join his informal referral network. Competing for the middle of the market—customers who wanted a clean, comfortable, and consistent offering, but at an affordable price—the strength of Guertin's business model was his innovation in design and content (an association of independent hotels that conformed to common standards but offered individual experiences) and his emphasis on reliability and relationships (he checked out potential members carefully and monitored existing associates to ensure consistency of quality and service). This is captured in Best Western's own assertion that its "uniqueness is found in each hotel's charm and local appeal while maintaining a commitment to quality, service and value."[9] Thus, for example, hotels must display the Best Western logo but can retain their old names. The result is that Best Western, unlike rival hotel chains such as Holiday Inn, has an integrated identity, blending the best of common Best Western and individual hotel characteristics.

A further interesting feature of the model's decentralized and autonomous approach is what has been referred to as a "Jeffersonian democracy" ethos, where it's not size that counts; the system operates on a principle of "one property, one vote," regardless of whether you own a 20-room or a 200-room property.[10] It is this unique combination of decentralized, democratic system design and variable product features—but with common standards—that makes Best Western's business model so effective. It is also what enables the model's successful internationalization; the common values, practices, and processes are service-led and lack any clear national orientation. On top of these, a Best Western hotelier can add features and support as he or she sees fit and therefore can easily tailor his or her offering to meet different national requirements.

By the early 1960s, the company had expanded rapidly, so that Best Western was the largest U.S. hotel chain. But the company —and the brand—really took off in 1964 when it ventured abroad for the first time, with Canadian hotel owners joining the system. This was the first of many waves of expanding-horizons breakout. As the company grew, its business model became more sophisticated. With its emphasis on cost efficiencies, features augmentation, relationship development, and brand enhancement, Best Western evolved to offer members the benefits of a global reservations system (including online bookings) and integrated marketing, advertising, purchasing, and training—as well as quality standards, of course.

As this story indicates, expanding-horizons breakouts assume that you can leverage your core competency to other geographic markets. Whether it is your superior cost management, branding, or innovation, to expand into other markets, you must bring something to the table that incumbent competitors do not have and ideally cannot replicate easily. For Best Western, it is innovation; for Starbucks, it is brand; for Wal-Mart or Tesco, it is cost; for CEMEX, it is reliability; for Apple, it is relationships; for Mittal Steel, it is channels. The key lessons are, first, that scalability, the essence of an expanding-horizons breakout, requires some advantage in the business model that is apparent to customers, be it cost controls that allow aggressive pricing or branding that conveys prestige, and second, that it must be difficult for competitors to easily replicate or imitate this advantage. For example, Cirque du Soleil has internationalized successfully on the basis of having an innovative product that has unique features, including an imaginative stage show that is based on music rather than words and therefore is easy to convey to international audiences. The experience of a Cirque du Soleil show is unique, and its restricted availability further adds to the attraction and international market demand.

One final point that cannot be overlooked is the downside of mismanaging the scalability requirement. While it is clear that an expanding-horizons breakout requires a business model that provides a competitive advantage across market boundaries, sometimes companies overestimate the applicability of some aspect of their business model. The costs can be enormous. For example, when Marks & Spencer expanded to Canada, the United States, and continental Europe in the 1980s and 1990s, it assumed that its stellar brand renown in the United Kingdom as the purveyor of clothes to Princess Diana and many others would extend to these other markets. Furthermore, the company underestimated the importance of its decades-long relationships with suppliers, resulting in their always putting Marks & Spencer first; this would be weakened and in some cases absent as the company expanded into other global markets. Marks & Spencer was seeking scalability, but its business model was not sufficiently robust to readily allow it. Hence successful breakouts of the expanding-horizons type are predicated on a company's ability to leverage its business model to other locations; companies contemplating such a move would be well advised to make the necessary investments in people, resources, relationships, and processes to ensure that they can deliver what they promise.

Shifting-Shape Business Models

Of all the breakout strategies possible, *shifting shape* is perhaps the most paradoxical. These large, often dominant companies boast enormous resources, deep pockets, or considerable intellectual capital, and sometimes all three. It seems that they have everything necessary to make any strategic shift work, yet they are overrepresented in the annals of corporate failure. Marconi, Vivendi, the U.S. locomotive industry in the 1940s and 1950s, the U.S. steel industry in the 1960s and 1970s, the U.S. tire industry in the 1980s—the list goes on and on. Some of the best-endowed companies in the business world falter because they don't understand and act on the opportunities that arise from new markets, new products, and new knowledge. To stay on top, leading organizations not only must be alert to potential opportunities for shifting shape, but also must build the infrastructure that will allow them to move toward exploiting these opportunities in a reasonable fashion. While we will have much more to say about the infrastructure for change in Chapter 8, there are important implications for how to think about business models that warrant consideration first.

One of the problems that would-be shape shifters confront is that their business models often are not attuned to the new realities that arise from this strategy. What once may have been a carefully constructed business model that was closely aligned with the value proposition will almost certainly become less relevant if it is left untouched. The challenge is daunting. To deliver the promise to customers, shape shifters must create a new business model that fits. There will be many business imperatives that result from this. There is a big risk of not coming through for customers, who, after all, don't really care that you may be going through such a transformational change.

As one illustration of just what is involved in making this type of breakout work from a business model point of view, consider HIT Entertainment's *early-adapter* shape shift back in the mid-1990s. As we discussed in Chapter 3, the children's entertainment business was evolving rapidly at that time, and HIT's role as a distributor of preschool children's TV shows was fast being taken over by larger, vertically integrated competitors. HIT shifted shape by retaining distribution rights and contracts while evolving into a more sophisticated entity, capturing more stages of the children's entertainment value chain. From a value proposition perspective, HIT was offering its customers a more integrated and original product.[11] By acquiring the rights to music catalogues and subsequently developing its own intellectual property (*Bob the Builder* and other characters), HIT was giving TV broadcasters a wider array of services and options to choose from.

From a business model standpoint, as HIT evolved, it had to adapt its six pillars. On cost, the company began to achieve efficiencies and savings as it increased its scale and its bargaining power with suppliers. These savings did not translate into price reductions; HIT's pricing remained toward the premium end of the market. But since the company now was developing its own product, much of the cash provided through cost savings had to be reinvested in R&D and new-product development.

Innovation was perhaps the part of the business model that had to change most dramatically. For a distributor, this was not crucial or even particularly necessary, and HIT's offering was distinguished more by reliability and relationships than by innovation. The business model became more complex when HIT shifted shape into other, more knowledge-intensive parts of the value chain. In developing its own products, the company had to strive for original characters and an original format. This came in the form of *Bob the Builder* and three-dimensional (3D) model animation, as well as acquiring various music back-catalogue rights, giving the company a wealth of original features.

From the beginning, HIT's value proposition had been built largely on excellent quality. It dealt only in the best products and with the premier program and character creators. It established a reputation for consistently delivering outstanding products to customers. As a result, reliability was, in many ways, the focal point of HIT's business model. The challenge in shape shifting was to retain this excellence and consistency as the company expanded and its markets became more varied and international.

In the area of relationships, HIT had traditionally been strong; it was known as a company that would go the extra mile to provide support to customers. Despite the company's small size, HIT's founder, Peter Orton, had a durable network of relationships and was an established and internationally regarded figure in the media business. Through effective management and leveraging these contacts and relationships, HIT became a respected and profitable distributor of television shows. Taking this to the next stage—distributing its own program content—was not as huge a stretch as it might have been, and it added to the choice and support offered to customers.

Availability always was going to be a challenge for a small player like HIT because channels were restricted by its geographic focus on the United Kingdom and its lack of brand equity that resonated with end users (children and their parents). Breaking into the United States was particularly difficult. As HIT's chairman, Peter Orton, told us,[12] when HIT first tried to enter a float in the Macy's Thanksgiving Day Parade in New York City, it was selling itself as a small British company and was discouraged from entering by the high price quoted. But the company overcame such setbacks, largely through acquisition. The purchase of Dallas-based Lyric Studios brought the company *Barney* and the U.S. market. When the company returned to the Macy's organizers as Barney, a mainstay of the event in recent years, the cost of entering the parade dropped dramatically. Added to this, the takeover of Gullane Entertainment brought the company *Thomas the Tank Engine* and a raft of other markets, both at home and abroad.

Finally, HIT had some distance to go on brand, particularly as it came into more direct competition with giants such as Disney.

HIT already had a respected reputation—it was known to offer fair deals and to be trustworthy. For example, it did not demand deep discounts from suppliers, as many competitors did. Also, it appealed to the creative talent (the producers of the TV shows) because it had a reputation as an approachable, independent mini-major that took pride in developing more personal relationships with its customers and suppliers. As we discussed in Chapter 6, though, HIT had little corporate brand value. The ultimate consumers of the product—preschool children and the parents who guided their choices—were not familiar with the company's reputation or didn't recognize the logo. This was a weakness because it meant that HIT had to provide a consistently successful product stream, whereas rivals such as Disney could sell even average products simply on the strength of their names. HIT was under constant pressure to increase brand awareness among end users, but this was a difficult task when the company was competing head to head with Disney, which enjoyed instant name recognition and infinitely deeper pockets.

Overall, the outcome was a business model that evolved successfully to meet the test of HIT's reengineered value proposition, but the challenge of effectively branding against the Disneys of the world highlights just how difficult it is to pull off a shape-shifting breakout. But in helping managers identify each of the key components of the business model that must be aligned with the value proposition, our framework helps to direct managerial attention and priority setting to the areas that are most in need of work.

Early adapters have another challenge to confront. By shifting into a new market space where they have had no presence, they may run smack into other breakout players who see the same opportunity, especially true originals and wave riders. The early adapter may well not have any clear advantage other than its ability to convert its business model expertise into delivering on the value proposition. HIT was fortunate in that it occupied the market space—particularly in 3D model animation—ahead of any taking-by-storm new entrants. But true originals such as Pixar were strong in the related field of 3D computer animation and were working in collaboration with Disney to commercialize their product, with the hugely successful *Toy Story* being the company's first market entry. Disney later acquired Pixar, driven by wave-rider logic and the need to catch up technologically in an industry that it had helped to found.

If all three types of breakout players—early adapters, true originals, and wave riders—see the same opportunity, who will win? When there is a first or very early mover advantage, as was the case for HIT Entertainment (early adapter), eBay (true original), and Ryanair (wave rider), speed is of paramount importance. But let us not overestimate the ability of early entrants to sustain an advantage. It is critical to build barriers to entry—something that makes it more difficult, or more expensive, for followers to gain traction in the market. For eBay, this meant creating a trading community that naturally benefited from the economics of its business—new buyers will go to where the sellers are, and new sellers will go to where the buyers are. Thus, eBay took advantage of a virtuous cycle that led to exponential growth for a time. Other barriers to entry with staying power might be brand (e.g., RIM's BlackBerry or Bob Dylan) and significant product or service differentiation (e.g., Nokia or Apple). So speed is very important, if not because being first is nearly always advantageous, then certainly because moving late requires a huge uphill battle that you will do well to avoid.

In addition to speed, early adapters can draw on their superior resources to grab market share. True originals and wave riders cannot bring the same heft to the market, yet here again there are countervailing difficulties for early adapters because their business models may be weighed down by bureaucratic forces or brand baggage. When E.&J. Gallo spotted the turning point in U.S. wine consumption and the trend toward a better-quality product, it wasted no time in segmenting its business and shifting part of that business to the premium end of the market. The company had the scale and resources to deliver on cost efficiencies; customized, technologically advanced features; better quality; more comprehensive customer support; and new channels to market. From a business model standpoint, the company seemed unassailable on most—but not all—dimensions.

The company's Achilles heel was brand. Because it chose to retain the Gallo name for its premium wines, the company had to struggle to convince wine drinkers and experts that these products were in a different league from the long-established low-priced Gallo table wine. As a result, strong challenges to Gallo were mounted from both above and below by both bigger and smaller companies. These included new entrants or emergent producers such as Deerfield Ranch Winery, Ravenswood, and Storybook Mountain Vineyards that took the wine business by storm, winning both awards and market share. It also included wave riders such as Brown-Forman Corporation, owner of Jack Daniels Tennessee Whiskey, which in the 1990s purchased Californian winemakers Fetzer Vineyards and Bonterra Vineyards, invested heavily in both brands, and put them in direct competition with Turning Leaf and Gallo of Sonoma. The outcome of all these machinations was that Gallo faced vigorous competition as the company shifted shape, forcing it to invest heavily in brand development to ensure that its business model could deliver on the new value proposition.

Finally, shape shifters in general and *power players* in particular bring to the plate a mix of business model expertise that may well vary in its appropriateness for a breakout of this type. Many power players will have tremendous skill in several elements of the business model, yet that deep expertise may not necessarily be an advantage. One can imagine, for example, a company with unmatched reliability and brand finding real value in bringing those skills to the growing market opportunity. However, the same degree of expertise in innovation (if it is limited to innovation in the older, already established product or service line) or in managing channels (again, if the channels are not the major drivers of the new opportunity) can be dysfunctional.

It is really a question of whether your business model is sufficiently flexible and robust to accommodate the type of shape shifting that is required to really reach breakout growth. Established pharmaceutical giants such as Pfizer and GlaxoSmithKline struggled initially to respond to biotechnology breakouts such as Amgen and Genentech and shift into the business areas created by the new technological applications. Through the vision and dynamism of breakout leaders such as Pfizer's Edmond Pratt, they ultimately leveraged their superior resources and adapted their business models to shift into and assume a leading power-player role in the emergent biotech market.

Conclusion

In this chapter, we have gone all out to convince you that, when it is approached in the correct way, the business model idea has enormous potential as a strategic management tool. This is the point at which executives must go beyond rhetoric and promises and start delivering. As we have seen, this is a challenge in all forms of breakout. It is a challenge not only because it may involve a scramble to develop or acquire new resources and capabilities, but also, often more tellingly, because managers fail to face up to home truths. Sometimes a business model is broken or flawed because its fundamental assumptions are outdated or off course, and a significant restructuring is needed to put it back on course to double-digit growth. It is critical not to become complacent; managers who do not realize or do not accept this transformational imperative are playing a very dangerous game.

The relationship between the inward-looking business model and the outward-facing value proposition is at the core of any breakout strategy. When a leadership team—or a single entrepreneur—understands this bipolar dynamic, it can do great things. The key lesson of this chapter is that managers must recognize that a business model is built on six pillars, all of which need time, energy, and resources. None can be neglected. A second lesson is that once you accept this premise, you must be willing to alter the configuration of your business model whenever the value proposition shifts or the market and the industry change. Complacency is the enemy of a dynamic and cutting-edge business model, and far too many managers delude themselves into thinking that all is well or stall for more time in implementing change.

We hope that by now you realize that the business model is the lynchpin of any breakout strategy. It builds on or takes its cues from the vision and value proposition that precede it, and it provides the foundation for the enactment of subsequent business projects and programs. Chapter 8 takes us even deeper into the challenge of execution and change, advancing a clear and dynamic method for putting a business model to work and achieving successful closure on breakout strategy.

Endnotes

1 A view similar to ours is that the function of a business model is to articulate the value proposition and define the structure of the value chain that is needed to deliver on it. See Henry Chesbrough and Richard S. Rosenbloom, "The Role of the Business Model in Capturing Value from Innovation: Evidence from Xerox Corporation's Technology Spin-off Companies," *Industrial and Corporate Change* 11(3):529–555, 2002.

2 Our approach differs from that of scholars who contend that strategies and business models are distinct or that a strategy is a subset of a business model (the opposite of what we argue). See, for instance, George S. Yip, "Using Strategy to Change Your Business Model," *Business Strategy Review* 15(2):17–24, 2004. Still other researchers argue that business models are mere abstractions of strategies, whereas we suggest that they are in fact the first step in realizing strategies. See, for instance, Peter B. Seddon, Geoffrey P. Lewis, Phil Freeman, and Graeme Shanks, "The Case for Viewing Business Models as Abstractions of Strategy," *Communications of the Association for Information Systems* 13:427–442, 2004.

3 This case discussion is based on research undertaken by Ramita Mohan under the supervision of Thomas Lawton.
4 "Hanging Up on Dell," *BusinessWeek Online*, October 10, 2005.
5 Franklin Grosvenor and Terrence A. Austin, "Cisco's eHub Initiative," *Supply Chain Management Review*, July–August 2001.
6 www.collinsclubs.com/history/.
7 Cited in Philip Siekman, "A Big Maker of Tiny Batches," *Fortune*, May 27, 2002.
8 Interview with Tom Higgins, president and CEO of Best Western, conducted by Sydney Finkelstein, February 25, 2004.
9 This is acknowledged on Best Western's home page, as well as in its annual reports.
10 "The Brand Wagon," HYPERLINK "http://www.theman ufacturer.com," January 31, 2004.
11 Interview with Peter Orton, chairman, and Rob Lawes, CEO, HIT Entertainment, conducted by Charles Harvey and Thomas Lawton, July 23, 2003.
12 Interview with Peter Orton and Rob Lawes, July 23, 2003. The Macy's Parade is a long-established event that occurs annually at Thanksgiving and takes place in New York City.

CHAPTER 8

EXECUTING BREAKOUT

Every breakout strategy represents, at least in some respects, a clean break with the past. Companies that step up to breakout are defining an inflection point in their history; they are taking command of an opportunity that they intend to translate into double-digit growth.

Breakout strategy starts with a clear, compelling vision that simultaneously supports and energizes stakeholders. The vision is the guide, but in many ways the creative leap involves a new, differentiating value proposition for customers. The six pillars of the value proposition tell the world: this is what we are, why we are special, and what we can offer you that our competitors cannot. It is critical to back up such a promise, and that is the purpose of the business model and the corresponding business imperatives. As we have seen, each of the six pillars of the value proposition corresponds to one of the six critical attributes of the business model, with business imperatives identifying critical needs that must be met to deliver the promise.

Even with all this, however, there is a fundamental element in bringing breakout to fruition that is missing—implementing the strategy. By *implementation*, we are referring to two interconnected processes: quick learning and adaptation to the demands of breakout (change management), and the development and delivery of a series of specific tactical projects and programs that are absolutely necessary if breakout is to truly take hold (strategy execution).

Most managers understand that great strategy—either of the breakout type or of a more pedestrian nature—necessitates a series of tactical maneuvers to translate ideas into action. This is not to say that the strategy itself should not offer the road map for implementation. As Sun Tzu famously wrote, "Strategy without tactics is the slowest route to victory. Tactics without strategy is the noise before defeat."[1] In this book, we have gone much further than just talking about strategy; we have explicitly laid out a way to think about your vision, value proposition, and business model. The key point here, however, is that if all this is to bear fruit, understanding how to design an implementation process is critical. That is the purpose of this chapter.

Effective implementation starts with quick learning. Why? Because, unlike developing a business plan, for instance, there are no hard-and-fast formulas for implementation. If we view implementation as a process of strategy enactment, there are many different requirements that must be met in order to reach the end goal. While we will shortly introduce a model that helps put all this into perspective, we must be careful not to imply that *all* activities can be prespecified once a breakout strategy has been designed. Thus, there is real value in promoting a learning environment, one that is flexible and can be adapted as the company's needs change. In fact, it would not be an overstatement to say that one of the most powerful competitive advantages any company can have is its ability to learn and adapt.

One company that learned from its business environment, recognized changing customer demands, and adapted accordingly is the global energy giant BP.[2] In 2000, the global oil company BP Amoco rebranded itself as "bp: beyond petroleum." This was in response to growing criticism, particularly in Europe, of the business activities and environmental impact of BP and other extractive industry giants. Recognizing earlier than its main competitors that broadening its appeal made business sense, BP transformed itself from an oil company into an energy company. To the casual observer, this is mere semantics, but BP quickly learned that in mature markets such as the United Kingdom or Germany, a significant—and growing—portion of the population factored ethics and environmental responsibility into its purchasing choices. By repositioning itself as an energy company, BP was emphasizing its solar energy projects and other initiatives aimed at eventually reducing the company's dependence on oil. The company adopted a new logo, a green, white, and yellow sunburst named after Helios, the ancient Greek sun god, that was intended to symbolize its new focus on the environment and alternative fuel sources.

Critics argued that this was merely a publicity stunt, similar to BP's previous attempt in the late 1980s to do much the same thing. Things were different this time, though. The company had learned from its previous efforts and the ridicule that it brought on itself. CEO John Browne intended to make it stick this time around—to ensure that the change of heart was implemented. He had already begun to enact it in 1997, when he pulled BP out of the Global Climate Coalition, a group of business interests that claimed that global warming was unproven and should not be tackled. He also made several public speeches that same year calling for action to combat greenhouse gases. For his unique stand in an industry that was opposed to any environmental activism, Browne even received praise from former foes, including Greenpeace

Whether this was real change or just really good spin, BP's share price and profits rose significantly as a result of the company's new, more ecofriendly image. What most people bought into was Browne's credible acknowledgment that his company had a long way to go, but that it was at least making a start at trying to reverse its massive environmental impact. He was pushing his industry to accept global warming as a fact, and he was candidly acknowledging the mistakes that BP had made in the past and would try to avoid in the future. In so doing, he displayed significant business acumen—recognizing the need to reposition his company, but at the same time adopting a practical and realistic approach to doing so.[3] By 2001, Browne had taken BP from the fifth largest and least profitable of the main petroleum companies to the second largest and most profitable. In the 2005 Fortune Global 500 list of companies, BP was ranked second in the world for turnover—just short of Wal-Mart in the number one spot. By this measure, it had become the largest energy company on the planet.

The story of BP illustrates another aspect of managing strategic change: it is often necessary to unlearn, or forget, some of what you did in the past in order to break out. If Nokia had not abandoned the practices of a diversified commodities manufacturer, could it have succeeded in the technology-driven, dynamic cell phone business? Compare Nokia with Motorola, the company that dominated the cell phone market throughout much of the 1990s, but was unable to let go of its analog heritage when the technology shifted to digital. Because it stuck with analog long past its useful life and was unwilling to unlearn the past, Motorola found its horizons contracting rather than expanding for a 10-year period beginning around the middle of the 1990s.

Unlearning and learning require open-mindedness on the part of leaders and an innovative mind-set on the part of organizations. It is hard to imagine any breakout strategy succeeding if these two attributes are not in high gear. By *innovation*, we are not referring only to the effect on the features you can offer in your value proposition. An innovative mind-set means that managers are looking for the right ways to change, are convinced of the importance of change, and are actively engaged in executing change. In the next section we introduce a model we have used extensively with companies that are implementing breakout strategies. This model does not just assume that the innovative mind-set is present; instead, it suggests specific ways to elicit and promote that mind-set. It doesn't stop at motivating change by pulling the key levers of the socio system in an organization; it also identifies specific process changes that are needed to transform your company into the kind of efficient, productive, and technically competent organization it must be if it is to execute a breakout strategy effectively.

Enacting Breakout Strategy

Peter Drucker, the famed management thinker, once remarked, "Strategy is a commodity; implementation is an art."[4] While we do not agree that strategy can be called a commodity (the number of failed breakout strategies, for one thing, suggests that this is wrong-headed), Drucker is absolutely right about implementation. Things start getting out of control when you reach the enactment stage. Most business leaders either flounder or rely on the sheer force of their personalities to deliver on strategy. Although this latter approach is often effective, it is far from foolproof, and it rarely works in the absence of the "enforcing leader." Few leaders succeed in turning the art of implementation into the science of enactment. Drucker was right in asserting that implementation is an art, but this does not mean that it cannot be formalized. Breakout strategy requires more than simply generating lists of things to do for implementation. We hold that the best leaders integrate the artistic and scientific sides of business.

A key feature of the breakout approach is its clear and comprehensive strategic enactment model. This starts from the premise that every organization *is a community dedicated to the maintenance and development of a value-creating system*. In order to implement a strategy, to deliver value, the individual elements of a business model must be built, maintained, and strengthened by keeping the artistic, or "soft" (socio), and the scientific, or "hard" (techno), determinants of organizational performance in balance. The model presented in Figure 8.1 demonstrates the necessity of endeavoring to realize an energized and productive socio system and an efficient and productive techno system simultaneously.

So what does this mean in practice? We are not using jargon for jargon's sake; there is a real purpose and practice behind our idea of the socio and techno systems. When it comes to change management and strategy delivery, there are two schools of thought: one that emphasizes the organizational process, structure, and system dimensions of the business (techno), and one that highlights the group culture, people skills, and management practices side of the enterprise (socio).

On the techno-system side, companies might focus on implementing packages and processes emphasizing customer relationship management (CRM), total quality management (TQM), supply-chain reconfiguration and the creation of virtual networks,

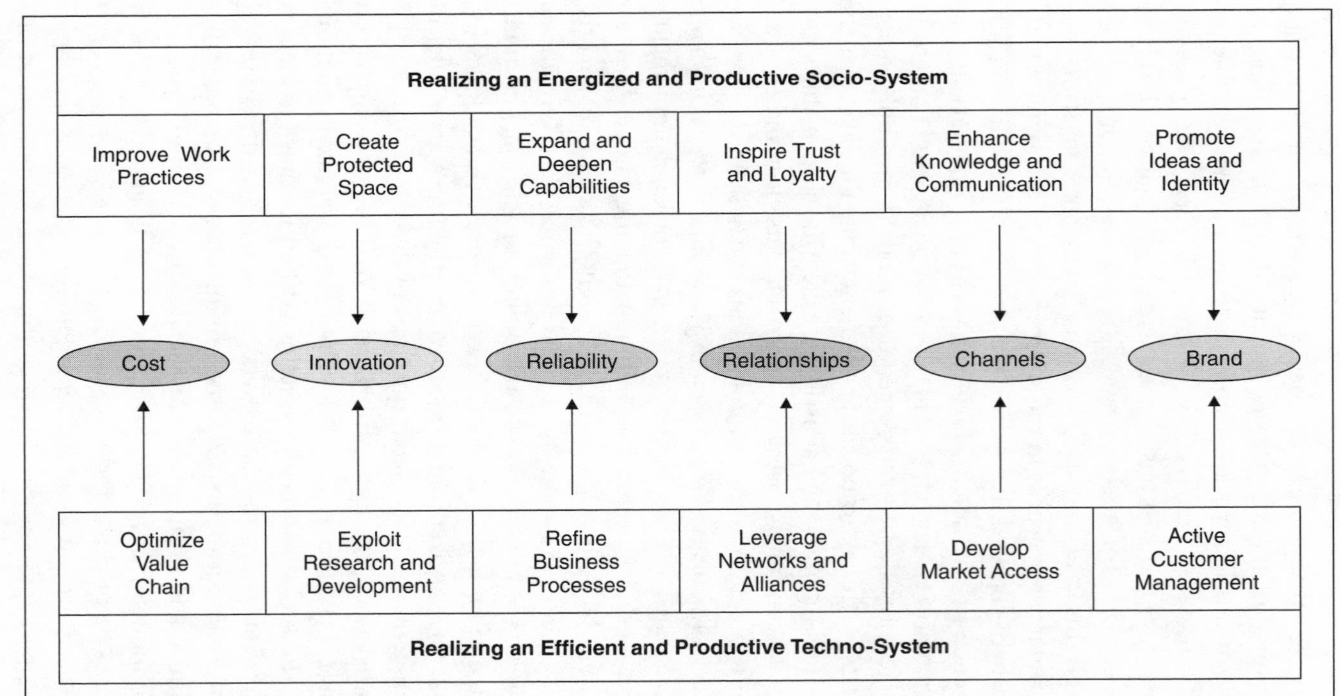

Figure 8.1 Delivering Strategy

and knowledge or innovation management. We are all familiar with such tools and techniques, and because they are often easy to understand and ready to use, they tend to appeal to many managers. Techno systems can be put to work right away through clearly defined projects and programs, and they deliver results that are easy to measure. As a consequence, strategy implementation is often techno-dominated, and the failure to fully recognize the socio, or community, aspect of implementation has led to the failure of numerous strategic initiatives.

On the socio-system side, the focus is usually on principles and practices that call attention to employee empowerment and commitment, human resource flexibility, creating communities of practice, dealing with chaos and complexity, shaping the learning organization, and fostering capable, responsive leadership and good governance. This is a lot of activity, and there aren't always clear methods for delivering it. Sure, techniques exist, but they are not always straightforward or widely applicable. More than that, before you can use these tools, you need to understand what makes your company tick, how to reconcile written and unwritten rules and routines, and what truly matters to your people at all levels of the organization.

We're sure you will agree that this is a rather daunting checklist. Beyond that, socio systems can take time to put into effect, and the projects and programs involved are often unclear in their objectives and deliver results that are difficult to measure and sometimes impossible to assess from a success or failure perspective. Is it any wonder that most entrepreneurs and managers prefer to use techno systems to deliver their strategy? But the point we are making is that a balance between the techno and socio systems is crucial and that to give one preference over the other risks weakening—if not derailing—an entire breakout strategy.

The difficulties that Bob Ayling encountered when he was chief executive of British Airways (BA) illustrate the problem of giving priority to the techno system at the expense of the socio system when implementing strategic change. When Ayling took the helm at BA in 1996, the markets and shareholders warmly welcomed his appointment. His vision and ability to generate strong strategic solutions made him the ideal replacement for the high-profile Colin Marshal, architect of BA's spectacular renaissance in the late 1980s and early 1990s. For stakeholders, Ayling's challenge was to maintain BA's position as industry leader and its image as "the world's favorite airline." For many within the company, this was not an easy task. The business had undergone a painful decade-long restructuring, resulting in a much leaner and more efficient organization than had existed at privatization. In addition, its service quality and brand had been pushed to a level higher than those of most competitors. What more could be done? Why not simply maintain the status quo?

To a strategic thinker like Bob Ayling, the answer was simple: BA had to continue to pursue its strategic transformation initiative relentlessly because new competitive threats meant that it could not afford the luxury of resting on its laurels. BA's breakout could not slow down and most certainly should not cease. Ayling was well aware that the deregulation of European air transport, completed at the end of 1996, soon would open the floodgates and allow dozens of new airlines to enter the industry. As had happened in the United States almost two decades earlier, this was likely to unleash a new breed of low-fare competitors. BA had to continue its cost-reduction drive and service innovation in order to take on the new budget airlines and retain its customer base. Ayling also realized that the industry was becoming increasingly globalized. Airlines were losing their national loyalties, and customers were demanding seamless service from anywhere on the globe to anywhere else. To respond to these dynamics, Ayling pursued an ambitious global alliance with American Airlines (AA), and he undertook a change of corporate identity, deemphasizing the company's British origins.

Ayling's initiatives made perfect strategic sense—from a techno-system point of view. He set about creating an efficient and productive techno system in BA through a set of projects and programs associated with each of the six core elements of the company's business model.

Cost was reduced through greater optimization of the value chain. Particular emphasis was placed on the reform of allowances and salary scales and the outsourcing of non-core activities such as routine maintenance and information technology. BA went deeper and wider in its outsourcing tactics than any other major airline in Europe.

Service *innovation* was enhanced through exploitation of research and development (R&D). For instance, the company spent money on ergonomic consultants to enhance the design and improve the comfort of business- and first-class seats.

Reliability was improved through a refinement in business processes. This included upgrading information systems across the company to give booking agents and check-in personnel integrated and up-to-the-minute computer systems that improved customer information and made the entire BA interface a better experience for consumers.

Relationships were enhanced by leveraging national and international networks and alliances. Most prominently, BA sought to deepen its association with AA, stopping just short of cross-ownership. This alliance also formed the basis of oneworld, a global multilateral airline alliance that subsequently emerged, with BA and AA at its heart. These moves ultimately were customer-facing, intended to strengthen and deepen the airline's relationship with and service to its customers.

In the area of *channels*, BA began to broaden its market access, both through the alliances just mentioned and through increased emphasis on direct bookings. To augment indirect access through travel agents, BA encouraged customers to approach the airline directly when they wanted to book tickets. This served a dual purpose: (1) it gave customers more choice in how they purchased the airline's products, and (2) it reduced cost by gradually increasing the number of tickets sold directly and therefore eliminating the fee charged by travel agents (as much as 10 percent of the ticket price in the 1990s). BA invested more resources in its central reservations system and in developing its nascent Internet-based online reservations system.

Finally, Ayling and his team raised the *brand* profile by placing particular emphasis on actively managing high-yield customers. They placed much of their emphasis on enhancing services for business-class passengers and ensuring that the BA brand was solidly associated with unmatched benefits and outstanding service for these passengers. The other element of this brand development effort was to attract more overseas customers. By moving the corporate identity away from a national association and toward a global image, Ayling hoped to attract more customers from the international markets to which BA flew. For instance, when customers were flying to Italy or India and BA was competing head to head with national carriers Alitalia and Air India, Ayling aimed to capture more of his rivals' customer base on such routes by projecting a transnational brand of excellence that appealed to everyone, regardless of country of origin.

These initiatives made perfect business sense and demonstrated Bob Ayling's understanding of the evolving industry structures and market trends. However, although the markets initially approved Ayling's agenda and its enactment, he ultimately failed to deliver the anticipated profit figures and shareholder value. So what went wrong?

Leaving aside Bob Ayling's leadership traits (more on that in Chapter 9), the fundamental flaw was in the enactment of the change strategy. As we have seen, BA placed considerable emphasis on delivering changes in the techno system. In most cases, these changes were not balanced by transformations in the socio system. By neglecting or underestimating the softer side of the business, Ayling did little to realize an energized and productive socio system based around his workforce.

For instance, in order to reduce costs further, Ayling needed to improve work practices and reform pay systems. He considered the airline's allowance scheme and pay scale for cabin crew too generous and felt that it was unsustainable in a future determined by cost efficiency and productivity maximization. However, his efforts to change pay agreements, introducing performance-related pay schemes and more flexible working hours led to a cabin crew strike during the summer of 1997 that brought the airline to a virtual standstill. Ayling handled the crisis poorly; he adopted a very tough position, closing the Heathrow office of the main cabin crew union and threatening to fire strikers and even sue them for breach of contract.[5] His tactics were a throwback to the acrimonious industrial relations of the early Thatcher years and did not fit with the agenda of the New Labour government that had just assumed power in the United Kingdom. Most people saw the company's confrontational stance as counterproductive. BA's top management team came across as bullies and turned even moderate staff opinion against them. The cost of the strike was estimated to be in the region of 125 million pounds ($200 million) in lost revenue. The damage to staff morale, customer service, and corporate reputation was far greater and difficult to measure accurately.

In exploiting R&D to deliver improvements in innovation, Ayling and his team did not provide the personnel involved with the protected space needed to think creatively. This is common in many organizations: management rarely shields those who are expected to come up with good ideas and new approaches from other responsibilities that eat up their time and energy and erode their creative flow.

Furthermore, to deliver on the new external relationships, Ayling needed to ensure internal trust and loyalty. Relationships between corporations may have legal underpinnings, but they cannot thrive without the human dimension. If Ayling's various external associations were to blossom, he had to have buy-in from his own people. Particularly in the early days, he devoted little time and capital to building this buy-in. He did not communicate effectively to the company's employees why BA needed to grow and strengthen its external linkages with other airlines. He did not convince them that the future of the company depended in part on the success of these alliances. He did not motivate them to be loyal to him and to sell the message on his behalf.

A final example of Bob Ayling's neglect of the socio system is brand development and the active customer management approach that was introduced to deliver on brand transformation. Many of BA's personnel neglected—or refused—to promote the ideas and identity that Ayling championed. They understood that business- and first-class passengers accounted for an inordinate share of the company's profits, but they did not agree with top management's almost exclusive focus on this customer segment. Most significantly, they did not want to abandon their British identity, opposing changes in tailfin design and the removal of the Union Jack from BA's livery. Again, Bob Ayling championed these changes on their rational business merits, but gave little thought to what some might describe as the more irrational and emotional issues associated with brand and identity change.

The moral of this story is that breakout vision and mastery of technical detail are not enough to deliver on strategy. Neglect of the socio system that underpins an organization can undermine a brilliantly devised and executed techno-system transformation. This happened at BA in 1997–1998, with the result that the chief executive's power and authority were undermined. Bob Ayling never regained the complete trust of his workers or the confidence of his investors, leading ultimately to his resignation in 2000.

So what are the keys to enacting strategy effectively? We've already noted the importance of quick learning and unlearning, something that requires a degree of open-mindedness to new solutions rather than an automatic regression to old ways of doing things. The role of leadership is of paramount importance, as we discuss in Chapter 9. Our research, as well our extensive experience working with companies on breakouts, indicates that a deep understanding of how you can use *both* the socio and the techno systems to your advantage cannot be underestimated.

A company that gets this point exceptionally well is the Mexican conglomerate CEMEX. In Chapter 3 we discussed the international market breakout of CEMEX, Mexico's leading provider and distributor of cement and ready-mix concrete products. We discussed how CEMEX successfully orchestrated its rise from a small cement manufacturer in Monterrey, Mexico, to the third-largest producer and distributor of cement in the world. How did CEMEX implement its breakout strategy successfully?[6] The identification and alignment of a vision, value proposition, and business model were crucial. But none of this could have delivered value without the balanced enactment of creative projects and programs for delivering the strategy.

CEMEX built a successful value proposition through a vision to serve the global building needs of its customers and to create value for its stakeholders by becoming the world's most efficient and profitable cement company. Its value proposition is modest; it aims to provide an average product at a competitive price, but with comprehensive customer support and universal availability. Consequently, the company is respected as a brand and a supply-chain partner. CEMEX delivers on this promise through a business model that is very cost-efficient and has basic features. But these factors alone are not going to give the company a market advantage. Where it excels is in its strict adherence to reliability to ensure a consistently high-quality product; deep and enduring relationships with its workers, customers, and supply-chain partners; a technologically advanced global distribution system that is second to none; and a brand that denotes reliability and integrity. This is all well and good, but how does CEMEX translate these principles into practice and ensure the successful conveyance of its breakout strategy?

Figure 8.2 details how CEMEX balances its socio and techno systems in the generation of business initiatives to deliver its business model.

CEMEX identifies the five keys to its success as (1) maintain capital-allocation discipline, (2) manage costs aggressively, (3) reinforce a commitment to continuous improvement, (4) get closer to the customer, and (5) develop your people. CEMEX delivers on these through a dual emphasis on investment in plants,

Business Model	Socio-System Projects and Programs	Techno-System Projects and Programs
Cost	CEMEX realized that in order to bring about innovation in a commodity business, cross-functional teamwork and cost-saving ability would be crucial. They incentivized managrs by allowing them to share cost savings directly and established a practice of team bonuses.	Established extensive information management system that brought about tremendous cost savings for the organization. Introduced Internet-based system called CxNetworks (for order tracking and placement), which brought about savings of $120 million a year.
Innovation	People at all levels and in all jobs are encouraged to think creatively in how the product is designed, packaged, and delivered. CEO Zambrano encourages ideas to bubble up from the bottom.	Through investment in R&D and IT, they perfected and institutionalized the seamless acquisition of new plants. The emphasis is on due diligence and postmerger systems integration.
Reliability	Continuous collection and processing of customer feedback Information. This is then displayed on charts and graphs for all employees to see. CEMEX also believes that the customer is king. A culture exists whereby a dissatisfied customer who calls always receives an apology.	CEMEX uses Mexico and some other markets to continuously test new business practices. Once perfected, they become part of "the Cemex Way"—a culture that blends flexible and enlightened management practices with cutting-edge technology—and are then replicated in all other markets.
Relationships	CEMEX maintains a safe and healthy working environment for its employees. This is important because as their manufacturing processes are hazardous by nature. Also, by establishing an entrepreneurial ethos, the company has ensured that people are rewarded for performance and given the freedom to come up creative solutions.	By bringing together experts in various fields, CEMEX has established comprehensive training programs for its employees that inspire trust and loyalty. These include classroom courses and an extensive Web-based training system, as well as an in-house "mini-MBA" to educate workers in areas outside their specialities.
Channels	The company's aggressive policy of international acquisition and increased availability is always accompanied by a postmerger consolidation of companies and their people into "the CEMEX Way." Global growth can only succeed if all employees share common values as well as practices.	CEMEX equips trucks with GPS navigational systems to ensure same day delivery and delivery within 20 minutes of the scheduled time. In logistically challenged developing countries, this communication efficiency is really appealing.

Business Model	Socio-System Projects and Programs	Techno-System Projects and Programs
Brand	Despite the business it is in, CEMEX tries to ensure that its processes are environmentally friendly. They also produce Cemex sustainability reports, reinforcing their commitment to green development. The company has sponsored community outreach events such as girls education in Egypt, further enhancing its market reputation.	CEMEX practices active customer management with the help of sophisticated IT systems. Leading-edge technology is a hallmark of the company and has given it a distinct identity within an industry that traditionally was low tech in its systems integration. These systems have helped the company to establish itself as a trusted brand.

Figure 8.2 System Balance and Strategy Delivery at CEMEX

equipment, information technology, and process efficiency and on fostering a common culture, ensuring responsive, caring leadership, and developing people and their commitment to the company. The CEMEX example also emphasizes the importance of breakout leaders in delivering strategy.

The synchronization of the techno and socio systems at CEMEX would not have happened without the vision and commitment of CEO Lorenzo Zambrano. When he assumed the top position in 1985, he was determined to make CEMEX the best-managed company in Latin America. When he ran up against cultural obstacles, not only within the company but also within its home country and within the industry, Zambrano persevered, and in less than two decades he had created a business that was not only a Latin American but also a global benchmark for best practices. Two decades after becoming CEO and a decade after being appointed chairman and CEO, Zambrano presided over a company that had grown from a midsized domestic business into a global colossus and was consistently the most profitable company in the industry, with sales in excess of $15 billion, 50,000 employees, and a market presence in more than 50 countries. Based on this track record, no one could doubt Zambrano's ability and CEMEX's capacity to execute breakout successfully.

Renewing, Not Replacing Culture

Enacting changes or improvements in the techno system is usually a clear and well-defined process, and a variety of ready-made tools and techniques are available to the enterprising business. This is not to say that every company can or will take the initiative to put these into effect. Even fewer will do so effectively. But progress on technical processes such as value-chain optimization and R&D exploitation is tangible and easy to comprehend. This is not true with the socio system, and particularly with its overarching premise of "culture."

Most business leaders recognize that when they are putting a new strategy in place or transforming an old one, cultural change is their number one challenge. Our view is in some ways similar and in some ways different. Culture certainly is a vital issue in transformation, and it is difficult for any leader to deliver value through strategy without a supportive culture, no matter how strong the logical foundations of the strategy itself may be. Successful strategic leaders recognize both the strengths and the limitations of the existing organizational culture and find means of both energizing the culture and climate of the business and improving them progressively. The evidence does not support the view that out-and-out cultural transformation should be a primary objective, but rather that successful leaders should recognize and build on what is already strong.

When Ed Zander was brought in to lead Motorola at the beginning of 2004, he instinctively recognized that Motorola's culture did not need replacing—it needed rejuvenation and reinvention. He observed that great high-technology companies of the recent past—Compaq, DEC, Wang, and others—had failed because they forgot to reinvent themselves.[7]

When Zander took over Motorola, it was a 75-year-old company that had seen better days. Despite having been a pioneer over the years in the design and production of the first car radios, then televisions, and then cell phones, Motorola had taken a few wrong turns, missing big technology bets such as the shift from analog to digital and failing at bold experiments such as the Iridium satellite phone technology project. Throw in the high-tech downturn of 2000, and you had a company that had lost its self-confidence.

A major corporate restructuring and a series of layoffs in 2002–2003 indicated that Motorola already had picked itself up by the time Zander came on board, but it had come back less courageous and less hungry. The new chairman and CEO realized that what was needed was not cultural change per se. Rather, he needed to get people to believe in themselves and revive the company's strong culture of quality, reliability, and status as a thought leader. He had to build on the existing culture, taking the good and making it better.[8] This involved improving and updating the socio system—he changed the performance system to link bonuses to performance, for example—but not fundamentally reconstituting it.

Zander's decision to renew rather than replace Motorola's socio system and overarching culture proved to be correct, as the company soon was back to double-digit growth and high profit margins. Within two years of Zander's appointment, Motorola had recaptured a leadership position across a range of product areas and was producing one billion units per year overall—a number that dwarfed the number of iPods, personal computers, and other consumer electronic goods being made by its competitors.

Zander's approach—and that of other cultural energizers such as Carlos Ghosn and Terry Leahy—can be captured by the model of cultural reproduction described in Figure 8.3.

Cultural assumptions are formed and expressed through a self-reinforcing system of cultural expression that, without intervention, tends toward reproduction. Naive attempts at culture change that see the existing culture as a problem are doomed to failure and often waste time and energy. In contrast, working with the grain of culture and building on strengths tend to liberate energies and fire people up to achieve and deliver on strategy. Zander proved this to be the case at Motorola, as did Ghosn at Nissan and Leahy at Tesco.

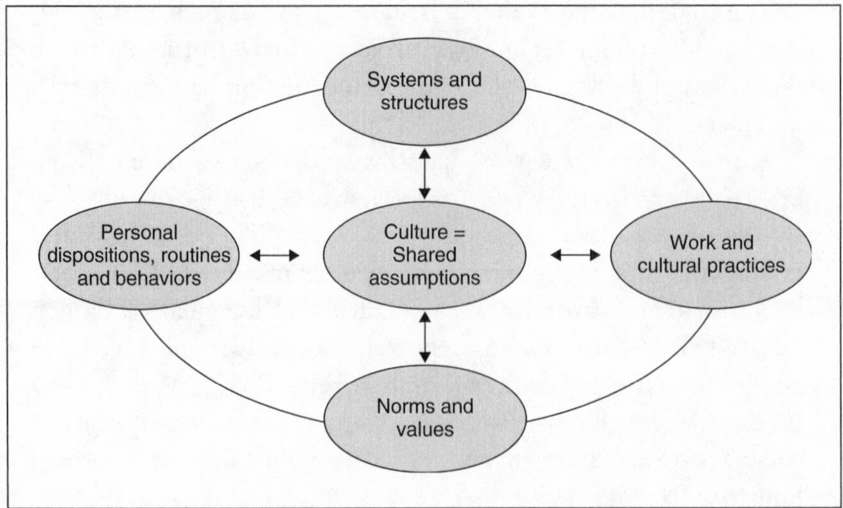

Figure 8.3[9] Organizational Culture and Cultural Reproduction

This cultural reproduction interrelationship is at the core of any strategic enactment. Unless strategic leaders have a deep and meaningful understanding of the culture of the organization they are leading, they will find it difficult—if not impossible—to embed their strategy in the enterprise's socio system. As Figure 8.3 illustrates, culture is multifaceted and inimitable. Not only is it about shared assumptions concerning what the stakeholders believe the enterprise is about and is trying to achieve, but it is also about the company's hard-and-fast systems and processes and its softer, less tangible norms and values. It is as much about the group-oriented work and cultural practices of the organization as it is about the more individual personal dispositions, routines, and behaviors. To understand and transform a company's socio system, you must have a feel for that company's culture. More than that, you must realize that the culture is multidimensional, encompassing not only what is codified but also what is uncodified (systems and structures on the one hand and norms and values on the other), including both individual and group cultures. Comprehension of this many-sided and dynamic interpretation of organizational culture is a basic ingredient of any successful strategy implementation process and is essential to executing a breakout strategy.

Implementing Breakout Strategy

In the following sections, we turn our attention to some specific conditions that arise in different types of breakouts, and also to further illustrations of each type. Perhaps even more than for other ideas in this book, understanding how different types of breakout strategy are enacted is important for the lessons we can draw concerning what to do and what not to do on the way to double-digit growth.

Taking-by-Storm Execution

Taking-by-storm breakout companies have both a big advantage and a big disadvantage relative to the other breakout types, and both stem from the same reality. These companies are smaller and more entrepreneurial in nature, and thus they do not have an installed base of systems and processes to either rely on or overcome. Alone among breakout companies, taking-by-storm companies have little to unlearn, at least from a corporate perspective. (Their leaders may need to battle the assumptions that they developed during their own past experiences in other companies, but that is another story.) These companies really have no "past"; the mere fact that they are attempting an entrepreneurial breakout implies a degree of innovation. Of course, companies that bring no innovation to the taking-by-storm strategy will never have a chance, so in some ways the innovative mind-set that is so important to strategic change is part of any serious attempt to execute taking by storm.

By the same token, however, this lack of history means that these companies have no infrastructure to rely on. There are no ongoing projects or programs that can be adjusted to meet the demands of breakout. With few exceptions (there are some taking-by-storm breakouts that evolve more gradually), the socio and techno systems that lie behind the implementation of breakout strategy must be created. Complicating matters, it is typical for these companies to have scarce resources, making it highly unlikely that the leader will have the people and capital needed to create a fully realized implementation plan. Despite these challenges, there are important pathways that breakout companies can follow to minimize the downside and maximize the upside that comes with newness. For example, when the Boston Beer Company started out in the mid-1980s, the founder, Jim Koch, recalls

> *I started the company on $100,000 cash of my own money, and then I raised $140,000 from a couple of clients and relatives. We started with no overhead. Two people. That was it. . . . There was just me and a secretary named Rhonda. We didn't even have an office. We ran it, we had an answering service, and we had a truck.*[10]

Koch took on multiple tasks. On Mondays, Tuesdays, and Wednesdays, he promoted and sold his new product, Sam Adams beer, and on Thursdays and Fridays he delivered it, driving the truck around Boston and carting a two-wheel trolley with five cases of beer weighing 190 pounds up and down the steep basement steps of old New England bars and restaurants. To make his first hire—his secretary, Rhonda—Koch had to lure her away from a well-paid secretarial job at his old employer, the Boston Consulting Group, attracting her with assurances of a new and exciting challenge and promises of a stake in the business. The company's breakout strategy was purposefully designed to minimize both socio- and techno-system resource needs, ensuring that successful implementation could be achieved without an extensive and expensive set of resource inputs.

Similarly, when The Body Shop started out, it solved the resource problem in a rather unusual manner. As we noted in

Chapter 7, this revolutionary put together a business model that avoided the high-cost characteristics of its competitors (simple packaging, no advertising, franchised retail shops) while leveraging the talents of a charismatic leader (CEO Anita Roddick was a tireless company promoter, generating massive, and mostly favorable, publicity by adopting prominent social causes, among other things).

In the same way, when wholesaler Costco first broke out, it dealt with resource constraints by employing a no-frills approach to strategy execution. The company operated out of low-overhead warehouses where the goods were not even removed from the pallets on which they were delivered. Shopping was self-service, and inventory was minimized by having a rapid turnover and a policy of not stocking many of the same goods twice in succession. On the people side, Costco spent more to get more, paying its people better than its rivals did and providing a range of added benefits, but receiving higher productivity and lower staff turnover as a result.[11]

Over time, however, even a taking-by-storm breakout requires extensive systems and processes, backed up by targeted programs and projects. Neglecting either the socio or the techno systems in a company is not a sustainable formula for success. The Body Shop's creative entry strategy, for example, eventually broke down because of massive inefficiencies in business processes. Sometimes a change in leader is needed to make the transition from initial breakout to sustainable breakout, as was the case with Kuala Lumpur–based AirAsia. Like Ryanair, AirAsia was launched initially as a full-service regional airline offering slightly lower fares than its main competitor, Malaysian Airlines. The company suffered losses until charismatic former music industry executive Tony Ferndandes took it over and transformed it into Asia's first successful low-cost, low-fare airline.

One final point here: strategic change for taking-by-storm companies is really all about breaking the rules in an industry.[12] This is as true for *revolutionaries* as it is for *true originals*. These companies see an entrepreneurial opportunity emerging from changes in a market space or envision the type of changes that could take place in a market space. They create a frame-changing value proposition; continuous learning and flexibility fine-tune the value proposition; the business model is often unique as well to match the demands of the value proposition; and then comes the challenge of effective implementation. Despite everything that is different about these breakouts, at the end of the day we return to the first principles of execution. There is no getting around the need for world-class socio and techno systems, no matter how innovative the core strategy may be. There is an irony in this. Learning, unlearning, and change are the key watchwords for effective implementation of all the other types of breakout strategies, but success in taking-by-storm breakouts—in some ways the most individual and original of all—depends on mastering the art and science behind basic business processes that seek to energize people at the same time as they emphasize efficient operations.

Laggard-to-Leader Execution

In previous chapters we described the challenges facing companies that look for breakout in a *laggard-to-leader* fashion. These are companies whose entire strategy is predicated on their ability to manage a very complex strategic change process. By virtue of their historically poor performance, they have much to unlearn.

Consider Japanese auto manufacturer Nissan Motors. On the verge of bankruptcy in the 1990s, Nissan was saved by Brazilian-born Carlos Ghosn, who already was skilled at getting companies to unlearn bad practices and overcome their laggard mind-set. It was this equal emphasis on technical improvement and cultural renewal that bolstered Ghosn's success as a turnaround maestro. He had honed his turnaround abilities first as president and CEO of Michelin North America, which he restructured successfully before being hired away by Renault in 1996. He masterminded a three-year cost-cutting campaign at Renault that did not transform it from laggard to leader, but did eliminate its losses and put it back on the road to profitability. It also enabled Renault to invest

$5.4 billion and take effective management control of Nissan in 1999, a decision that then-executive vice president Carlos Ghosn played an instrumental part in making.

Ghosn's surprise appointment as Nissan's COO and subsequently as its president and CEO (no foreigner had ever before run a large Japanese company) proved to be the turning point for the ailing company. Within two years, he had transformed Nissan, revitalizing its product portfolio, slashing costs by more than $9 billion, and bringing its crippling debt under control (reducing it from $22 billion to $6.4 billion in three years). His approach was two-pronged: he tackled Nissan's techno-system inefficiencies and its complacent socio system simultaneously. His first step in getting the company to unlearn bad practices and negative ways was to set up cross-functional teams to examine every area and function of the company and develop a set of recommendations that were ambitious but achievable.[13]

The outcome had implications for all elements of Nissan's strategy execution. For instance, in the techno system, Ghosn sought much greater effectiveness in the exploitation of R&D. Nissan had unlearned how to innovate, particularly in product design. Its cars, trucks, and SUVs had become boring and unattractive to consumers. As laggard-to-leader companies in other industries, such as Gucci, had done, Nissan rediscovered and relearned design innovation by hiring new talent and giving these people the space and the resources to come up with the goods. In this case, Ghosn hired Shiro Nakamura from Isuzu and put him in charge of Nissan's design revival. Also on the techno side, costs were reduced dramatically through making cuts and efficiencies across the value chain (by centralizing global purchasing, for example), adopting more technologically advanced business processes, leveraging networks and alliances (particularly with Renault), and developing market access (again, mostly in partnership with Renault).

In reforming and reviving Nissan's socio system, Ghosn faced challenges—not least because his cost-cutting initiatives also involved the loss of 21,000 jobs. This was especially challenging in Japan, where the "job for life" concept had not yet been challenged seriously by any sizable corporation. Ghosn reduced the social fallout in part by ensuring that most of the reduction in headcount would come about through natural attrition, increased numbers of part-time employees, the spin-off and outsourcing of noncore activities, and early retirement packages. But he also knew that reforming Nissan's culture and the resulting socio-system projects and programs were where he faced the greatest challenge.

In addition to a sense of complacency—perhaps caused by the job-for-life tradition—Ghosn faced problems similar to those that Ed Zander faced at Motorola. Nissan had gone through a decade of decline, and morale was at an all-time low. The new boss knew that he had to restore a sense of confidence and pride in Nissan workers before he could achieve any improvements. He did this first by creating a protected space for the design team, as just mentioned. This had an impact right across the company because employees had lost confidence in the brand and its products, viewing them as being behind the times and unattractive market offerings. He also expanded and deepened capabilities and enhanced knowledge and communication by bringing in a small team of people from Renault, whose job was to coach and encourage change across business functions, but not to force it on employees in a top-down, unexplained style. Ghosn led from the front, too, speaking plainly and directly, conveying his vision for Nissan, establishing a sense of urgency, and impressing upon workers that if his strategy was not implemented fully and effectively, they all might lose their jobs.

This approach—and the results he delivered—inspired considerable trust in Ghosn and loyalty to him among workers, supply-chain partners, and, ultimately, customers. The flawless execution of Ghosn's laggard-to-leader breakout soon was evident: Nissan was profitable in 2000, and within five years, it had become the world's most profitable carmaker. In 2005, PricewaterhouseCoopers named Nissan the world's best turnaround.

For other best-practice examples, we could do worse than turn to the world of private equity. While private equity financing—in which investor-supported financial buyers acquire public companies, take them private for a time while pushing performance improvements, and then exit by either selling the company to another buyer or taking it public through an initial public offering (IPO)—has become so big that it is difficult to isolate just one methodology, it is fair to say that turnaround is a central feature of most deals. Hence many private equity buyers are in the business of playing the laggard-to-leader breakout game.

What lessons emerge from private equity? First, these buyers place major emphasis on finding the right management team to lead the turnaround. Indeed, we have noted in several places just how important leadership is to breakout, and in the final chapter of the book, we provide some guidance on how to make this happen in your own organization. Second, and this may be surprising to some, the best private equity buyers pay attention to both the socio and techno systems that are in place, with special emphasis on upgrading their quality and reliability.

Perhaps it is easier to imagine financial buyers paying attention to optimizing value chains, refining business processes, managing customers more effectively, and the like. For example, when a group of private equity buyers led by Bain Capital acquired Burger King in 2002, they dissected every aspect of the business to look for places where they could improve efficiency, methods, and productivity. This analysis led to changes such as franchisee restructuring (upgrading market access), improved service quality and delivery (active customer management), and new systems for international expansion (refining business processes). At the same time, they paid tremendous attention to bringing in new talent (expanding and deepening capabilities), energizing franchisees (enhancing knowledge and communication), and installing performance measurement systems (improving work practices).

The importance of managing the socio system cannot be overestimated. One of the fallacies that managers in laggard-to-leader situations sometimes hold is the belief that it is the people within the company who have not performed well enough to keep the company on top. Of course, this is sometimes true, and wholesale changes may well be needed. But often a large stratum of managerial talent has been held down by the lack of vision and leadership at the very top. Few laggard-to-leader breakouts will succeed without new leadership, but this does not necessarily mean that middle- and upper-level managers also must be removed. In truth, it is hard to imagine doing so in a comprehensive manner in a company of any significant size. It is important to realize that many managers and employees who lived through the lean years have been left with some degree of disillusionment, and that energizing those people is critical to a successful turnaround.

This lesson became clear to Alec Gores, chairman of Gores Technology Group, after its acquisition of the Learning Company, a unit that had wildly underperformed while it was part of Mattel Corporation. On the first day after the deal closed, Gores realized that he needed to reach out to people and begin the process of reenergizing:

> *We called for a town hall–type meeting to openly communicate with employees and set the pace for our management style and plans. We were amazed at how upset and negative the attitudes of the employees were. They had been involved with something that had gone from billions of value to being an industry scar. . . . Frustrations with the parent and the process had left the employees extremely disillusioned.*[14]

Laggard-to-leader breakouts often stumble because insufficient attention is given to the mechanics of turnaround, and it is here that our model of the socio and techno systems in organizations can be extremely valuable as a template for managing strategy change. Private equity acquirers have a track record in precisely this type of change, and, as these examples suggest, some of the same discipline that characterizes our approach has been part of the private equity playbook for years. While it is sometimes difficult to see just what goes on in private companies, the model we've laid out in this chapter should help to make clear what the key tasks and challenges are.

Expanding-Horizons Execution

How do companies expand their horizons? Organic growth can certainly help, and some of our breakout companies have continued to move in this direction as they expanded their horizons across regional and national boundaries—Best Western, Starbucks, and Zara come to mind. Many others, however, especially *conquistadores*, use mergers and acquisitions as their vehicle for growth. Indeed, the huge vision of conquistadores cannot be fulfilled easily without some degree of buyout activity. Energy giant BP, for example, has grown to be the world's second-largest company in part through a series of well-chosen and perfectly executed acquisitions. Takeovers of long-established, respected companies such as Burmah Castrol, Aral, Arco, and Amoco strengthened and deepened BP's core businesses, while at the same time increasing the company's global reach and presence.

If strategic change comes to many *expanding-horizons* breakouts via mergers and acquisitions (M&As), it seems critical that these companies develop tailored expertise in how to execute. This is not an easy task. The track record for M&As of any type borders on the abysmal, with many studies putting the success rate at between 30 and 50 percent.[15]

While overpaying generally is not the most effective way to make a strategy of breakout via acquisition work, the most common flaw occurs during postdeal integration. During this process, the two firms must be melded in some way; the previously independent managerial groups must learn to coordinate and cooperate so that the hoped-for synergies can be realized. We believe that the framework in this chapter can be a particularly useful tool for merging companies to rely on during integration. For example, when Air France and KLM merged in 2004, the integration of the French and Dutch flag carriers was executed in textbook fashion and added considerably greater value more quickly than even the staunchest supporters of the merger anticipated.

What made the merger so successful? The answer can be found by examining the postmerger integration strategy and its execution. The new entity, controlled by a Paris-based joint holding company, succeeded in delivering both techno-system cost savings and process efficiencies (such as joint purchasing and maintenance contracts, as well as network rationalization) and socio-system governance harmony and shared identity (KLM shareholders received 40 percent more than their shares were worth to sweeten what was in fact a takeover, and Amsterdam's Schiphol Airport was retained as a core hub within the new dual-identity organization). The concept of one company (Air France–KLM Group), two airlines, and two hubs proved a winner from both a techno (operational) and a socio (cultural) perspective.

Whether they are expanding their horizons via M&A or not, conquistadores are remarkable for what they are trying to accomplish. Imagine this: a large company, competing in established markets, seeks to break from the slow-growth days of the past. It sees an opportunity to restructure and integrate its industry on a more global basis. How does it move forward? The image that comes to mind is that of a supertanker slowly moving its rudder in a new direction. What kind of culture is formed when once-distinct markets and companies are folded together? Such breakouts involve a change from being a national company—or a nationally oriented industry—to a global one, creating new problems that even may include geopolitical concerns.

Mittal Steel (then known as Ispat International) embarked on just such a breakout during the 1980s and 1990s, gobbling up failed or failing national steel companies, turning them around, and rejuvenating a declining industry. It ran into trouble, however, when it tried to acquire its closest rival and the world's second-largest steel company, Arcelor. Several European governments had a stake in the company, either through shareholding or because of the number of their nationals that Arcelor employed. Underestimating the scale and force of resurgent protectionism in Europe, Mittal emphasized in its negotiations the benefits that the acquisition would bring to shareholders through the increased cost efficiencies and process improvements that Mittal would bring to its European rival. In so doing, the steel giant was focusing almost exclusively on the techno system.

However, in an emotional and politically charged context in which job security had become a massive social issue, Mittal needed to put more emphasis on the socio-system side of its planned takeover. Seeing the millions of people who took to the streets all across France in the spring of 2006 to protest against French government efforts to introduce a modicum of flexibility into the labor market—by passing a law allowing employers to fire young workers during their first two years on the job without giving a reason—you could not help but be aware of the sensitivity surrounding employment rights. Mittal was ultimately successful, but despite the fact that much of the opposition to its takeover bid was irrational and couched in regressive protectionist rhetoric, the company might have made its task easier if it had given relatively equal weight to technical and social issues when drawing up and executing its takeover game plan.

We don't want to leave this section without pointing out that while *boundary breakers* tend not to operate on the same scale as conquistadores, they too are confronted with the same types of issues concerning organization building. They must put in place the formal structure, systems, and processes needed to control their now far-flung operations. Coordination between units in different regions or countries becomes important. Marriott, McDonald's, Starbucks, and many others have undertaken boundary-breaker breakouts that encounter the same challenges as companies such as Mittal Steel face in ensuring balanced strategy implementation across their different national markets.

The advantage these companies have over conquistadores is that their internationalization often is partly or wholly undertaken through franchise agreements. Companies such as McDonald's have tended to pursue a replication approach,[16] transferring knowledge from the franchisor to the franchisee in such a way and to such an extent that the franchisee's identity is defined or redefined as a result. In the fast-food business, the emphasis is on creating new outlets with local production capability—what has been cleverly labeled "the mass production of organization."[17] At McDonald's, creating restaurants around the world that have equal or similar capabilities for local production requires the transfer of an extensive set of techno-system routines and practices. It also involves the transfer of many socio-system components, such as techniques for work practice improvements and schemes for employee training and development.

Other boundary breakers tackle breakout execution by combining a global brand and best practices with local knowledge, customs, and cultural understanding. Although it is an association rather than a franchise, Best Western combines these with optimal impact, effectively splitting techno- and socio-system responsibilities between the association and its locally owned members. Acknowledging the advantages of not imposing a socio system from the center, Best Western's now former President and CEO Tom Higgins told us[18] that he is constantly aware that a global company should not be run with an American mind-set. There should not be a complete separation of roles and responsibilities—Best Western has views on brand identity and work practices, for instance—but combinations of the two occur where they make the most sense. The company's global breakout therefore is most often a balance between Best Western value-chain efficiencies, R&D, business processes, networks and alliances, market access, active customer management processes, the local owners' work practices, incentive schemes for employee innovation, service-delivery capabilities, loyalty initiatives, communication efforts, and ideas and identity. As we saw in the last chapter, this approach to breakout execution has proven extremely effective.

Shifting-Shape Execution

The fourth and final breakout type—the *shape shifter*—has its own challenges when it comes to enacting strategy. These too must be understood if we are to have at our disposal all the lessons on what do to and what not to do on the road to double-digit growth. How often and how exactly does a company shift shape? Is this a breakout strategy that companies can return to whenever they need a burst of growth?

Well, it is tempting to think so, but the reality is that shifting shape is among the most difficult of all breakout strategies. Consider the typical pattern of a company over time. At its founding, especially if it's a very successful start, the first breakout has occurred. Taking by storm would be an appropriate blueprint. Then, as time passes, there is a natural convergence in systems, processes, and even culture, to a point where much of the change that occurs is incremental in nature. Some companies never break out of this stage and either fall by the wayside when the market turns sufficiently against them or continue to hang on in a low-growth world.

It is really because so many companies find themselves mired in the past and are searching for a way to escape to double-digit growth that we wrote this book. This is all the more true for shape shifters—large companies with dominant positions in the market, but with unattractive growth prospects. What are the key issues for companies like this to consider when they are looking for strategic change?

Since history indicates that most companies converge around a strategy over time and change only rarely after that, the necessity to be alert to shifts in markets is paramount. Nokia saw the rise of cell phones and a huge market and made the shift. Gallo realized that the exciting and growing market was in higher-end wines and made the shift. IBM understood that the old model of hardware first was dying and moved aggressively into the knowledge-intensive market of integrated information technology (IT) solutions for customers. Samsung knew the difference between selling commodity products that never could yield growing profits and the upside in highly differentiated, branded consumer electronics. Each of these shape shifters was open to change, looked for the opportunity to change, and was rewarded handsomely for its effort.

When companies undertake a shifting-shape breakout, they must understand that their established systems and processes will be disrupted. There is a period of flux during which the right set of programs and processes is not crystal clear. In this situation, creativity and innovation are critical, and here we mean that these must be directed toward the socio and techno systems that will need to be in place if breakout is to be implemented effectively. Certainly, learning and unlearning are key attributes as well. It is also vital to monitor industry discontinuities closely for potential disruptions, because they often hold the seeds of major change and opportunity. Anticipating what is about to happen or responding early is critical. Some of the key early indicators to pay attention to are[19]

- Substitute product and process technologies, such as jet engines and digital technology
- Major economic and social changes, such as oil prices, demographics, and geopolitical issues
- Product life-cycle shifts
- Changes in emerging economies, such as China, India, and Vietnam
- Your own company's size and stability, which has natural limits that no company has ever surpassed indefinitely

The shape shifters we studied saw the changes coming, decided to view them as opportunities rather than threats, and were willing to make tough decisions that entailed a nontrivial degree of risk. We know that this is not an easy formula to follow. The consequences of not making the shift, however, are significant. Even when the decision to change in this dramatic way has been made, there are still huge challenges to overcome. But it can be done. Paying attention to the socio and techno systems provides a blueprint for executing any breakout strategy, including shifting shape.

When Tony Blair was elected leader of the British Labour Party in 1994, he took the party in a radical new direction and was determined to make tough decisions that would ensure the party's reelection at the central government level. He was the most prominent advocate of a rightward shift in European social democracy, championing so-called third-way politics and the occupation of a middle ground between socialism and conservatism. Shifting shape by abandoning a wide range of outdated policy positions and political priorities was the only way Labour could break out and gain power again. Blair began to refer to the party as "New Labour," symbolizing a rightward shift of the party and a move away from the "Old Labour" associations with left-wing causes such as pacifism, nuclear disarmament, and the redistribution of wealth. The name "New Labour" signified a rebranding of the party and was intended to appeal to British voters who were in the center or slightly left of center, many of whom had drifted away from the Labour Party when it moved further left under the leadership of Michael Foot in the early 1980s.

The change that Blair saw coming was a post–Cold War "end of ideology" among many British voters, with most being somewhere in the center and looking for politicians who were practical and adaptable rather than dogmatic. Taking his cue from Bill Clinton's "New Democrats" presidential victory less than two years earlier, Blair adopted the politics of pragmatism, shifting his party toward the center on everything from defense and foreign policy to taxation and labor law. One of his first actions as Labour leader was the rewriting of Clause IV of the party's constitution, removing the commitment to public ownership. Although it was a purely symbolic act, it signaled a new era in British politics, a willingness to break the shackles of the past and the emergence of a real alternative to the Conservative Party, which had run the country since the election of Margaret Thatcher in 1979.

Blair's risk paid off: he won a landslide victory in 1997, and his reelection four years later was the first time a Labour prime minister had won two general elections in a row. What factors best explain the success of this shape-shifting breakout for Blair and his party? In addition to an astute reading of the changing political landscape of modern Britain and a willingness to make tough decisions and risky shifts to make his party electable, Blair and his senior colleagues had an unbeatable strategy. The vision was clear and inspiring, the value proposition was appealing, and the business—or party—model was efficient and effective.

Above all, though, Blair paid attention to execution and the need to balance the hard and soft dimensions. For instance, on the socio-system side, New Labour espoused a stakeholder society, promoting ideas and an identity based on a balance between rights and responsibilities. On the techno side, the party launched a more aggressive and targeted approach to winning votes, courting the media—including previously antagonistic daily tabloid newspapers such as *The Sun*—to get its message and new brand across to noncore and nontraditional Labour voters.

In the area of relationships, Blair and his shadow Chancellor of the Exchequer, Gordon Brown, reached out to the business community, assuring business leaders that Labour would be a competent manager of the economy and would adopt policies that would help and not hinder the business community. In the Labour Party Manifesto for the 1997 general election, Blair and Brown explicitly embraced globalization and rejected economic protectionism, and when they gained power, one of their first acts was to give the Bank of England decision-making independence from the government. These actions inspired trust and loyalty in Blair among people who had previously been skeptics, particularly in the corporate world and the financial community. New Labour also leveraged networks and alliances, attracting sponsorship and support in the business community even before winning office. For instance, David Sainsbury, chairman of J Sainsbury, the food retail giant, donated 2 million pounds (close to $4 million) to the Labour Party in 1996—and more than triple that amount during the next five years. As an indication of New Labour's acceptance of big business, Sainsbury received a peerage in 1997—becoming Lord Sainsbury—and was made Minister for Science in 1998.

We could go on, but the point has been made. New Labour consistently demonstrated how effectively it had unlearned the practices of the past that had kept the party out of power for 18 years. It created a powerful party machine and a political message that proved capable of reaching out beyond its core constituency—market, if you will—and achieving double-digit growth in the number of new voters—or "customers"—that it won. Putting aside your own political position and your assessment of the eventual results, you have to acknowledge that under Blair's stewardship, New Labour delivered on a business model that ensured the party's political breakout. It combined discipline and efficiency, creativity and modernism, competence and effectiveness, conviction and partnership, dialogue and reach, and beliefs and reputation—realizing an energized socio system and an efficient techno system. The rest is history and is best left to other scholars to assess.

Conclusion

In this chapter, we have shown that to execute breakout successfully, an enterprise must be adaptable, nimble, and balanced in its approach. More specifically, the implementation lessons are

- Effective execution begins with quick learning and a willingness to adapt to meet new challenges or changing circumstances.
- Not only must you learn, but you also must unlearn. For some breakout types, forgetting some or even most of what you did in the past and how you did it is essential if you are to make the transition to breakout.
- To execute breakout and deliver double-digit growth, the six elements of a business model must be built, maintained, and strengthened by keeping the socio and techno determinants of organizational performance in balance.
- Most businesses that encounter problems in implementing strategic change do so because they focus on the techno system and neglect the socio system.
- Working with and renewing an existing corporate culture is often more effective than seeking to change the culture completely. This approach builds on and extends organizational strengths, releases energies, and motivates people to achieve and deliver on strategy.

Building and remodeling the techno system of an enterprise is a lot easier than doing the same for the socio system. For most businesspeople, renegotiating purchasing agreements, introducing a TQM process, or setting up CRM software is a lot simpler than bringing in new incentives aimed at increasing employee productivity, designing skills-development programs, or motivating a dejected workforce and reviving a lackluster company identity. Which set of processes would you prefer to tackle? Unfortunately, you do not have a choice—you and your team must deal with both the project and program dimensions of the business model. And you must do so with equal enthusiasm and balanced consideration of their interaction and mutual impact.

In the last four chapters, we have built on the stories, generalizations, and insights of Chapters 2 and 3 to demonstrate that breakout businesses have good strategic habits, each of which is culturally embedded and is played out time and time again. This gives stability, a sense of confidence and continuity, and the flexibility needed to keep pace with rapidly changing markets.

We next move on to discuss the fifth and final essential practice for double-digit growth—breakout leadership. In Chapter 9, strategy is placed more securely within the context of leadership. You will be brought to reflect on your own practices and how you might bring the lessons of breakout strategy to bear within your own organization. Most of all, we will look at how everything we have discussed so far is shaped and guided by the thoughts and actions of strategic leaders. The key to breakout success—and the reason for failure—is always found at the door of those who run the business.

Endnotes

1 Sun Tzu, *The Art of War*. Philadelphia: *Running Press*, 2003.

2 It also changed to lowercase letters—bp—because company research indicated that the old BP was too austere for many modern customers.

3 The importance of business acumen in successfully incorporating external trends into internal strategy is emphasized by Ram Charan in "Sharpening Your Business Acumen," *Strategy + Business* 42:49–57, 2006.

4 For this and other pearls of wisdom from Peter Drucker, see Peter Drucker, *The Essential Drucker: The Best of Sixty Years of Peter Drucker's Essential Writings on Management*. New York: *HarperBusiness*, 2001.

5 "Industrial Relations at British Airways—Setting a New Course?" European Foundation for the Improvement of Living and Working Conditions, *European Industrial Relations Observatory Online*, www.eiro.eurofound.eu.int.

6 Thanks are due to Pranav Bhanage, Tak Wai Chung, Cesar Galan, and Javier Romero, Tuck 2005, for their input into this case study.

7 Ed Zander, chairman and CEO, Motorola, Inc., talking at the Tuck School of Business at Dartmouth, March 28, 2006.

8 Ibid.

9 Here, we apply the original model presented by Mairi Maclean, Charles Harvey, and Jon Press in *Business Elites and Corporate Governance in France and the UK*. London: Macmillan, 2006, pp. 41–43.

10 Interview with Jim Koch, founder and chairman of Boston Beer Company, conducted by Thomas Lawton, April 6, 2006.

11 A 2004 *BusinessWeek* study found that Costco has one of the most productive and loyal workforces in all of retailing and attributes this in large part to the salaries it offers, with Costco's average hourly wage being 40 percent higher than that of archrival Sam's Club. On top of this, Costco spends significantly more than rivals on workers' health and retirement benefits and runs a successful profit-sharing scheme (BusinessWeek Social Issues Commentary, "The Costco Way," *BusinessWeek*, April 12, 2004).

12 The rule-breaking idea was originally advanced by Gary Hamel in "Strategy as Revolution," *Harvard Business Review*, July–August 1996, pp. 69–82.

13 Gary Witzenburg. "How to Turn Around a Car Company," Automotive Industries, November 2003, www.ai-online.com.

14 Interview with Alec Gores, chairman of Gores Technology Group, conducted by Charles Harvey, April 12, 2002.

15 Michael A. Hitt, Jeffrey S. Harrison, and Duane R. Ireland, *Mergers and Acquisitions: A Guide to Creating Value for Stakeholders*. Oxford, England: *Oxford University Press*, 2001.

16 Sidney G. Winter and Gabriel Szulanski, "Replication as Strategy," *Organization Science* 12(6):730–743, 2001.

17 This term was coined by J. L. Bradach, "Using the Plural Form in the Management of Restaurant Chains," *Administrative Science Quarterly* 42(2):276–303, 1997.

18 Interview with Tom Higgins, president and CEO, Best Western International, Inc., conducted by Sydney Finkelstein, February 25, 2004.

19 Michael L. Tushman, William H. Newman, and Elaine Romanelli, "Convergence and Upheaval: Managing the Unsteady Pace of Organizational Evolution," *California Management Review* 29(1):29–44, 1986.

Chapter 9

BREAKOUT LEADERSHIP

Breakout strategy requires leadership. Fundamental decisions with long-lasting impact must be made, and these choices are made by the people leading the organization toward the goal of double-digit growth. In truth, one of the most difficult challenges is creating a momentum for change, a new agenda designed to transform an organization from second-tier player to industry leader.

Let's consider some of the challenges facing leaders in each type of breakout. *Taking-by-storm* breakouts are made by relatively smaller companies with weaker competitive positions in the marketplace. Often the leaders of these companies are entrepreneurs, who by definition are rule breakers[1] with tremendous self-confidence and aspirations. The challenge is to take advantage of the power of the entrepreneurial leader who is out to reconceptualize value for consumers, and to surround the founding entrepreneur with other talented individuals who can temper any extreme tendencies on the entrepreneur's part, while adding complementary capabilities of their own to the mix. Sustaining such breakouts almost always involves building bench strength so that the company can make the inevitable transition from ad hoc management to more sophisticated systems.

In companies of this type, breakout strategy may well be a multiperiod game. Even initial taking-by-storm breakouts can falter when more powerful competitors respond, as the traditional cosmetics makers did to Anita Roddick's The Body Shop and the large breweries to Jim Koch's Boston Beer Company. Winning one round does not necessarily mean that the next round is already won. Companies without sufficient leadership talent cannot stay in the breakout game for long.

Laggard-to-leader breakouts present a different set of leadership challenges. At some point, laggards are faced with a classic inflection point where they can either descend into a downward spiral or embrace the trauma of turnaround. Because the latter choice, while clearly better than the former, is incredibly difficult to bring about, most successful laggard-to-leader breakouts follow a change in leadership at the top, as with Carlos Ghosn at Nissan, Rose Marie Bravo at Burberry, Clay Jones at Rockwell Collins, Ed Zander at Motorola, Terry Leahy at Tesco, Robert Louis Dreyfus at adidas, and Richard Teerlink at Harley-Davidson. All of these executives came into a difficult situation and spearheaded the laggard-to-leader turnaround.

In addition, the burgeoning business of private equity almost always involves bringing in new executive talent to lead turnarounds. As we discuss later in this chapter, many of the key leadership capabilities of breakout leaders tap into such underlying characteristics as open-mindedness, creativity, and inspiration, attitudes that are often in short supply among long-time CEOs and other senior executives, who mistakenly believe that they have seen and heard everything and therefore know everything there is to know about their business.

An *expanding-horizons* breakout involves a huge strategic leap, and the leaders who have been successful with it are almost always outward-looking, bold, and energizing. These leaders not only need to be able to see opportunities, but also must be capable of formulating a plan to exploit those opportunities. In some ways they are also entrepreneurial, as they are attempting to expand the scope of their businesses.

There is some risk that these leaders will be too confident of their abilities and fall into some of the traps that we have identified elsewhere—arrogance, inability to learn new things, and underestimating the difficulties of making it all work.[2] The balance of leadership capabilities that our research has identified as critical for breakout strategy tackles these challenges directly.

Finally, because *shifting-shape* breakouts are so unusual, their leaders tend to be exceptional. As we discussed earlier, there are not as many shape-shifting breakouts as there are other types simply because leaders of large companies with often-dominant positions seldom wish to accept the inherent uncertainty that comes with change and transformation. These leaders are truly forward-thinking, and many of the leadership techniques we describe in this chapter can be of particular value to would-be shape shifters. In addition, each of the leadership capabilities at the heart of breakout strategy—while no doubt unlikely to be equally abundant in all such leaders—is of paramount importance in shape-shifting breakouts because of the innate challenges of this strategy.

Leadership for Breakout Strategy

Transformational activities cannot occur without a dynamic and focused leadership. Breakout strategy starts with leadership, but what precisely does this mean? The answer is that breakout leaders need to possess, at least to some degree, a set of distinct but complementary capabilities that enable them to identify, craft, and implement breakout strategy. Our research, as well as years of working with senior executives, points to five key leadership capabilities that every company needs; we call these *positive*, *negative*, *conceptual*, *creative*, and *relational capabilities* (Figure 9.1).

The central part of this chapter describes each of these capabilities, provides illustrations of how each plays out in breakout, and offers techniques and insights on how to enhance your own capability level. As we discussed in Chapter 4, tools such as capital accumulation are important enablers of successful breakout leadership. But the most effective breakout leaders also have the

Capabilities	Associated Behavior	Significance
Positive	Visioning. Articulating. Inspiring. Persuading. Deciding. Resolving. Selling.	Positive projection of the future, inspires confidence, belief, and commitment.
Negative	Waiting. Listening. Thinking. Testing. Feeling. Absorbing. Debating.	Enables engagement with complex issues and maintenance of focus when uncertainty is rife, preventing dispersal into unfocused activity.
Conceptual	Analyzing. Auditing. Appraising. Planning. Researching. Theorizing.	Well grounded and realizable strategies follow from the application of abstract reasoning and the evaluation of evidence.
Creative	Experimenting. Interacting. Harmonizing. Patterning. Imagining. Questioning.	Enterprise and innovation follow from creative engagement with market and other business imperatives.
Relational	Communicating. Empathizing. Building solidarity. Reaching out. Giving. Demonstrating competence.	Trust, confidence, and reputational gain are the products of relational excellence. Each is vital to the effective management of networks and alliances.

Figure 9.1 Breakout Leadership Capabilities

balance of capabilities needed to see and to seize market opportunities and advantages.

When most of us think of the characteristics of a leader, we think first of the inspired and inspirational element—the person knows his or her own mind and knows how to win others over to his or her view of the world. This is absolutely right, and these traits are vital elements of leadership. We group them together under the collective label *positive capabilities.* Positive capabilities enable transformational qualities such as vision or direction setting and value demarcation. From a transactional point of view, they facilitate behaviors such as the raising of financial capital and the effective execution of performance and control mechanisms.

The flip side of positive capabilities is a less-explored area of leadership. The management literature and the world of business are poorer places as a consequence. The old saying, "The quiet ones are the ones to watch" holds true, and leaders such as media-shy Sir Terry Leahy of Tesco and introverted Michael Dell are great examples. The term *negative capabilities* can be misconstrued: it does not refer to aptitudes that can lead you astray or cause you to make bad judgment calls; instead, it involves the ability to deal with negative situations, people, and contexts. People with negative capabilities listen and watch and can anticipate or spot problems and fix them before they escalate into a crisis. These people have the ability to live with paradox and ambiguity, protecting change initiatives despite pressures to the contrary. This is an essential ingredient of any leadership system.

As you can imagine, there are few people out there who fully embody both of these somewhat paradoxical types of capabilities. The concerned listener who is also a fast-talking salesperson is as rare as the decisive, action-oriented boss who takes the time to contemplate his or her actions and consider different approaches. Yet our research has found consistently that many of the most impressive breakout leaders, people such as Carlos Ghosn (at Nissan) and Ed Zander (at Motorola), consciously try to combine the best of both sets of capabilities. No one will score 100 percent on both dimensions, but paying attention to the yin and yang of positive and negative capabilities to make sure that one never completely dominates the other is critical.

Conceptual capabilities are found in people who believe in mastery of existing systems, processes, and procedures and standardized organizational behaviors. These traits lead an individual to pursue an evidence-based approach to leadership and to shy away from gut instinct-based risk. Calling such people technocrats or number crunchers would be an unfair assessment; a fairer assessment might be to see them as calculated risk takers.

Creative capabilities are the polar opposite. These are found in people who think outside the box each and every day, who believe instinctively that success can happen only if you jump in at the deep end before you know if you can even swim. Serial entrepreneurs such as Sir Richard Branson spring to mind. These people are idea maestros, but usually they are either not interested in or not aware of the specifics involved in realizing their schemes. They need people with conceptual capabilities to deliver on their vision, and conceptual people need the ideas people!

The final set of leadership capabilities is relational. None of the preceding types matters much without the skills and aptitude required to build trust and confidence and relate to people. *Relational capabilities* extend across a company—downward to every worker and across to your managerial peers. They reach along a value chain, embracing suppliers, distributors, and outsourcing partners. They shape the business's interaction with investors, analysts, and regulators, and, of course, they define customers' perception of and interaction with the enterprise. They are by nature multifaceted and complex. A leader with well-developed relational capabilities instinctively knows the importance of understanding and committing to systemic relationships and organizational purpose and can connect with individuals effortlessly, even without extensive contact.

If you pause for a moment and reflect on these five capabilities, you will realize two things. First, it is unusual for any one person to possess all five capabilities. How many people do you know who are articulate and inspirational, attentive and patient, analytical and methodical, inventive and enterprising, and empathetic and trustworthy? A rare few come close. Michael Dell, despite his natural shyness, meets many of the criteria. Herb Kelleher, cofounder of Southwest Airlines, was best known for his positive and relational capabilities but did have elements of the other competencies. But even these corporate legends realized their limitations and surrounded themselves with people who provided complementary capabilities. Colleen Barrett, who succeeded Herb Kelleher as president of Southwest, had been with the company from the early days, and had regularly tempered Kelleher's natural exuberance and shored up his deficiencies in negative and conceptual capabilities. This is one of the main reasons that these leaders will be remembered long after most others have faded into obscurity.

In Chapter 8, we described what happened during Bob Ayling's failed tenure as CEO of British Airways (BA). The five-capabilities approach is a useful prism through which to look at what went wrong at BA under Ayling's leadership. He had positive capabilities externally in that he could project a vision to investors and inspire confidence in the market. Internally, he was singularly unable to inspire confidence, belief, and commitment among his workers.

He was weak on negative capabilities, being poor at listening, absorbing, and testing. This was evident not only in his confrontational management of industrial relations disputes, but also in his corporate rebranding and tailfin redesign, which did not sit well with many customers. In the area of conceptual capabilities, the former lawyer was clearly strong. Interestingly, he was also strong in creative capabilities, being a visionary who was not afraid to take risks. This combination is not easy to find and was probably a major reason for his rise to the top in the first place. Finally, in relational capabilities, as with positive capabilities, he was good externally but less successful at building trust, solidarity, and confidence within the company.

What does all this tell us? It indicates that a leader such as Bob Ayling needs people around him who complement his personality and style, plugging the gaps in his own leadership capabilities. He needs top-management team members from whom he can take advice and criticism and whom he could respect and treat as equals.

This did not emerge at Bob Ayling's BA. Instead, he surrounded himself with competent and clever people, but not with people who were strong on negative capability or internal positive and relational capabilities. He brought in outsiders, often with little airline experience and usually with no ability to connect with BA employees. In short, he fashioned an imbalanced top-management team, one that was highly competent in areas such as analysis, planning, and vision creation but very weak in listening to or absorbing stakeholder needs, internal problem solving, building solidarity among the disparate elements of BA, and reaching out to disaffected people and groups (such as trade unions). A company run by an imbalanced leadership team always will run into problems sooner or later, and is unlikely to survive to create long-term value and shareholder return.

The second thing you should recognize from the five-capabilities approach is your own personal shortcomings. Hard as it may be to admit, you can't read a list like that found in Figure 9.1 without recognizing your own strengths and weaknesses. Acting on them is a different matter. Bob Ayling clearly did not do so, but Herb Kelleher did. The leadership lesson is clear: identify your deficiencies in capabilities, accept them, and shore them up by leveraging the complementary capabilities of others. A top-leadership team should lead by design, with a clear intent to combine all five capabilities successfully so that they can be deployed in the formulation and implementation of breakout strategy. In this way, the leadership team can ensure that the company breaks out of its industry context rapidly and decisively to establish fast-track business growth.

In the following sections, we discuss each of these five leadership capabilities and how they can enhance breakout opportunities and breakout strategies. There is no one leadership "style" or "approach" that works in all situations. One thing we can be sure of is that the corporate leader who follows an unnatural style because he or she sees others adopting such an approach successfully is almost certainly doomed to failure. Each leader must be true to him- or herself. It's not about style; it's really about capabilities. Breakouts never happen without strong leadership, and our framework of breakout leadership capabilities drives this point home.

Positive Capabilities

Of the five capabilities, in many ways this one is the easiest to understand. However, demonstrating positive capabilities is much more difficult. Consider Paul Pressler, who took over as CEO of the megaretailer Gap in 2002. A big part of his turnaround strategy was to install world-class management processes in a company that had had a more entrepreneurial style for years. Thus, rather than sit with clothing designers and debate what he did and didn't like (something that actually is not that unusual in the fashion business), Pressler asked questions that forced people to consider basic business principles, such as what the consumer did and didn't like. While this would not be revolutionary in many companies, to be sure, an emphasis on what the marketplace was demanding, as opposed to what the internal staff wanted the marketplace to demand, was an essential mind-shift.

Unfortunately, Gap's attempt to break out under Pressler so far has not been successful. Fashion retailing requires having fashion taste, making the right design calls, and staying hot in the minds of consumers, and Gap has yet to increase its capabilities in these areas. This example is instructive because it indicates that positive capabilities in the absence of execution often are not enough.

Two quick side notes: first, the idea that a company knows more than its customers almost always leads to failure. While there are occasions when customers need to be educated on what a provider can do for them (this was true in the earliest days of fiber optics, for example), most of the time this attitude arises from the leadership's arrogance and narrow-mindedness. Many high-tech companies have fallen into this trap over the years, including Motorola (believing that customers preferred its analog mobile phones when digital technology was beginning to take off), Cabletron (assuming that its customers wanted to buy technology as a product, not as a solution to their networking problems), and Iridium (the satellite communications company that assumed that customers would flock to its gee-whiz technology despite outrageous prices and inherent equipment limitations). Would-be breakout leaders will do well to dispel such notions right from the beginning.

Second, as we discussed in Chapter 8, the ability to manage change effectively is an essential part of the breakout leader's capability set. Despite the hard slogging, many of Paul Pressler's changes at Gap were long overdue—they really were a prerequisite for change. In much the same way, other recent turnarounds have put breakout CEOs front and center in leading change. And this is where positive capabilities—the ability to recognize when something is not working, the internal strength of character to resolve to do something about it, and the capacity to articulate and inspire people to follow this lead—do play a big role. Mark Hurd, the breakout leader at Hewlett-Packard (HP) who has been quickly transforming that former laggard to a new leadership position in information technology and consumer electronics, puts it this way:

> *When things weren't right in the past, they were fixed. If things aren't right now, we've got to fix them. If that's countercultural to the past few years, so be it. We're just trying to run the fundamentals of a sound business.*[3]

A leader's ability to inspire, to set a vision that others care about, is among the most important positive capabilities. Breakout leaders have primary responsibility for the visioning process described in Chapter 5. Furthermore, central to any inspirational leader are the highest of ethical values. We need not be reminded of what can happen to an organization when its senior leaders allow their ethical compass to go off kilter, even when the organization has many other positive, perhaps even stellar, attributes. Breakout involves, by definition, considerable change and transformation. It is not a status-quo event, so there are many balls in the air and competing demands to address. In this environment, it is essential for a leader to remain vigilant and to actively promote ethical conduct and values. In truth, when the pressure is on, there are temptations (think WorldCom), and the most effective breakout leaders channel their awareness of the inherent risk into real vigilance.

Breakout leaders also must build commitment to change in their organizations. The reason why many companies don't embrace breakout, but rather remain on the sidelines or as laggards, is that their leaders allow it to happen. As Ed Zander, the CEO of Motorola who is in the midst of a classic laggard-to-leader breakout, puts it, leaders often don't "want to shake things up; they prefer to remain in their comfort zone." He relates how the demise of many of the companies in the old Route 128 high-tech corridor around Boston—DEC, Wang Labs, Honeywell, and Compaq—was due to their unwillingness to reinvent themselves in the face of changing markets.

We have demonstrated that changing markets create huge opportunities for breakout—whether for *true originals* jumping into a new market space, *wave riders* migrating refined value propositions and business models, or even *conquistadores* actively seeking to restructure markets—but nothing can happen without leaders who are willing and able to see the opportunity. This is a lot of what we mean by positive capabilities—leaders who can both articulate an inspirational vision and mobilize resources toward realizing that vision.

For laggard-to-leader breakouts, CEOs such as Ed Zander focus on getting people to believe in themselves again, restoring the company's positive culture and confidence, and generating commitment among managers and employees alike. Zander crafted a card that all employees now carry to remind them of what the company stands for and what the commitment is: customers, innovation, principles ("doing the right thing"), one Motorola ("cooperation and not 'warring tribes' "), and performance ("I'm here to win").[4] Breakout leaders don't just choose a direction and expect people to follow; they inspire others to want exactly the same thing. The best breakout leaders have followers, it's true, but those followers have completely embraced the same vision as their leader. Any way you look at it, this is a pretty powerful combination for change.

Accountability is another key attribute of successful breakout leaders. To generate confidence among internal and external stakeholders, an organization must back up what it promises to do with real actions. This was a big theme in the discussion of how to deliver the promise of a value proposition, but for leaders it goes even further than that. Accountability means that there is a performance orientation at work, that people know that there are high expectations that must be met, and that leaders hold their people to those expectations.

It is hard to imagine how a breakout strategy can take hold in an organization that cannot back up its talk with meaningful action. For example, one of CEO Mike McGavick's first priorities when he joined Safeco Insurance in 2001 was to instill a renewed sense of responsibility into management and employees after the Seattle-based property and casualty insurance company had chalked up five straight years of declining return on equity. He said it was essential to "hold the people and their organizations accountable for what we say we will do. We develop a plan together, people go off and do their work, then it's my job to make sure there's a pattern of accountability to that and a process of discovering results relative to the promises."[5] This was a laggard-to-leader breakout, but there is no doubt that a focus on accountability is a key positive leadership capability in all types of breakout.

Finally, an important characteristic of breakout leaders with positive capabilities is their resolve in seeking out new opportunities. These leaders are not afraid to make decisions, even tough decisions that entail a nontrivial degree of risk. Such was the case at CEMEX under CEO Lorenzo Zambrano, who spearheaded the classic conquistador breakout that we profiled in earlier chapters. From a base in Mexico, the company has expanded around the world through mergers and acquisitions. As Zambrano puts it, "If there's an opportunity, either you grab it or you let go. If you let go, you don't grow."[6] Resolve in the face of tough decisions is a key part of breakout, and positive capabilities are essential to this. We will return to the challenge of seeking and capitalizing on opportunities later in this chapter when we consider how the other leadership capabilities play a role as well.

Negative Capabilities

Negative capabilities[7] are perhaps the most difficult for executives to understand. How can a leader be negative? Isn't "negative thinking" one of the best ways to fall out of favor in most companies?

Well, unbridled negative thinking is not ideal, to be sure, but can you imagine an organization that contains only positive thinkers? Where will the debate, the challenge, come from? How will an organization be able to adapt to change if no one is asking the tough questions? Is breakout even possible when the entire executive team speaks with one voice on all issues, even in private?

We believe that the most successful organizations are the ones in which there is open discussion and analysis. Many of the famous failures of the last five years—Enron, Tyco, WorldCom, Vivendi, and Parmalat—were characterized by a remarkable degree of unanimity at the top. The executives of these companies really believed that they had it all figured out; as a result, there was little real debate and analysis. In particular, the CEOs in these companies were able to take advantage of the culture of silence to make decisions that ended up costing shareholders billions of dollars and employees their livelihoods.

In contrast, breakout leaders pick up on emerging trends, see opportunities when others see problems, fear not acting more than they fear acting, and have the balanced confidence to lead. This latter point is an important one, and one that is not always fully understood. Leadership certainly requires a significant degree of confidence, yet there are many examples—particularly in recent history—of leaders whose confidence turned into arrogance. Leaders such as Jeffrey Immelt of General Electric (GE), Alan Lafley of Procter & Gamble (P&G), and Ed Zander of Motorola are not afraid to make big changes to their businesses, in part because they have the confidence to see a reasonable picture of the future and to energize others to seek that future. However, unlike Jeffrey Skilling at Enron, Martin Glass at Rite-Aid, and Maurice Saatchi at the old Saatchi & Saatchi—each of whom also saw a future, but one with unlimited potential that provoked them to unbridled aggressiveness that was devoid of balance—these leaders are aware of their own and their organizations' limitations. Ed Zander calls this "confidence without arrogance." There is a fine line between appropriate confidence and over-the-top arrogance, and the best breakout leaders inherently understand that they can't cross that line.

Some of the most compelling examples of great breakout leadership in recent years—Michael Dell at Dell Computer, Andy Grove at Intel, Margaret Whitman at eBay, Herb Kelleher at Southwest Airlines, and Lou Gerstner at IBM, to name a few—have precisely this type of balance. Anyone who has ever met any of these CEOs and now former CEOs certainly would not say that they didn't believe in themselves and their companies, but at the same time, few would ever call them arrogant. They started with an understanding that their organizations were vulnerable and that things sometimes do go wrong, and this humility fired up a culture that was all about excellence in ideas and execution.

Take Michael Dell, for instance. Almost 10 years ago, when his company was not quite the powerhouse it has become, he explained his philosophy in an interview in *Industry Week* magazine:

> *You have to be self-critical to succeed. If you sat in on our management meetings, you would find that we are a remarkably self-critical bunch with a disdain for complacency that motivates us. We are always looking to do things more efficiently. We are 99 percent focused on what is going to happen and what could change the business in the future. We ask ourselves what are the risks to the business, what could go wrong.*[8]

Why is this significant? Because this type of self-analysis and questioning sends the entire management team the clear message that overconfidence is out and careful attention to reality is in. Breakout leaders benefit from this mind-set because it helps to keep them grounded and, in fact, may help to generate new ideas about what is possible if the logic is applied to competitors. Remarkably, Michael Dell tells the same story today, an indication that the "balanced confidence" approach to breakout pays dividends:

> *We think about failure all the time. We've been able to simulate failure in our minds before it happens and avoid extinction or disastrous consequences because we've thought through all the bad things that could happen.*[9]

Negative capabilities are not limited to open-mindedness and adaptability, as important as these characteristics are for breakout success. Organizational life is characterized by significant ambiguity, paradox, and change. Managers and employees look to their leaders for guidance on how to operate in such a world. The best leaders are able to cope with anxiety-provoking situations, with uncertainty, and with resource constraints. Instead of jumping to quick and often not-well-thought-out solutions to problems, they are comfortable enough with ambiguity to promote testing, evaluating, and absorbing behaviors.[10]

World-class negotiators have understood this logic for years—often the best response is to wait out your opponent, learn more, ask questions, and look for answers that go beyond the obvious. When Michael Dell pushes his leaders to ask the tough questions, he is implicitly saying that the answers are not obvious; we need to listen and understand better, and if we do so, we will be in a better position to act when the time comes.

Finally, how do you know whether the leaders in your organization are capable of doing what we are advocating here—asking tough questions, displaying open-mindedness, learning from mistakes, and listening carefully to others? One of the efforts we have undertaken with a variety of organizations in the United States, Europe, and Canada is to develop an "early-warning system" that, in part, addresses precisely this question.[11] Through a series of carefully validated questions, we are able to assess the extent to which managers display these skill sets and suggest areas for improvement if there are shortfalls. Here are some examples:

- To what extent is your management team open-minded in seeking answers to the problems you have?
- Do you do a good job of learning from past mistakes to avoid their recurrence?
- Do you sometimes rely on solutions from the past even when the challenges you face are different?
- Do you expect everyone on the management team to express 100 percent agreement with a strategy?

- Does your management team do a good job at not just accepting the surface answer but pushing for more information when required?

These questions are part of a larger battery of questions that make up the early-warning system for breakout strategy. They identify whether a management team is well positioned to take advantage of strategic opportunities that offer breakout possibilities. It is critically important to understand that no matter how great the breakout opportunity may be "in theory," it simply can't be pursued successfully without world-class leadership. Breakout strategy requires breakout leaders, and the often-overlooked set of negative capabilities that we have discussed here is an important part of what is required.

Conceptual Capabilities

In addition to having the mind-set of asking tough questions and avoiding overconfidence, where else can leaders who are contemplating breakout turn for guidance? One of the most promising opportunities, we believe, arises from applying the discipline of *questioning assumptions.* The assumptions that companies adopt—and assumptions about customers, markets, competitors, technology, and people, among other things, are the underlying drivers of strategy—often turn out to be wrong. Even if the assumptions were reasonable when they were first adopted, the world changes, markets change, and products evolve. When companies' assumptions are kept in place beyond their useful life, the result is vulnerabilities that savvy competitors can exploit. In fact, many of the breakout strategies we have described succeeded because the breakout company's competitors stuck with old assumptions that no longer made sense.

Consider these examples. Leaders at eBay, a true original, developed a value proposition and business model that cleverly took advantage of limiting assumptions in industries as varied as auctioning, newspapers, and retail. While not all brick-and-mortar companies have fallen prey to Internet start-ups, eBay is the perfect example of a company that developed a taking-by-storm breakout designed to take full advantage of the incumbent industry players' constraints. More recently, true-original Google shot to fame by challenging the assumption that an operating system and an office suite of software were all that PC users needed to organize their work.

Revolutionaries are probably the classic example of a breakout strategy that is all about breaking a marketplace's established rules and assumptions. We've already discussed how The Body Shop turned the traditional cosmetics business on its head, challenging its most fundamental assumptions about what to sell and where to sell it. And Boston Beer Company, which we introduced in Chapter 2, is a great story of breakout as well. Founder Jim Koch put to the test two long-held beliefs—that foreign imports were necessarily of superior quality, and that an American company could not produce high-quality beer. With those assumptions put to rest, Koch described his ultimate goal to us:

> *My big goal is to change the way the world, Americans included, thinks about our beer, in the same way that people like Robert Mondavi and Jess Jackson and all those wonderful wine makers in California over the last 40 years have begun to change the way the world thinks about American wine. . . . That's why I export Sam Adams. It is not a lot of volume, you don't make any money on it, but it's the beginning statement of the paragraph that a small American brewery like Sam Adams can actually make arguably the best portfolio beer in the world.*

Both types of laggard-to-leader breakout also can capitalize on incorrect or inappropriate assumptions. The laggards often find that the incorrect assumptions are ones that they themselves, not their competitors, have made. The most effective leaders see that their assumptions have gone stale and seek to rejuvenate the entire company with a new set of guiding principles. Carlos

Ghosn at Nissan is a perfect example. When Ghosn came to Nissan, the company had been through several terrible years and was falling further and further behind not only Toyota, but Honda as well. As we described in Chapter 8, Ghosn was analytical, demanding, engaging, and logical in his turnaround plan. He is probably an example of that rare leader who possesses all five capabilities in abundance, but nothing could have happened if he had been unable to come up with a realistic formula for turnaround.

Expanding-horizons breakouts often begin by identifying faulty assumptions. For Zara, it was the assumption that the lead time between the design of a fashion line and its delivery to stores must be measured in months, not weeks (or even days). For Starbucks, it was the assumption that in Europe, high-quality coffee could be found only in small, one-of-a-kind cafés with inconsistent service and delivery and was not subject to world-class consistency and efficiency. For Mittal Steel, it was the assumption that sovereign borders limited consolidation opportunities because of nationalistic sentiment and tradition when, in fact, the global steel industry was ripe for just this type of breakout strategy.

Finally, successful shape shifters do what few other companies do—they identify the outdated assumptions in their markets and develop new approaches that capitalize on the resulting new opportunities. It is this type of breakout that shows just how difficult it can be for leaders to confront assumptions with an action orientation. It is so difficult that a company usually requires new leadership before it can begin the task.

This was certainly the case at IBM in the 1990s, when the former world beater was standing pat with the same old strategy in the face of a sharp erosion in mainframe pricing and the rise of new technology (client-server architecture) that was challenging IBM's supremacy in the data center. It wasn't until IBM booked an $8 billion loss and faced a rapidly deteriorating cash position that the board moved toward new leadership—Lou Gerstner.

When Gerstner and his team looked at the situation with fresh eyes, it was clear that some of the underlying assumptions behind

IBM's strategy had run their course. Mainframes were not going to be the engine of future profitability and growth as they had been in years past. A focus on sales at the expense of tight cost control was no longer a sustainable strategy. And competitors had caught up with, and in some instances surpassed, what IBM could offer to customers. Gerstner's solution included superior execution and continuous prodding of the company's culture to enable faster decision making, but the real breakout came when he decided to blow up those long-held but increasingly dangerous assumptions.

IBM adopted a strategy focused on being a global integrated solutions provider, leveraging the company's scope, scale, and customer base and distinguishing itself from the rest of the technology industry by pursuing a "best of breed" approach to product sourcing. As Gerstner said in reflecting on the challenge, "My view is that the company had been so successful for so long it stopped comparing itself with competitors and started gauging itself by internal measures. That's a recipe for trouble."[12]

How can executives and other leaders in an organization go about this questioning of assumptions that is so important for breakout? There are two steps: First, it is critical to know what to look for, and second, there is a process that can not only identify the dangerous assumptions but also increase the chances that you will do something about them. Our research and our consulting work with more than 40 companies around the world on this topic have allowed us to identify the following five strategic assumptions that are most likely to lead to problems at some point in time and that create opportunities for breakout if leaders know what to look for:

- Have companies in your industry settled on one dominant principle or model of competition, even though that might not be the only way to play the game? For example, in the 1980s, General Motors spent literally billions of dollars to increase automation in its factories because it believed that low-cost manufacturing was the key to success. The company was wrong on two counts. First, styling, branding, design, reputation and image, technology, and managerial competence are all major factors that lead to success or failure in the automobile industry. And second, a company cannot achieve low-cost manufacturing simply by replacing people with machines. The Toyota production system—which focuses not only on automation, but also on people skills, motivation and training, just-in-time delivery, supply-chain efficiencies, and several other factors—shows that removing people from factories pales in comparison with tackling the problem in a more comprehensive way. In fact, a big part of Toyota's initial breakout when it entered the U.S. and European markets with low-cost cars was due to its refusal to adopt the dominant assumption that influenced not only GM but also Ford, Chrysler, and Rover, among others, at the time.

- Are competitors and potential competitors assuming that what has worked for them in the past continues to be what they need to do today? In many ways, this is the archetypical assumption that breakout companies look for in a marketplace when they are seeking opportunities to exploit incumbents' weaknesses. Big improvers in particular look to this assumption for insight into how to differentiate themselves from the pack. Bill Clinton in the 1992 Democratic primaries is an example. Not everyone remembers that the forty-second president of the United States was considered a long shot for his party's nomination in the months leading up to the primaries. There were bigger names (Senator Edward Kennedy and Governor Mario Cuomo), and there were established power bases with traditional Democratic Party values that favored these candidates. What Clinton saw—and his competitors did not—was that these traditional party values had lost at the polls for 12 years. Calling himself a "new Democrat" and placing himself firmly in the political center, candidate Clinton became President Clinton by breaking with traditional views of what a Democratic candidate should look like.

- Are your competitors' ideas of what your customer needs based on limited models or experience? Incumbent players often narrow their vision of what customers want to what they typically deliver to those customers, without considering the possibility that a new value proposition is just what these customers have been waiting for. While this can create opportunities for any type of breakout, successful expanding-horizons breakouts often take full advantage of these narrow competitive mind-sets. For example, when Chairman Howard Shultz and then-CEO Orrin Smith began their aggressive campaign to establish Starbucks stores throughout Europe and Asia, they were not only leveraging their own capabilities in high-quality coffee and retail customer experience, but also capitalizing on a narrow view of customer needs that prevailed in most of the countries they entered. This narrow view may have had different characteristics in different countries, but virtually none of the new markets that Starbucks entered had coffee retailers that offered not just coffee but a branded coffee-drinking experience. The reputation of the brand and the quality of the coffee were important differentiators for Starbucks in its global breakout as competitors discovered that customers were attracted to these attributes of Starbucks' value proposition. The fact that competitors could not easily replicate the brand in particular has made the breakout all the more successful.
- Are players in the industry focusing on the right competitors; in particular, are they paying attention to newcomers? In the heat of competitive battle, some companies become so attuned to their traditional competitors that they leave themselves vulnerable to new entrants that come to market with a new value proposition and a new business model that change the face of competition. This opportunity can arise in any type of breakout. It is easy to see how taking-by-storm breakouts, almost by definition, blindside incumbents. But the same impact is also possible when companies are expanding their horizons (e.g., who knew Lakshmi Mittal until

recently?), shifting shape (e.g., did winemakers expect Gallo to move up in reputation and quality?), or moving from laggard to leader (e.g., what legacy carriers anticipated the challenge posed by AirAsia or Ryanair?).

- Have the companies in a target marketplace given enough thought to the ways in which their entire industry could be transformed suddenly or even become irrelevant? Competitors with static business models are sending signals to breakout leaders that opportunity exists. Sometimes companies are slow to see the changes coming, as was the case with Fruit of the Loom after the North American Free Trade Agreement (NAFTA) eliminated trade barriers in North America in 1995. It was next to impossible to compete on costs once tariffs on clothes were removed, necessitating a new business model that emphasized either innovation or outsourcing. Other times the preponderance of static business models creates opportunities for niche players. For example, Boston Beer Company, the maker of award-winning Sam Adams beer, started with the notion of producing a high-quality beer that would bypass the Anheuser Busches of the world. While no one would say that the big-time mass-market beer makers are doing poorly, their static business models left open an opportunity that a revolutionary breakout such as Boston Beer was able to take advantage of.

These assumptions can best be analyzed with what might be called a *strategic assumption analysis.* The process involves eliciting from each member of the management team the primary assumptions that the member believes lie behind the company's strategies and those of its competitors. Then, through facilitated discussion, the results are compared and contrasted. Two insights typically emerge: First, different people tend to identify different assumptions, and second, points of vulnerability and points of opportunity are identified. The best breakout leaders will use these discussions to push people toward a deeper understanding of the marketplace and their company's position within it. Doing so encourages involvement—which is critical for subsequent implementation—and bypasses ad hoc analysis in favor of a disciplined approach. In many ways, this is the essence of what we mean by conceptual capabilities. Analyzing, appraising, evaluating, planning—these are all essential skill sets of successful breakout leaders.

Creative Capabilities

It should be clear from our discussion throughout this book that there is a strong element of creativity and innovation in successful breakout strategies. Breakout strategies really are breakout ideas that are expertly executed. For example, Boston Beer founder Jim Koch had just left the Boston Consulting Group and was looking for an opportunity when he turned to the beer business. Actually, this wasn't such an out-of-the-box notion because his father, his grandfather, and even his great-grandfather all had been brewmasters. What was original was his idea that he could brew a high-quality premium beer at a facility in the United States. The fact that microbreweries were barely a blip in the market at that point is relevant, but so is Koch's insight:

> *Mass domestic beers, which are very well made, are consistent, inexpensive, perfectly designed for the mass market. There is no point in trying to compete with them. It would be like trying to sell french-fries next to McDonald's. If that is what you want to do, you can't do that better, but then the high-end of the market was owned by imports and they were skunky from the green and clear bottles, they were stale. Most of them weren't great beers where they came from. So there was an opportunity. . . . I knew I could make great beer here in the United States. There is no physical impediment to that. I can make beer in the United States and I knew from my consulting that if you have a truly better product, you have a viable business.*

What Jim Koch did was come up with an idea—one that no one had really had before—and execute it. This was the classic revolutionary breakout strategy in action.

With commentators arguing that the knowledge economy has been replaced by the creativity economy,[13] CEOs such as Alan Lafley at P&G and Jeffrey Immelt at GE are increasingly leveraging their creative capabilities. Immelt notes that "creativity and imagination applied in a business context is innovation." Soon after Lafley took on the top job at P&G in 2000, he began to invest heavily in his design team, quadrupling the number of team members even while laying people off in other areas of the business. Increasing resources (including hiring the best and the brightest from creative companies around the world), combined with listening to and watching customers more closely (to determine their "unmet, unarticulated" needs), made a significant contribution to P&G's product innovation and customer satisfaction, leading to a 58 percent rise in the company's stock price within three years of Lafley's taking over as CEO. By 2006, P&G had entered the top 20 of *Fortune* magazine's most profitable companies in the world. For his part in this transformation, in 2006 Lafley was named one of the best CEOs in America in a survey of analysts and portfolio managers at more than 400 money management companies, conducted by *Institutional Investor* magazine (Immelt also made the list).

Whether the product involved is consumer goods (GE and P&G), beer (Boston Beer), wine (Gallo), cement (CEMEX), or steel (Mittal), breakout leaders have the ability to imagine something different. They encourage others in their own organizations to seek new answers. They look for patterns among a myriad of factors to see what is emerging and what is changing. And they interact with people far and wide to try to identify the changes as they are happening. We've already discussed how the conceptual leader can question the assumptions of competitor companies when seeking opportunities, but the creative leader can do even more. The best breakout leaders are creative coaches, promoting innovative thought and action in their organizations.

There is certainly some degree of art to all this, but our experience in working with senior executives also suggests a more structured approach to seeing opportunities in the marketplace, opportunities that might lead to breakout strategies. In fact, we have used a set of probing questions to help management teams expand their thinking and encourage others to do so as well.[14] These questions are aids to engendering creativity and innovation, and while there can be no guarantee that such an exercise will lead automatically to breakout ideas, it seems clear that just sitting on the sidelines and waiting for that "Aha!" experience is a rather low-probability approach.

The first question we ask is, "To what other uses could this be put?" The *this* could be your technology, your processes and systems, your physical assets, your people, or your core competence. In some ways the question asks, "How can you leverage your core competence?" but it does so in a way that all managers can understand. Expanding-horizons breakouts in particular can be jump-started with this question. Starbucks, Zara, McDonald's, and other retail breakouts all were based on leveraging a good idea in new places.

"What could we add to make it more valuable?" This is the second question to think about. At this point in this book, it is clear that the value proposition framework can be a perfect complement to this type of creative searching for new ideas, but the process has to be started, and that is where a leader's creative capabilities come in. Consider the following example. For a number of years, many credit cards offered an annual written summary of all a customer's expenditures, neatly arranged in categories. But the banks that offered customers this service never thought about ways to make it even more valuable. Why not send the written statement every quarter so that customers would have the data sooner? Why even use hard copy? The Internet is perfect for this. Why not make the data available via the Internet whenever customers want them? And why not organize the data on expenditures in a way that is automatically readable by your Quicken budgeting software? Well, the first company to introduce a credit card with all these features was Intuit, the maker of Quicken software. Companies in the bank-credit-card business certainly knew more about their customers than a software provider did, but it was the outsider that first came up with the best way to "make it more valuable."[15]

"What can we borrow and adapt to our needs?" This question is not about a copycat strategy—breakouts don't result from following the pack. What this question is getting at is the value of looking in other industries, sectors, or walks of life for ideas that you can apply—often with some adjustment—to your own marketplace. One of the classic stories of this type of behavior involves the time when the U.S. Marines and Wall Street traders visited each other's "work sites" to see what they could learn. What could these two groups have in common? It turns out that both are all about how to create structure and seek advantage in the midst of chaos.

Cirque de Soleil, the Canadian entertainment company, fueled its breakout by adapting traditional entertainment industry practices to business, including novelty, constant innovation, delighting customers, and sourcing talent on a global scale. And Alice Waters, the founder of the culinary mecca Chez Panisse in Berkeley, California, started a breakout not only for her own business but also for the entire high-end restaurant industry in the United States by relying on only organic products, purchased almost entirely from local purveyors. Where did the idea come from? Anyone familiar with culinary tradition in countries such as France, Italy, and Spain knows that organic farming and the use of organic ingredients were standard practice in those countries for years. Yet it wasn't until Alice Waters had the creative spark and passion to import this idea to America that the industry changed.

"How can we change the pattern or rearrange the process?" This question implicitly recognizes that breakout strategies often disrupt established methods and business patterns. Thus, for example, revolutionaries almost by definition disrupt established ways of doing business in a marketplace, whether it is Jim Koch's high-quality beer made in America, Costco's Jim Sinegal selling high-end products to sophisticated consumers at a discount, or Anita Roddick at The Body Shop spearheading the use of natural ingredients in cosmetics. Each of these breakout leaders was a pattern disrupter.

One of the best examples is Howard Schultz at Starbucks. Where did people in the United States go to buy coffee before Starbucks revolutionized the industry? Corner coffee shops (as in the hit sitcom *Seinfeld*), Dunkin' Donuts, and coffee carts or convenience stores. And what did they pay? Perhaps 50 cents or a dollar. Starbucks changed the pattern of what buying a cup of coffee is all about. Now there are cool stores with music, soft lighting, and comfortable seats; richer coffee and more choice of espresso drinks; a brand that tells people that you are a discerning coffee drinker; and an atmosphere that is less about buying your coffee and moving on and more about enjoying the coffee-drinking experience. And the coffee now costs \$2, \$3, or even more. Leaders with creative capabilities are in a much stronger position to initiate breakout because they see things that others do not. And, just as important, they promote innovative thinking in their organizations.

There is one other benefit that accrues to breakouts built on creative capabilities—the sustainability of the breakout. Johnson & Johnson (J&J) in the cardiovascular stent market is a cautionary example. J&J went to market with the first stent—a small cylindrical device used in angioplasty procedures—in 1995 and quickly dominated the market. By 1996, J&J owned 90 percent of the market—an overwhelmingly successful taking-by-storm breakout. However, competitors were quick to respond, and because of the nature of the market—customers (especially cardiologists) had zero brand loyalty, were extremely demanding and powerful, and did not like suppliers to dictate terms to them—it was not difficult for these competitors to take share away from J&J. To sustain the breakout and overcome the brand-loyalty problem, it was absolutely necessary for J&J to continue to innovate and bring better products to market quickly.

Unfortunately, the innovative capability needed to meet these market demands was missing—the leaders of the division were going to the bank with profits from stents and paid little attention to developing the next generation of products. The result was predictable: the company's market share plummeted (actually to less than 10 percent by 1998), and the breakout was quashed prematurely. Without breakout leaders who had the creative capabilities that the market demanded (and remember, this means not only being creative yourself but promoting creativity and innovation in your entire organization), J&J was unable to sustain its breakout strategy. Once again, the theme is the same—successful breakout strategy requires breakout leaders.

Relational Capabilities

Relational capabilities help breakout leaders to execute their breakout strategies because they inherently support both people and culture, the two cornerstones of execution. For example, CEO Scott Edmonds has pushed the Florida-based retailer Chico's to become one of the leading chains in the United States by emphasizing culture and getting the job done. This required effective communication, the ability to empathize with others in the organization, and the ability to engender trust and confidence throughout the organization. In Chapter 8 we saw that both the socio and techno sides of change are necessary for success, and this is no different for breakout leaders.

Consider this example: with the rise of powerhouse big-box retailers such as Wal-Mart, Target, and Kohl's, traditional department stores have floundered. While Eddie Lampert's remake of Kmart and Sears is scoring some quick financial wins, the turnaround at JC Penney may be even more remarkable. Founded in 1902 by James Cash Penney, the retail chain adopted formal practices that defined its culture for years. Bosses always were addressed as "Mr.," "Miss," or "Mrs."; people at the head office rarely dressed in anything but the traditional suits and ties or dresses; and cubicles and offices were devoid of personal effects and remained sterile. These symbols of formality extended to the company's thinking, and it fell further and further behind, with outmoded stores and unchanging strategies in the face of massive industry restructuring.

All this began to change when Mike Ullman, only the second outsider in the company's history, became CEO in 2004. His first order of business was to shake up the culture and bring in new blood. First names were emphasized (he even developed a "Just Call Me Mike" campaign to reduce the resistance of long-time employees who were accustomed to the old ways). Casual attire became the norm. Restrictions on where employees could be seen at headquarters were removed. The company's famous art collection was sold and was replaced by photos of employees. While Penney's breakout involved much more than a change in culture (it also included newly designed stores, upgraded merchandising, and tighter financial controls), little would have happened if the troops hadn't been inspired to change. In just two years the stock was up 80 percent, and profits have more than doubled. Sometimes the relational capabilities displayed by CEOs such as Mike Ullman can make all the difference for breakout.

Relational capabilities are especially important when your breakout strategy takes you to new terrain with new people and systems. Whether this comes about through alliance, merger or acquisition, or some other method, the ability to bring people from other worlds into your orbit and help them to see the advantages of staying there is critical. Consider the breakout of Best Western, the U.S.-based hotel chain that has expanded throughout Europe and Asia in recent years. When we spoke to Tom Higgins, then president and CEO of the company, he told us how Best Western's mind-set had had to accommodate the vast array of talent that the company found in other countries:

> *I think the level of expertise has expanded. One of the things that we need to continually do better is not think that a global company has to be run, if you will, from a North American perspective. There is a huge amount of talent around the world that we try to tap into and capitalize on, even though these individuals are operating through our affiliates in Europe . . . [There are] tremendous technological skills, in our particular instance, in Italy . . . [and] especially in Scandinavia, so we try to take an*

> *approach that respects and learns from these managers. We also try to tap into the skills that our affiliates have within their organizations around the world.*[16]

The value of relational capabilities extends beyond their impact on employees. You are really building the reputation of the entire enterprise as you interact with a wide variety of stakeholders. Earlier, in Chapter 5, we emphasized that key stakeholders were at the heart of the visioning process. Here we can close the loop on that point by noting that it is breakout leaders who take primary responsibility for understanding the needs of those various stakeholders and seeking ways to accommodate them. Once again, the experience of Tom Higgins at Best Western is instructive. In building its affiliate network throughout Europe, the company had to learn how to address the sensibilities of longtime hoteliers who were used to traditional practices and had a deep commitment to their family name. Higgins understood that

> *It was a different country, a different culture, different business practices, and the consumer buying habits are different. So if you were learning how to do business in these places, if the cultural history of the hotel business in a place like Europe has been very, very family oriented, "our name's been on this building for the last 250 years" type of business model, for us to all of a sudden go in there and say, "Well, that's nice, but everywhere you have your name, we want our name" . . . that's kind of a hard sell, and so the people have to be educated as to what it means to be a branded piece of a much larger chain.*[17]

Note that Higgins didn't say that he was stepping away from a major part of the breakout strategy (the brand); he simply said that it was important to understand what these affiliates were thinking and feeling and to make the effort to convey the logic of the relationship. This is what winning breakout leaders do on a regular basis—being empathetic and reaching out are not about giving up the raison d'être of your strategy when stakeholders come at the problem in a different way; they are about doing everything you can to bring those stakeholders on board.

When we studied and consulted with these breakout leaders, we found that time and again, relational capabilities were critical to the success of their strategies. Expanding-horizons breakouts such as Best Western couldn't work unless leaders were sensitive to cultural differences and built talent in the new markets. And foreign-born executives were brought into senior leadership positions in companies such as PepsiCo and McKinsey as they expanded globally.

Companies going from laggards to leader could not possibly have made the transition without breakout leaders who could build confidence and trust among employees who may have felt beaten down after years of subpar performance. Carlos Ghosn made it a priority to convey real hope to the people at Nissan, spending countless hours in front of groups of employees and answering any questions they fired at him. He realized that honesty and empathy were necessary prerequisites to reenergizing the base. In many ways, this is the essence of political campaigns; it was something that Ronald Reagan excelled at as he spent the years after Ford's defeat in 1976 preparing the ground for his run in the 1980 Republican Party primaries.

Shape shifters are perhaps the most dependent on the relational capabilities of senior management. To move a company from a reasonably strong position to a new place, even when that place has the potential for exponential growth, is a scary assignment for any leader. Ensuring that you have the right people, motivated and energized, confident and trusting, to succeed at this transition is at the top of the "to-do" list. Thus companies such as P&G have expanded their search for talent to sources outside the company. Yahoo! brings in people steeped in entertainment industry know-how to help it manage the shift from Internet portal to entertainment hub. Gallo, Nokia, and IBM all faced huge resistance to change as they undertook their shifting-shape breakouts. In each of these instances, breakout leaders paid special attention to the relational issues that can make or break this strategy.

Even leaders of taking-by-storm breakouts—which because of the often entrepreneurial nature of these ventures are the least attuned to relational issues—frequently pay attention to building their internal and external reputations. In many ways, Cisco's treatment of the people it brought in through acquisition was the key to its success. In contrast to our example of J&J earlier in this chapter, Cisco made a concerted effort to retain the talent it had acquired, recognizing that sustaining its breakout required more than just technology and systems.

Overall, relational capabilities are important for breakout success regardless of the nature of the breakout strategy. As a result, all five of the key leader capabilities we have discussed here play a vital role in breakout success. In a very practical sense, companies should be screening managers at all levels of the organization for these capabilities and should use those screens as part of their leadership assessment programs. Similarly, leadership development programs should emphasize the acquisition of these capabilities. As we have argued throughout this chapter, breakout leaders are the key to breakout strategy, and there are concrete sets of skills or capabilities that characterize leaders of successful breakouts that all companies must attend to.

Conclusion

This last chapter takes us full circle to where we started in Chapter 1. Breakout strategy is all about the principles and practices that we have identified, through our research and consulting activities, as being the real differentiators between companies that are struggling and those that craft a winning strategy for their marketplace. In some ways, we have been describing how a company can go from an inferior position in the marketplace to one that is substantial and sometimes dominant.

The breakout strategy formula is important not only because it can provide guidance to leaders who are seeking to resurrect weak brands and positions, but also because it is fundamentally forward-looking and therefore is of value to managers and leaders in all sorts of organizations. And it is important because it documents what is needed to generate double-digit growth as a matter of course.

When one delves into the nuts and bolts of breakout strategy—as we have done here—an encouraging story emerges. There is not just one path to success. What is possible for any organization depends in part on that organization's existing market position, particularly in terms of its initial scope and industry standing. With this as a backdrop, however, many breakout strategies are possible, and, indeed, breakout leaders have implemented a wide variety of strategies. Throughout this book, using stories and vignettes as well as a set of battle-tested models and frameworks, we have sought to identify the major breakout patterns that companies have followed on their way to double-digit growth. We have paid special attention to specific techniques, ideas, and insights that can help you to apply the lessons of breakout to your own organizations.

The story ends with great optimism. There are many ways to get on the track to breakout. Which one makes sense for your company depends on what you have when you start, your ability to identify the shifts and discontinuities that give rise to big opportunities, and your discipline in constructing breakout strategies. And it depends on how well you can manage the capital-accumulation cycle to your advantage. Regardless of the type of breakout, however, the five essential practices that are at the heart of this book will remain paramount. All breakouts start with a realistic, stakeholder-driven visioning process. All breakouts require a compelling value proposition that will attract customers to your offerings. All breakouts must have a robust business model to deliver the promise you make to customers. All breakouts focus on both the socio and techno sides of execution. And all breakouts have at the helm breakout leaders who bring, in some measure, all five of the key leadership capabilities that we discussed in this chapter to transform their businesses. This is the blueprint for double-digit growth that has worked for many companies and may well hold the potential for your own breakout as well.

Endnotes

1 The term *rule breakers* was originally advanced in the strategic management literature by Gary Hamel in "Strategy as Revolution," *Harvard Business Review, July–August 1996, pp. 69–82.*

2 Sydney Finkelstein, *Why Smart Executives Fail*. New York: Portfolio, 2003.

3 Adam Lashinsky, "The Hurd Way: How a Sales-Obsessed CEO Rebooted HP," *Fortune*, April 17, 2006, p. 100.

4 The comments attributed to Ed Zander in this section are from a speech at the Tuck School of Business, March 28, 2006.

5 Colette A. Frayne and Robert E. Callahan, "Safeco CEO Mike McGavick on Leading a Turnaround," *Academy of Management Executive* 18(3):144, 2004.

6 Diane Lindquist, "From Cement to Services," *Chief Executive*, November 2002, www.findarticles.com/p/articles/mi_m4070/is_2002_Nov/ai_94145241.

7 The notion of "negative capabilities" was first developed in Peter Simpson, Robert French, and Charles E. Harvey, "Leadership and Negative Capability," *Human Relations* 55(10):1209–1226, 2002.

8 Michael A. Verespej, "Michael Dell's Magic," *Industry Week*, November 16, 1998, pp. 58–64.

9 Thomas A. Stewart and Louise O'Brien, "Execution without Excuses," *Harvard Business Review* 83(3):102–111, 2005.

10 Simpson, French, and Harvey, "Leadership and Negative Capability."

11 Sydney Finkelstein, "Seven Habits of Spectacularly Unsuccessful Executives and How to Spot Them," *Ivey Business Journal*, January–February 2004, pp. 1–6.

12 Tim Stevens, "Deja Blue," *Industry Week*, November 17, 1997, pp. 82–88.

13 "Get Creative! How to Build Innovative Companies," *BusinessWeek*, August 1, 2005.

14 Our thinking on the right questions to ask when trying to engender greater innovation and creativity has been influenced by Alex Osborn, *Your Creative Power*. Schaumburg, IL: Motorola University Press, 1991.

15 Eventually, of course, major credit-card-issuing banks replicated Intuit's features, but the point remains that opportunities for breakout depend heavily on leaders who can engender creativity and innovation in their organizations.

16 Interview with Tom Higgins, president and CEO of Best Western, conducted by Sydney Finkelstein, February 25, 2004.

17 Ibid.

CASES RESEARCHED FOR BREAKOUT STRATEGY[1]

adidas
Aer Lingus
AirAsia
Airbus
Air France–KLM
AOL
Apollo Group (The)
Apple
Award Technology
Bacardi
Bankers Trust
Beiersdorf
Best Western International
Bill Clinton
Bob Dylan
Body Shop (The)
Boston Beer Company
Boston Red Sox
BP
Bridgestone
British Airways (BA)
Burberry
Carnegie Steel
CEMEX
Chez Panisse
Chico's
Cirque du Soleil
Cisco Systems
Computer Sciences Corp. (CSC)
Costco
Dell
Direct Line
Disney
Dyson
E.&J. Gallo Winery
EADS
easyGroup
easyJet
eBay
EMI Music
Gap
Genentech
General Electric (GE)
General Motors (GM)
GlaxoSmithKline (GSK)
Google
Gores Technology Group
Gucci

Harley-Davidson
Hewlett-Packard (HP)
HIT Entertainment
Horace Green & Co.
HSBC
IBM
IDEO
IKEA
Inditex (Zara)
JC Penney
jetBlue
Johnson & Johnson (J&J)
Krispy Kreme
Labour Party (The)
L'Oréal
LVMH
Marks & Spencer (M&S)
Marriott International
Matsushita
McDonald's
McKinsey
Michelin
Microsoft
Mittal Steel
Morris (William) & Co.
Motorola
Nestlé
Netflix
Nokia
Paul Reed Smith Guitars
Pfizer
Porsche
Procter & Gamble (P&G)
Psion
Reed Executive
Renault-Nissan
Rio Tinto
Ritz-Carlton
Rockwell Collins
Rubbermaid
Ryanair
Safeco
Samsung Electronics
Singapore Airlines
Smith & Nephew
Sodexho
Southwest Airlines
Standard Oil
Starbucks
Swift Trade
Tesco
Texas Instruments (TI)
Toyota
Triumph
Unilever
U2
Virgin
Vivendi
Vodafone
Volkswagen
Wal-Mart
Webvan
W.T. Grant
Yahoo!
Zara (Inditex)

Endnote

1 Not all case examples are corporate. Notable exceptions are our discussion of Bob Dylan's breakout and briefer examples of breakouts by President Bill Clinton, the Boston Red Sox, and U2. Please note that some cases have been drawn on much more heavily than others. Also, we have extracted information from multiple data sources, including interviews and company observations. Published case studies are cited in the endnotes only when they have formed the principal source for the case.

INDEX

Accenture, 200
accountability, leadership and, 305–306
acquisition. *See* merger and acquisition
Adidas, 31, 116, 155, 182, 296
AEG, 67, 68
Aer Lingus, 49, 50, 91–94, 99, 211, 220
aerospace industry, 3, 4, 85 , 87–88, 228
aerospace, 240–243, 240
Air France, 283
Air India, 266
Air Liquide, 67
AirAsia, 29, 277, 316
Airbus, 3, 87–88, 166
airline industry, 6, 19, 22, 29, 49, 50, 52, 55, 91–94, 99, 124, 155, 164–167, 201, 233–234, 263–268, 277, 283, 300–302
alignment. *See* strategic alignment
Alitalia, 266
Amazon, 219
American Airlines, 264
America Online (AOL), 16
Amgen, 254
Amoco, 76, 258, 283
Amstrad, 97
Andersen Consulting, 200
Anheuser=Busch, 43
Apax, 95
Apollo Group, 29, 34–35, 63, 151
Apple, 4, 19, 76–77, 97, 171, 186–190, 123, 216, 232, 252. *See also* iPod/iTunes
  business model for, 247
  as magnet companies, value propositions for, 181–182
Aral, 283
Arcelor, 284
Arco, 283
Armani, Giorgio, 132, 133
Artzt, Edwin, 53. *See also* Procter & Gamble
Asian Tigers, 69
assumption analysis , strategic, 316–317
Aston Martin, 52
AT&T, 34
Australia, 46, 60, 137
automotive industry, 19, 23, 31, 35, 51–52, 55, 69–71, 248
availability, business model for, 187, 229–230, 232
Award Technology, 108–111, 113–114, 121, 123, 125, 140, 141
Ayling, Bob, 263–268, 301–302. *See also* British Airways

Babe Ruth, 59
Bacardi, 204–205, 216
Bailey, Christopher, 31
Bain Capital, 281
balanced=scorecard approach, vision and, 152
Bank of England, 290
Bankers Trust, 52–55, 61
banking and investment industry, 6, 52–55, 61, 128–130, 174
Barclays, 67
Barrett, Colleen, 300
Barsalona, Frank, 115
BASF, 67
Bausch & Lomb, 111, 124
Bayer, 67, 77, 120
Beatles, The, 170, 171
beer, 8
Beiersdorf, 230, 232

Bell Telephone, 34
Bellon, Pierre, 8, 36
Ben & Jerry's, 193–194, 209
benefits to customer, tangible and intangible, 182–183
Benetton, 74
Bershka. *See* Benetton
Best Buy, 36, 69
Best Western, 19, 79, 83–84, 119
  business model for, 245–247
  executing breakout in, 283, 286
  leadership of, 323–325
  vision and, 173–174
Bettmann, Siegfried, 57. *See also* Triumph
big improvers
  business model for, 237
  fast track breakout and, 36, 55–63
Birmingham Small Arms (BSA), 57, 58
Blackberry, 34, 252
Blair, Tony, 131
  and New Labour party, executing breakout in, 288–291
Bloor, 58. *See also* Triumph
BMW, 52, 67
Body Shop, The, 132, 200, 236–237, 296, 311
  executing breakout in, 276–277
  leadership of, 320
  vision and, 155
Boeing, 3, 87, 166, 243
Bombay Gin, 204
Bonterra Vineyards, 253
Boomtown Rats, The, 114
Boots, 121
Booz Allen Hamilton, 5
Borders Bookstore, 200
Borders, Louis, 200
Bosack, Leonard, 116–117, 141. *See also* Cisco Systems
Bosch, 67
Bosnia, 86
Boston Beer Company, 8, 29, 34, 43, 118, 122, 151, 296, 311, 316, 317
  executing breakout in, 276
  leadership of, 318
Boston Red Sox, 59–60, 333
boundary breakers, **73**, 74–75, 78–84, 119
  business model for, 245
  executing breakout in, 285
  value proposition and, 207
Bower, Marvin. 128. *See also* McKinsey
Bowie, David, 170
Boyer, Herbert. *See also* Genentech
BP, 8, 67, 76, 119, 130–131, 258–260, 283
branding, executing breakout in, 266
Brando, Marlon, 57
Branson, Richard, 182, 201, 300
Bravo, Rose Marie, 31, 296
Brazil, 75
breakout defined, 3
breakout dynamics, 107–143
  capital positioning and, 117–118
  cash flow and, 115–116
  expanding horizons and, 128–131
  historical perspectives on, 133–139
  human capital and, 112, **113**, 115–116
  laggard to leader in, 125–128
  organizational capital and, 112, **113**, 115–116
  process of breakout and, 116
  shifting shape strategy and, 131–133
  social capital and, 112–113, **113**, 116
  symbolic capital and, 113–114, **113**, 116
  taking by storm and, 120–125
breakout strategy, 1–28
  acquisition and, 8
  boundary breakers in , **73**, 74–75, 78–84, 119, 207
  breakout defined for, 3
  building, process for, 7–8
  business model refinement for, 10–11, 14–15, **14**, 219–256, 257
  business planning vs. strategy in, 13
  commitment to, 12
  competitive edge and, 2, 3, 4, 27
  Conquistadores in, **73**, 75–76, 84–90, 119, 208
  consistent leaders and. *See* staying out in front
  culture, organization, and company realities in, 8–9, 272–275, **274**
  customer relations and, 2, 7
  cycle of, 14–15, **14**
  defining, 3–6
  dominant companies and, 23
  dynamics of, 107–143. *See also* breakout dynamics
  early adapters, **73**, 76–77, 90–99, 211
  executing, 257–292. *See also* executing breakout
  expanding horizons strategy for, 19, 26, 74, 90–91, 128–131, 128
  failure and. *See* success vs. failure
  financial commitment to, 18
  five essential practices in, 9–12
  global competition and, 27
  growth and market expansion using, 4–6, 8, 15–16
  historical perspectives on, 133–139
  holistic view of, 15
  implementing the strategy for, 13–14, 257
  importance of, 2
  industry dynamics and, 8
  innovation and, 2, 8, 260
  lack of, in general business climate, 2
  laggard to leader firms and, 19, 21–22, 26, 31–32, 35, 118, 119
  leadership and, 8–9, 295–329. *See also* leadership
  learning environment for, 258

breakout strategy (*Cont.*):
logic behind, 19–20, **20**
magnet companies and, 179–218. *See also* magnet companies
major players using, 3–5
perspectives on, 6–9
power player in, **73**, 77–78, 99–103, 119, 211
product and process nature of, 12–16
projects and programs in, 14–15, **14**
research foundations for, 24–25
resource management and, 11
shifting shape strategy as, 19, 23, 26, 74, 131–133, 209–215
simplicity of, 6–7
strategic alignment and, 15
strategic definition and, 15
strategic enactment and, 15
strategic thinking and, 14–15
strategy defined for, 13
success vs. failure with, 5–6, 29, 69–71
supply=chain management and, 2
tactics for, 258
taking by storm strategy as, 18–19, 21, 26, 29–31, 196–200
types of, 16–23, **20**
value creation through, 2, 4, 7, 10, 14–15, **14**
value proposition and , 180–190, 257
vision and, 7, 9–10, 14–15, **14**, 36, 145–178, 257. *See also* vision
Breyers, 193–194
Bridgestone, 194
Brin, Sergey, 41, 42
Britain. *See* United Kingdom
British Airways, 49
executing breakout in, 263–268
leadership of, 301–302
British Leyland (BL), 71, 72
Brooks Brothers, 81, 82–83
Brown, Gordon, 290
Brown=Forman Corporation, 253
Browne, John, 8, 76, 131, 259. *See also* BP
BSA Group. *See* Birmingham Small Arms (BSA), 58
BTG, 108
Buckner, Bill, 59
building a breakout strategy, 7–8
Buitoni, 102
Burberry, 4, 19, 31, 32, 36, 61, 296
Burger King, 281
Burmah Castrol, 283
Burne=Jones, 40
Bush, George H., 240
business imperatives, business model for, 232–233
business models, 10–11, 14–15, **14**, 219–256
Aer Lingus and, 220
Apple and, 247
availability and, 229–230, 232
business models (*Cont.*):
Beiersdorf and, 230
Best Western and, 245–247
big improvers and, 237
Body Shop, The, 236–237
boundary breakers and, 245
breakout strategy to deliver, 233
business imperatives and, 232–233
CEMEX and, 247, **279–281**
Cirque du Soleil and, 222, 236, 247
components of, **221**
Costco and, 235
Dell and, 229
E&J Gallo and, 220, 252–253
early adapters and, 249, 251
eBay and, 236, 245, 252
executing breakout in, 257
expanding horizons firms and, 244–248
Google and, 234–236
HIT Entertainment and, 249–252
importance of, 220
innovation and, 231
laggard to leader firms and, 237–243
Marks & Spenser and, 247–248
Marriott International and, 228
Mittal Steel and, 247
needs analysis and, 226–233, **227**
Nestlé and, 244
power players and, 253
Procter & Gamble and, 244
quality and, 228, 231
resource allocation and, 230–231
revolutionaries and, 235
Rockwell Collins and, 228, 238–243
Rubbermaid and, 238, 239
shifting shape firms and, 248–254
Smith & Nephew (S&N) and, 224–226
Southwest Airlines and, 233–234
Starbucks and, 245, 247
support and, 229, 231–232
taking by storm firms and, 233–237
Tesco and, 247
true originals and, 236, 251–252
value proposition and, 220, 222–226, **223**
Wal=Mart and, 247
wave riders and, 237
business planning vs. strategy, **13**
BusinessWeek, 53
Byung Moo, Lee, 180. *See also* Samsung

Cabletron, 303
Canada, 60, 75, 86, 137
capabilities essential to breakout leadership, 297–302, **298**
Carnation, 102
Carnegie Steel, 84, 88
Carnegie, Andrew, 84, 85, 86
Carrefour, 46
case studies used in the book, 25 , 331–332
Case, Steven, 16

cash flow, breakout dynamics and, 115–116
Casio, 97
Cayenne SUV (Porsche), 51
CBS Records, 114
cement industry, 3, 8, 19, 86–87, 88, 268–271
CEMEX, 3, 8, 19, 85–88, 130, 140
  business model for, **247, 270–271**
  executing breakout in, 268–271, **270**
  leadership of, 306, 318
  system balance and strategy delivery at, **270–271**
Chambers, John, 122, 141
channels , 265–266
Chez Panisse, 320
Chico's, 322
China, 69, **75, 288**
Chronicles (Dylan), 38
Chrysler, 314
Cirque du Soleil
  business model for, 222, 236, 247
  leadership of, 320
Cisco Systems, 3, 17–19, 34, 69, 116–117, 122, 125, 127, 140, 141, 232, 326
Citigroup, 174
clarity and consistency, magnet companies, value propositions, and, 185, 188
Clash, The, 114
Clayton, Adam, 114
Clinton, Bill, 240, 289, 314
clothing and fashion industry, 4, 19, 32, 36, 61, 74, 79–83, 195, 202–203, 302–303
Clubcard, 56
Coca=Cola, 22, 68
cognitive mapping, vision and, 151–152
Cohen, Jack, 56. *See also* Tesco
Colgate, 72
Collins Radio, 238, 239. *See also* Rockwell Collins
Collins, Arthur, 239–241. *See also* Collins Radio; Rockwell Collins
Columbia Records, 37, 39
commitment to breakout strategy, 12
Commodity Futures Exchange Commission, 54
communications industry, 34, 198–199, 228, 238–243
Compaq, 272, 305
competition, 2, 3, 4, 27
  leadership of, 314–316
  value propositions and, leveraging up, 185–190, **189**
  vision and, 152–153
computer industry, 3–6, 17–19, 23, 31, 34, 63, 76, 77, 96–103, 116–117, 126–128, 152, 169, 172–173, 211, 229, 308–309, 312–313
Computer Sciences Corporation (CSC), 126–128
conceptual capabilities, leadership and, 299, **310–317**
Conde Nast Traveler magazine, 166
conquistadores, **73**, 76–76, 84–90, 119
  executing breakout in, 283
  leadership of, 305
  value proposition and, 208
  vision and, 174
consolidation, 75–76
consulting firms, 128–130
consumer electronics industry, 4–6, 18, 23, 31, 34, 36, 47, 48, 77–78, 96–98, 101, 180–181, 186, 196–197, 212–215, 252
  in Japan, wave rider nature of, 47–55
consumer goods industry, 72–73, 77, 238. *See also* retail
contact lens, 108
CooperVision, 108
Copisarow, Alcon, 130. *See also* McKinsey
cosmetics industry, 8, 77, 131–133, 230, 236
Costco
  business model for, 235
  executing breakout in, 277
  leadership of, 320
creative capabilities, leadership and , 299–300, 317–322
cultural sclerosis as cause of failures, 70
culture, organization, and company realities, 8–9, 271–274, **274**
Cuomo, Mario, 314
customer relations, 7
  Apple and, 180–181
  availability and, 187
  breakout strategy and, 2
  clarity and consistency ensured to, 185, 188
  competitive advantage and , 185–190, **189**
  customer relationship management (CRM) and, 179, 261, 292
  executing breakout in, 261, 272–275, **274**, 292
  explaining your offerings to, 183
  magnet companies and, 179–218. *See also* magnet companies
  price and, 185, 188
  quality and, 185–186
  reputation and, 187
  Samsung and, 179–180
  support and, 187
  tangible and intangible benefits to customer in, 182–183
  value proposition and , 180–190
  value propositions in, multiple and simultaneous families of, 190–195, **191**
customer relationship management (CRM), 179, 261, 291. *See also* customer relations

cycle, of breakout strategy, 14–15, **14**
Czechoslovakia, 86

Dalle, François, 131–132, 133, 141.
See also L'Oréal
Datamonitor, 25
De Sole, Domenico, 202–203.
See also Gucci
Dean, James, 57
DEC, 272, 305
Deerfield Ranch Winery, 253
delivering the promise. *See* business models
delivery or enactment model, for executing breakout, 260–271, **262**
Dell Computer, 5, 182, 299, 300
business model for, 229
leadership of, 308–309
vision and, 172–173
Dell, Michael, 299, 300 , 308–309
Deming, W. Edward, 48
Deutsche Bank, 55
Deward, 204
Diageo, 205
Direct Line, 35, 45, 198–199
Disaronno Amaretto, 204
Discovery Channel, 95
Disney, 5, 94, 122, 190–192, 251, 252
dominant companies and breakout strategy, 23
dot=com business boom, 219
Dreyfus, Roubert Louis, 155, 296.
See also Adidas
Drucker, Peter, 260–261
Duncan, Val, 137–138, 139, 141.
See also Rio Tinto
Dunkin' Donuts, 60
DuPont, 67, 127
Dylan, Bob, as example of a true original, 37–42, 252
dynamics. *See* breakout dynamics
Dyson, 4, 18–19, 29, 35, 43–44, 46–47, 118
Dyson, James, as example of revolutionary, 43–44

E&J Gallo, 19, 93–94, 99, 287, 316
business model for, 220, 252–253
leadership of, 318, 325
EADS (European Aeronautical Defense and Space Company), 85, 87–88
early adapters, **73**, 76–77, 90–99
business model for, 249, 251
value proposition and, 211
vision and, 170
Eastwood, Clint, 57
easyGroup, 236
easyJet, 22, 91, 124, 155, 165
eBay, 19, 29, 34, 35, 199, 219
business model for, 236, 245, 252
leadership of, 308, 310–311
value proposition and, 206–207
economies of scale, 75–76
Edgar Thompson Works, 85
Edison General Electric, 34
Edison, Thomas, 68
Edmonds, Scott, 322
eHub, 232
Electricite de France (EdF), 130
EMI Music, 169–172
enactment. *See* strategic enactment and
energy industry, 8, 76, 84, 85, 119, 130–131, 258–260
Engibous, Tom, 167–168.
See also Texas Instruments
England. *See* United Kingdom
Enron, 307
entertainment industry, 5, 94–95, 99, 122, 190–192, 197, 222, 249–252
Epstein, Theo, 59–60. *See also* Boston Red Sox
Ericsson, 98
essential practices in breakout strategy, 9–12
European Commission, 49
European Union, 50
Evans, Dave, 114
executing breakout, 257–292
Air France/KLM and, 283
AirAsia and, 277
Best Western and,286
Blair, Tony and New Labour party as example for, 288–291
Body Shop, The and, 276–277
Boston Beer Company and, 276
boundary breakers and, 285
BP and, 258–260, 283
branding and, 266
British Airways and, 263–268
business models and, 257
CEMEX and, 268–271, **270**
channels and, 265–266
conquistadores and, 283
cost and, 265
Costco and, 277
culture and, 272–275,. **274**
customer relations and, 261, 292
delivery or enactment model for, 260–271, **262**
expanding horizons firms and, 283–286
implementing the strategy for, 257
innovation and, 260, 265
laggard to leader firms and, 278–282
learning environment for, 258, 278
McDonald's and, 285, 286
mergers and acquisitions and, 283
Mittal Steel and, 284–285
Motorola and, 271–272
Nissan and, 278–280
Nokia and, 260
private equity firms and, 280–281
quality and, 261, 292
relationships and, 265

executing breakout (*Cont.*):
reliability and, 265
revolutionaries and, 277–278
shifting shape firms and, 286–291
socio= and techno systems involved in, 261, 263–268
supply chain management and, 261, 263
tactics for, 258
taking by storm firms and, 275–278
true originals and, 277–278
value proposition and, 257
vision and, 257
expanding horizon firms, 19, 74, 26, 90–91
breakout dynamics and, 128–131
business model for, 244–248
executing breakout in, 283–286
leadership of, 296–297, 312, 325
magnet companies, value propositions, and, 205–209
value proposition and, 205–209
vision and, 150, 172–174
ExxonMobil, 130–131

Fairtrade, 57
fast track breakout, 29–65
big improvers in, 36, 55–63
growth and market expansion using, 29–31, 32
laggard to leader strategy in, 31–32, 35
methods used to get on, 32–37, **33**
revolutionaries in, 34–35, **33**, 42–47, 118, 196–197
taking by storm strategy in, 29–31
true originals and, 32–34, **33**, 37–42, 196
vision and, 36
wave riders in, 35–36, **33**, 47–55, 201
Federal Reserve Board, 54
Ferrari, 52
Fetzer Vineyards, 253
Fiat, 52
Fidelity, 6
Fielding, Charles, 136, 138, 139, 141. *See also* Rio Tinto
financial commitment to breakout strategy, 18
Firestone Tire and Rubber Company, 194
food and drink production/service industry, 4, 5,7, 8, 19, 22, 29, 34, 36, 43, 56, 57, 60–63, 74, 77, 79–82, 93–94, 99, 102–103, 118, 173, 204–205, 244, 245, 252–253, 286, **320**
Forbes magazine, 243
Ford, 52, 68, 314
Ford, Tom, **202–203.** *See also* Gucci
Fortune magazine, 61, 318
rankings of business by, 69
France, 67, 86, 87, 285, 320
Franco, Francisco, 72
Frazee, Harry, 59
Friends Reunited, 34
Fruit of the Loom, 316
furnishings and home decor, 5, 44–47, 63

Gallo of Sonoma, 253
Gallo, Ernest, 93. *See also* E&J Gallo
Gap, 150, 302–303
Garnier, 132
Gates, Bill, 63, 122
Geddes, Auckland, 137–141. *See also* Rio Tinto
Genentech, 196, 254
General Dynamics, 127
General Electric, 34, 48, 67, 68, 77, 101–103, 111, 119, 133, 307, 318
General Motors, 23, 68, 70, 206, 209, 314
Germany, 67, 68, 75, 86, 87, 198, 230, 258
automotive industry of, 71
Gerstner, Lou, 101, 103, 120, 152, 242, 308, 312–313. *See also* IBM
Ghosn, Carlos, 272, 273, 278–280, 296, 299, 311–312, 325. *See also* Nissan
Glass, Martin, 307
GlaxoSmithKline, 35–36, 254
Global Business Browser, 25
Global Climate Coalition, 259
global competition, breakout strategy and, 27
Goldman Sachs, 200
Goodyear, 67
Google, 5, 20, 29, 34, 35, 40–42, 63, 111, 122, 199, 216, 219
business model for, 234–236
leadership of, 311
true original status of, 40–42
value proposition and, 196
Gores Technology Group, 282
Gores, Alec, 282
Graham, Bill, 114
Great Escape, **The** (movie), 57
Greenbury, Richard, 149. *See also* Marks and Spenser
Greenpeace, 259
Grey Goose, 204
groups/holding companies, value proposition and, 194
Grove, Andy, 308
growth and market expansion, 4–6
breakout strategy and, 8, 15–16
fast track breakout and, 32
taking by storm and, 29–31
Gucci, 202–203, 230
Guertin, M.K., 245. *See also* Best Western
Gullane Entertainment, 250
Guthrie, Woody, 38

Hamilton, Ron, 108–111, 121, 123, 124, 141. *See also* Award Technology
Harley=Davidson, 19, 22, 36, 58, 243, 296

Harley=Davidson (*Cont.*):
competition from Japanese producers and, 160
culture of, 157, 161
current market statistics for, 163–164
diversification of, 158–164, **159 , 160, 161**
joint visioning process in, 162–163
leadership of, 161–162
merchandising of image of, 157
state transitions in developing vision of, 158–164, **159, 160, 161**
supply chain management and, 160
vision and, 145–146, 155, 156–164
Hastings, Reed, 197. *See also* Netflix
health care industry, 35, 108–111, 121, 124, 146–147, 224, 254
Heinz, 68
Hennes and Mauritz (H&M), 150
Henson International Television. *See* HIT Entertainment
Henson, Jim, 94, 122
Hepburn, Audrey, 202
Hewlett=Packard, 97, 304
Hewson, Paul, 114
Higgins, Tom, 286, 323–324. *See also* Best Western
historical perspectives on breakout dynamics, 133–139
HIT Entertainment, 94–95, 99, 122, 140, 191–192, 211–212
business model for, 249–252
Hitachi, 47, 67
holistic view of breakout strategy, 15
home appliances industry, 18, 29, 34, 35, 43–44, 46, 118
Home Depot, 36, 69
Honda, 312
Honeywell, 305
Hoover, 34, 182
Horace Green & Co., 118–119
hospitality industry, 19, 30, 32, 34, 83–84, 119, 173–174, 228, **245–247**
Hot Press, 114
HSBC, 22, 67, 174
human capital, breakout dynamics and, 112, **113**, 115–116
Hurd, Mark, 304

IBM, 18, 19, 23, 67, 77, 100–101, 103, 119, 120, 126, 182, 211, 212, 215, 242, 287
leadership of, 308, 312–313, 325
vision and, 152, **169**
Icon magazine, 46
IDEO, 75
IKEA, 5, 44–47, 63
Immelt, Jeffrey, 101, 307, 318. *See also* General Electric
imperatives, business, 232–233
implementing breakout strategy, 13–14, 257
India, 69, 288
Inditex, 74, 79, 80, 94, 122
industry dynamics and breakout strategy, 8
innovation
breakout strategy and, 2, 8
business model for, 231
executing breakout in, 260, 265
insurance industry, 198
Intel, 69, 182, 308
Internet, 20, 29, 34, 35, 63, 199, 245
Internet services, 5, 16, 19, 40–42, 196, 197, 206–207, 219, 234–236, 310–311
Intuit, 319
iPod/iTunes, 171, 181–182, 186, 190
Ireland, 49, 50, 114
Iridium, 303
Ispat International, 284. *See also* Mittal Steel
Isuzu, 279
Italy, 132, 198, 320

J Sainsbury, 56, 290
Jack Daniels Tennessee Whiskey, 253
Jaguar, 52
James, Bill, 60
Japan, 46, 67, 83, 97, 132
automotive industry of, 71
consumer electronics industry of, 77–78
wave rider electronic companies of, 47–55
JC Penney, 90, 118, 230, 322
jetBlue, 4, 19, 182
vision and, 155, 164–167
Jobs, Steve, 123, 186
Johnson & Johnson, 321–322
Jones, Clay, 228, 230–231, 240–243, 296. *See also* Rockwell Collins
Jones, Fletcher, 126. *See also* Computer Sciences Corporation (CSC)
JP Morgan, 127
Junkins, Jerry, 167–168. *See also* Texas Instruments
JVC, 77

Kamprad, Ingvar, 44–47, 63. *See also* IKEA
Kawasaki, 58
Kazakhastan, 86
Kelleher, Herb , 300, 308. *See also* Southwest Airlines
Kelly, Grace, 202
Kennedy, Edward, 314
KFC, 74
Kiehle, 132
Kings Supermarkets, 81–82
KitKat, 102
KLM, 283
Kmart, 46, 90, 322

Koch, Jim, 8, 34, 43, 122, 151, 276, 296, 311, 317, 320. *See also* Boston Beer Company
Kodak, 206
Kohl's, 322
Krispy Kreme, 60–63

L'Oréal, 8, 67, 77, 119, 131–133, 140, 141
lack of breakout strategy, in general business climate, 2
Lafarge, 86
Lafley, Alan, 307, 318
laggard to leader firms, 19, 21–22, 31–32, 26, 118, 119
  big improvers in, 36, 55–63
  breakout dynamics and, 125–128
  business model for, 237–243
  executing breakout in, 278–282
  fast track breakout and, 35
  leadership of, 296, 325
  magnet companies, value propositions, and, 200–205
  value proposition and, 200–205
  vision and, 149, 167–169
  wave riders in, 35–36, **33**, 47–55, 201
Lamborghini, 52
Lampert, Eddie, 322
Lancome, 132
leadership, 295–329
  accountability and, 305–306
  breakout strategy and, 8–9
  capabilities essential to breakout in, 297–302, **298**
  competition and, 314–316
  conceptual capabilities in, 299, 310–317
  conquistadores and, 305
  creative capabilities and, 299–300, 317–322
  expanding horizon firms and, 296–297, 312, 325
  laggard to leader firms and, 296, 325
  negative capabilities in, 299 , 306–310
  positive capabilities in, 298–299, 302–306
  relational capabilities and, 300, 322–326
  revolutionaries and, 311
  shifting shape firms and, 297, 325
  strategic assumption analysis and, 316–317
  taking by storm firms and, 295–296, 326
  true originals and, 305
  wave riders and, 305
Leahy, Terry, 8, 56–57, 272, 273, 296, 299. *See also* Tesco
learning environment, executing breakout and, 258, 278
Lee, Kun=Hee, 212–213. *See also* Samsung
Lerner, Sandy, 116–117, 141. *See also* Cisco Systems
leveraging up to gain competitive advantage, 185–190, **189**
Levy, Alain, 170, 172. *See also* EMI Music
Live Aid concert, 115
logic behind breakout strategy, 19–20, **20**
Lucier, Charles, 5
Lyrick Studios, 95, 250

Madox=Brown, 40
magnet companies, 179–218
  achieving status of, via breakout strategy, 195–196
  Apple as 181–182
  availability and, 187
  defining, 180
  expanding horizons firms and, 205–209
  laggard to leader firms and, 200–205
  price and, 185, 188
  quality in, 185–186
  reputation and, 187
  Samsung as, 179–180
  shifting shape strategy as, 209–215
  support and, 187
  taking by storm firms and, 196–200
  tangible and intangible benefits to customer in, 182–183
  value proposition and, 180–190
  value propositions in, multiple and simultaneous families of, 190–195, **191**
Malaysian Airlines, 277
Marconi, 8, 206, 248
market expansion. *See* growth and market expansion, 8
market segment, value proposition and, 193
MarketLine, 25
Marks & Spenser (M&S), 81–83
  business model for, 247–248
  vision and, 149–151
Marks, Alfred, 30
Marriott International, 228, 285
Marshal, Colin, 264
Martini & Rossi, 204
Maslow, Abraham, 162
Massimo Dutti.. *See* Benetton
Matheson, Hugh, 134–139, 140, 141. *See also* Rio Tinto
Matrix, 132
Matsushita, 47, 77–78
Matsushita, Konosuke, 77. *See also* Matsushita
Mattel Corporation, 282
Maybelline, 132
MCA, 78
McConnell, Bill, 61
McDonald's, 74, 173
  executing breakout in, 285, 286
  leadership of, 319
McGavick, Mike, 306
McGuinness, Paul, 114

McKinsey , 128–130, 325
McQueen, Steve, 57
Menichetti, Robert, 31
Mercedes, 52, 67
mergers and acquisitions, 8, 283, 284
methods used to get on the fast track, 32–37, **33**
Mexico, 3, 60, 86
Michelin, 35, 67, 133
Michelin North America, 278
Microsoft, 3, 6, 17, 63, 69, 98, 122, 182, 199, 215
Miller, 43
Mini Cooper, 69
mining industry, 134–139
Mitchell, William B. (Bill), 167. *See also* Texas Instruments
Mitsubishi, 67
Mittal Steel, 85–86, 88, 119, 130, 140
  business model for, 247
  executing breakout in, 284–285
  leadership of, 312, 318
  value proposition and, 208–209
Mittal, Lakshmi, 85–86, 315–316. *See also* Mittal Steel
Moet Hennessy=Louis Vuitton (LVMH), 194, 195
Monterrey Tech, 86
Morgridge, John, 117
Morris, William, as example of a true original, 39–42
motorcycle industry, 19, 22, 36, 57–59, 62, 145–146, 155, 156–164
Motorola, 98, 197, 209, 212, 215, 260, 273, 279, 296, 299, 303
  executing breakout in, 271–272
  leadership of, 304–305, 307
Mullen, Larry, 114
music industry, 37–42, 114–115, 169–172, 185–186

Nakamura, Shiro, 279
Napster, 170
National, 77
NEC, 47, 67
needs analysis, business model and, 226–233, **227**
Neeleman, David, 165, 166. *See also* jetBlue
negative leadership capabilities, 299, 306–310
Nestlé, 5, 77, 102–103, 119, 244
Netflix, 197
New Labour party as example of executing breakout, 267, 288–291
New York State Banking Commission, **54**
New York Times, 38
New York Yankees, 59
Nicoli, Eric, 170. *See also* EMI Music
Nissan, 243, 273, 296, 299
  executing breakout in, 278–280
Nissan (*Cont.*):
  leadership of, 312, 325
Nokia, 76, 98, 215, 252, 287
  executing breakout in, 260
  leadership of, 325
Nordstrom's, 166
Nutt, Roy, 126. *See also* Computer Sciences Corporation (CSC)

O'Donnell, Christopher, 224. *See also* Smith & Nephew (S&N)
O'Leary, Michael, 49–51. *See also* Ryanair
Oakland Angels, 60
oil industry, 8, 76, 84, 85, 88, 119, 130–131, 258–260
Oracle, 127
organic foods, 320
organizational capital, breakout dynamics and, 112, **113**, 115–116
Ortega, Amancio, 80–81, 122. *See also* Inditex
Orton, Peter, 94–95, 122, 140, 250. *See also* HIT Entertainment
Otis Elevator, 67
Owen=Jones, Lindsay, 8, 132, 141. *See also* L'Oréal
Ozley, Lee, 162. *See also* Harley=Davidson

Page, Larry, 41, 42, 63
Palmcomputing, 97–99
Palmisano, Sam, 100, 101. *See also* IBM
Pan Am, 201
Panasonic, 77
Parmalat, 307
Paul Reed Smith Guitars, 185–186
PDAs, 96–99
Penney, James Cash, 322
PepsiCo, 325
Perrier, 102
perspectives on breakout strategy, 6–9
Pfizer, 146–147, 254
Phillips, 77
Pier 1, 46
Pixar, 251–252
Poland, 86
Polygram, 170
Porsche, 51, 55
positive leadership capabilities, 298–299, 302–306
Potter, David, 96. *See also* Psion
power players, **73**, 77–78, 99–103, 119, 211, 253
Pratt, Edmond, 146–147, 254. *See also* Pfizer
Premier Talent, 115
Pressler, Paul, 302–303
price, magnet companies, value propositions, and, 185, 188
private equity firms, executing breakout in, 280–281
process of breakout, 116

Procter & Gamble, 53–55, 67, 68, 72–73, 77, 119
business model for, 244
leadership of, 307, 318, 325
value proposition and, 192–193
product and process nature of breakout strategy and, 12–16
projects and programs, breakout strategy and, 14–15, **14**
Psion, 96–99
Pull and Bear, 74. *See also* Benetton
Putin, Vladimir, 131
PwC Consulting, 18, 101

Quaker Oats, 68
quality
business model for, 228, 231
executing breakout in, 261, 292
magnet companies, value propositions, and, 185–186
total quality management (TQM) and, 261, 292
Quicken, 319

Randolph, Mark, 197. *See also* Netflix
Ravenswood, 253
Reagan, Ronald, 325
Redken, 132
Reed Executive, 30, 32, 34
Reed, Alec, 30–31
relational capabilities, leadership and, 300, 322–326
relationships, executing breakout and, 265
reliability, executing breakout and, 265
Renault, 67, 278, 279, 280
Renault=Nissan, 31
reproduction of culture, **274**
reputation, magnet companies, value propositions, and, 187
research foundations for breakout strategy, 24–25
Research in Motion (RIM), 34, 252
resource allocation
breakout strategy and, 11
business model for, 230–231
retail industry, 6, 31, 46, 69, 88–90, 118, 149–150, 210, 230–232, 302–303, 322
revolutionaries, 118
business model for, 235
executing breakout and, 277–278
fast track breakout and, 34–35, **33**, 42–47
leadership of, 311
value proposition and, 196–197
Rhodesia (Zambia), 72, 136, 137
Rhokana Corporation, 137. *See also* Rio Tinto
Riedel, Hans, 51–52. *See also* Porsche
Rio Tinto, 67, 72, 134–139, 140, 141
RiteAid, 307
Ritz Carlton, 166, 231
RMC, 87
Rockefeller, John D., 84, 85
Rockwell Collins, 228, 231, 238–243, 296
Rockwell International, 239, 241
Roddick, Anita, 200, 236, 277, 296, 320. *See also* Body Shop, The
Roddick, Gordon, 236–237. *See also* Body Shop, The
Romania, 86
Rose, Stuart, 150. *See also* Marks and Spenser
Rosetti, 40
Rothschild, 136
Rover, 314
Royal Bank of Scotland, 56
Rubbermaid, 238, 239
Russia, 76, 130–131
Ryanair, 6, 49–52, 55, 91, 165, 252, 277, 316

Saatchi & Saatchi, 307
Saatchi, Maurice, 307
Safeco Insurance, 306
Sainsbury retail, 150
Sainsbury, David, 290
Saint=Gobain, 67
Saint=Laurent, Yves, 133
Saks Fifth Avenue, 31
Sam Adams beer, 43. *See also* Boston Beer Company
Samsung, 5, 23, 209, 216, 287
magnet companies, value propositions, and, 179–180
value proposition and, 212–215, **214**
Sanford, Charles, 53. *See also* Bankers Trust
Santana, Carlos, 186
SAS, 127
Schmidt, Eric, 41
Schneider, 67
Schueller, Eugene, 132. *See also* L'Oréal
Schultz, Howard, 79–80, 122, 123, 321. *See also* Starbucks
Scotland, 56
Scottish Enterprise, 121
Sculley, John, 97
Sears, 90, 322
Securities and Exchange Commission, 54, 62
Seden, Bill, 108–111, 121, 124, 141. *See also* Award Technology
Sequoia Associates, 117
Shaheen, George, 200
Sharp, 97
shifting shape firms, 19, 23, 26, 74, 91
breakout dynamics and, 131–133
business model for, 248–254
executing breakout in, 286–291
leadership of, 297, 325

shifting shape firms (*Cont.*):
magnet companies, value propositions, and, 209–215
value proposition and, 209–215
vision and, 169–172
Shu Uemura, 132
Shultz, Howard, 315
Siemens, 67, 68, 77, 120, 133
Sinclair Computers, 96
Sinegal, Jim, 320
Singapore Airlines, 201
Skilling, Jeffrey, 307
Smith & Nephew (S&N), 224–226
Smith, Orrin, 315
Smith, Paul Reed, 185–186
social capital, breakout dynamics and, 112–113, **113**, 116
socio= and techno systems involved in executing breakout in, 261, 263–268
Sodexho, 8, 19, 36, 130
Softsheen=Carson, 132
Sony, 47, 77, 201, 215
Southwest Airlines, 6, 49, 165, 166, 182, 300, 302
business model for, 233–234
leadership of, 308
vision and, 155
Spain, 72, 74, 80, 87, 150, 198, 320
Sperling, John, 63, 151. *See also* Apollo Group
sport utility (SUV) market and Porsche, 51
sports franchises, 59–60
Springsteen, Bruce, 115
St. Louis Cardinals, 59
stakeholder needs and aspirations, vision and, 153–156
Standard & Poor's (S&P) 500 Index, 164
Standard Oil, 84, 85, 88
Stanford University, 40, 86, 117
Star Alliance, 201
Starbucks, 4, 7, 19, 74, 79–80, 122, 123, 182, 216, 285
business model for, 245, 247
executing breakout in, 283
leadership of, 315, 319, 321
value proposition and, 207
vision and, 173
state transitions specified in vision, 156, 158–164, **159** , **160**, **161**
staying out in front, 67–105
boundary breakers in, **73**, 74–75, 78–84, 119, 207
Conquistadores in, **73**, 75–76, 84–90, 119, 208
early adapters in, **73**, 76–77, 90–99, 211
expanding horizons strategy and, 74, 90–91
power player in, **73**, 77–78, 99–103, 119, 211
shifting shape strategy and, 74, 91
strategies for, 72–78, **73**
steel industry, 84, 85–86, 88, 119, 208–209, 248, 284–285
Storybook Mountain, 253
Stradivarious. *See* Benetton
strategic alignment, 15
strategic assumption analysis , 316–317
strategic definition, 15
strategic enactment, 15
strategic thinking, 14–15
strategic vision , 148. *See also* vision
strategy defined, 13
success vs. failure of breakout strategy, 5–6, 29, 69–71
Sun Tzu, **258**
Sun newspaper, 290
supply chain management
breakout strategy and, 2
executing breakout in, 261, 263
vision and, 160
support
business model for, 229, business model for, 231–232
magnet companies, value propositions, and, 187
Suzuki, 58
Swanson, Robert, 196. *See also* Genentech
Sweden, 150
Swift Trade, 75
Symbian, 98
symbolic capital, breakout dynamics and, 113–114, **113**, 116

T=Mobile, 171
tactics for executing breakout, 258
taking by storm firms, 18–19, 21, 26, 29–31
awakening to, 31
breakout dynamics and, 120–125
business model for, 233–237
executing breakout in, 275–278
growth and market expansion using, 29–31
leadership of, 295–296, 326
magnet companies, value propositions, and, 196–200
revolutionaries in, 34–35, **33**, 42–47, 118, 196–197
true originals and, 32–34, **33**, 37–42, 196
value proposition and, 196–200
vision and, 164–167
tangible and intangible benefits to customer, 182–183
Target, 46, 322
Technics, 77
technology industries, 68
Teerlink, Richard, 161–162, 296. *See also* Harley=Davidson
Templeton, Rich, 168. *See also* Texas Instruments

Tesco, 4, 6–8, 36, 56–57, 63, 118, 150, 151, 230, 243, 247, 273, 296, 299
Texas Instruments, 31, 36, 212
  value proposition and, 202
  vision and, 167–169
Thatcher, Margaret, 289
Thomson=Houston, 34
Tide detergent, 72–73. *See also* Procter & Gamble
Time Warner Cable, 215
TJ Maxx, 230
TNK=BP, 131
Toshiba, 47, 67
total quality management (TQM), 261, 292
Toyota, 19, 116, 133, 312, 314
Trinidad, 86
Triumph, 57–59, 62–63
true originals
  business model for, 236, 251–252
  executing breakout in, 277–278
  fast track breakout and, 32–34, **33**, 37–42
  leadership of, 305
  value proposition and, 196
Turck=Paquelier, Patricia, 131–132, 133. *See also* L'Oréal
Turning Leaf, 253
TWA, 201
Tyco, 307
types of breakout strategy, 16–23, **20**

U2 , 114–115
Ullman, Mike, 323
UMIST, 121
Unilever, 72, 119, 192–194, 209, 216
United Kingdom, 4, 35, 36, 44, 49, 50, 56, 57, 58, 60, 67, 71, 75, 81, 87, 96, 108, 115, 131, 198, 250, 258, 267, 289–291
  automotive industry of, 69
University of Nebraska at Omaha, Aviation Institute, 166
University of Phoenix, 35, 151

value creation through breakout strategy, 2, 4, 7, 10, 14–15, **14**
value proposition
  availability and, 187
  Bacardi and, 204–205
  breakout strategy to deliver, 233
  business model for , 222–226, **223**. *See also* business models
  clarity and consistency ensured in, 185, 188
  competitive advantage and, leveraging up, 185–190, **189**
  eBay, 206–207
  executing breakout in, 257
  expanding horizons firms and, 205–209
  explaining your offerings in, 183
value proposition (*Cont.*):
  failure to create, consequences of, 199–200
  families of, multiple, simultaneous, 190–195, **191**
  groups/holding companies and, 194
  Gucci and, 202–203
  laggard to leader firms and, 200–205
  magnet companies, value propositions, and, 180–190
  market segment and, 193
  Mittal Steel and, 208–209
  price and, 185, 188
  Procter & Gamble, 192–193
  quality and, 185–186
  reputation and, 187
  Samsung, 212–215, **214**
  shifting shape strategy as, 209–215
  six pillars of, 183–190, **184**
  Starbucks and, 207
  support and, 187
  tangible and intangible benefits to customer in, 182–183
  Unilever, 192–194
Van Ronk, Dave, 38
video recorders, 77–78
Vietnam, 288
Virgin Group, 182, 194–195, 201
vision, 36, 145–178, 257
  Adidas and, 155
  balanced=scorecard approach to, 152
  Best Western and, 173–174
  Body Shop, The, and, 155
  breakout strategy and, 7, 9–10, 14–15, **14**, 145–178
  cognitive mapping and, 151–152
  competition and, 152–153
  conquistadors and, 174
  Dell Computer and, 172–173
  determining, 148, 152, 154–156
  dynamic approaches to, 151–152
  early adapters and, 170
  easyJet and, 155
  EMI Music and, 169–172
  expanding horizons strategy and, 150, 172–174
  Harley=Davidson and, 145–146, 155, 156–164
  HSBC and, 174
  IBM and, 152, 169
  jetBlue and, 155, 164–167
  joint visioning process in, 162–163
  key requirements for, 175
  laggard to leader firms and, 149, 167–169
  Marks and Spenser (M&S) , 149–151
  Pfizer and, 146–147
  rules for formulating, 148–149
  shifting shape strategy, 169–172
  Southwest Airlines and, 155

vision (*Cont.*):
  stakeholder needs and aspirations in, 153–156
  Starbucks and, 173
  state transitions specified in, 156, 158–164, **159** , **160**, **161**
  static and dynamic (combined) approach to, 155–156
  strategic vision and, 148
  taking by storm companies and, 164–167
  Texas Instruments and, 167–169
  translating into practice, 151–153
  understanding the concept of, 147–151
  visionaries and, 148–149
  wheel or segments of, 154–156, **154**
Vivendi, 248, 307
Vodaphone, 196–197
Volkswagen, 52, 71–72

W. Frank Barton School of Business, Wichita State, 166
W.T. Grant, 88–90
Wal=Mart, 6, 69, 150, 210, 230, 238, 247, 260, 322
Wall's, 193
Walsh, Willie, 91–93. *See also* Aer Lingus
Walt Disney World, 222
Wang Labs, 272, 305
Waters, Alice, 320
wave riders
  business model for, 237
  fast track breakout and, 35–36, **33**, 47–55
wave riders (*Cont.*):
  leadership of, 305
  value proposition and, 201
Weber, William P. (Pat), 167. *See also* Texas Instruments
Webvan, 199–200
Welch, Jack, 101. *See also* General Electric
Western Electric, 48
Western Union, 126
wheel or segments of vision, 154–156, **154**
Whitman, Margaret, 308
Who, The, 115
William Morris, 29, 34, 39–42
wine, 93–94
World Series (baseball), 59
WorldCom, 304, 307

Yahoo, 200, 215
Yamaha, 58
Yeager, Bill, 116. *See also* Cisco Systems
Yong, Yun Jong, 213. *See also* Samsung

Zambia, 72, 136
Zambrano, Lorenzo, 8, 86, 270–271, 306. *See also* CEMEX
Zander, Ed, 272–273, 280, 296, 299, 304–305, 307. *See also* Motorola
Zara, 80–81, 150. *See also* Benetton; Inditex
  executing breakout in, 283
  leadership of, 312, 319
Zinc Corporation, 138
Zippo, 58